SPORTS AND GAMES OF THE 18TH AND 19TH CENTURIES

Recent Titles in
Sports and Games Through History

Sports and Games of the Ancients
Steve Craig

Sports and Games of Medieval Cultures
Sally Wilkins

SPORTS AND GAMES OF THE 18TH AND 19TH CENTURIES

Robert Crego

Sports and Games Through History
Andrew Leibs, Series Adviser

Greenwood Press
Westport, Connecticut · London

Library of Congress Cataloging-in-Publication Data

Crego, Robert, 1961–
     Sports and games of the 18th and 19th centuries / Robert Crego.
        p.   cm.—(Sports and games through history)
     Includes bibliographical references and index.
     ISBN 0–313–31610–4 (alk. paper)
        1. Sports—History—18th century.   2. Sports—History—19th century.
     3. Games—History—18th century.   4. Games—History—19th century.   I. Title.
II. Series.
     GV576.C74   2003
     790′.09—dc21   2001040590

British Library Cataloguing in Publication Data is available.

Library of Congress Catalog Card Number: 2001040590
ISBN: 0–313–31610–4

First published in 2003

Greenwood Press, 88 Post Road West, Westport, CT 06881
An imprint of Greenwood Publishing Group, Inc.
www.greenwood.com

Printed in the United States of America

The paper used in this book complies with the
Permanent Paper Standard issued by the National
Information Standards Organization (Z39.48–1984).

10 9 8 7 6 5 4 3 2 1

Every reasonable effort has been made to trace the owners of copyright materials in this
book, but in some instances this has proven impossible. The author and publisher will be
glad to receive information leading to more complete acknowledgments in subsequent
printings of this book, and in the meantime extend their apologies for any omissions.

▦ CONTENTS

⣿ SERIES FOREWORD

I am pleased to introduce Greenwood Publishing's Sports and Games Through History. I feel this new series offers readers the greatest geographical breadth and historical depth of any study on the games we play, how we play them, and what they tell us about the variations and the resounding similarities of the world's cultures.

The first four volumes in this series explore the sports, games, and physical activities during important periods in world history: from the first ancient Olympiad to the Fall of Rome (776 B.C. to 476 A.D.); from the start of the Dark Ages to the invention of printing (476 A.D. to 1450); from the beginning to the end of the Renaissance (1450 to 1649); and from Colonial America to the first modern Olympiad (1700 to 1896). The world's seven major regions (Africa, Asia, Europe, Latin America, the Middle East, North America, and Oceania) are all represented, though one of the series' great discoveries is how often sports and games cross geographic boundaries and historical time lines.

In the series' opening volume, Steve Craig notes that some sports, such as archery and wrestling, are indigenous to every culture in the ancient world. From the Pyramids of Egypt to the ruins of Rome, antiquity is strewn with references to, and artifacts from, what look like many sports and games we still play today. Although the lack of detailed accounts and written rules often prevents absolute knowledge of sport history, the knowledge compiled by scholars such as Craig provides valuable insight into the nature of games played in the ancient world.

Each entry in the series provides a detailed description of sport, game, or activity, traces its development, explains how essential equipment can be made or adapted, and provides the rules of play. One goal of the series is to include enough information so students can re-create an activity as well as read about it.

Along with the simultaneous development of sports around the world, the shaping powers of military and cultural imperialism are the driving force behind the series' final volume, on the eighteenth and nineteenth centuries. Bob Crego's book demonstrates the inexorable influence of Great Britain, both for the games they carried across their empire (the World Cup is awarded in soccer, not baseball), as well as the native games and traditions they banned while building colonies.

Above all, sports and games from all cultures offer insights that help us understand our own culture. One sees casinos on reservations differently after reading Sally Wilkins' book on the Middle Ages, where we learn about the vital role that games of chance played in the spiritual and emotional lives of most Native American tribes.

Entries on major modern sports such as baseball and basketball are included, but the series ends with the first Modern Olympiad in 1896. Thus, the series sets the stage for the twentieth century, during which sports were transformed by economic, cultural, and political realities into industries and their own myths, each needing its own encyclopedia.

One of the best things to take into the reading of this series is your own knowledge and love of the sports and games you play, watch, and follow. The ensuing pages offer many adventures in learning where these came from and thus provide ideas on how to have the most fun as you explore the universe of play.

Andrew Leibs
Series Adviser

▦ INTRODUCTION

OVERVIEW

Beginning in the mid- to late 18th century in England, the process of industrialization transformed traditional societies throughout Europe and North America. Life became more urban and less tied to farming and the land. Sports that originally had links either to fertility/harvest rituals or to agriculture and hunting in general (e.g., soccer, polo, jai alai) were taken out of their original contexts and modernized. The concept of time—when to wake up and go to work, when to come home—became ingrained in modern society as jobs and employment were separated from the home and land. While sport in many traditional cultures had been an integral part of life (e.g., running, jumping, and throwing as a part of hunting, or skiing and skating as essential modes of transportation), in an increasingly modern, industrial society sports became identified with and reserved for leisure time. Given the limited amount of time in which they could be played, many sports and games became formalized with the writing of rules and guidelines.

Some of our most popular sports and games today—football, baseball, basketball, and hockey—were originally played in the 19th century. Sports with older roots, like soccer, swimming, golf, wrestling, and fencing, were standardized with the creation of rulebooks. These rules governed competition between two teams or individuals, which bought into the concept that sports and games would have winners and losers. This is another new concept linked to modern industrial society. Victory or defeat—the final outcome—was emphasized over the process of sport.

The strength of the British Empire, which would form colonies and protectorates in Africa, Asia, and North and South America, was founded on its industry and economy—a capitalist economy based on the principles of free enterprise and competition. Not surprisingly, English sports (cricket, field hockey, boxing, soccer, rugby, rowing, track and field, etc.) reflected this competitive ethos.

Given the magnitude of England's world influence in the 18th and 19th centuries, one can begin to understand the widespread impact that British sports had throughout its empire and in Europe and North America. Though much of England's activity abroad was connected to business and government, the thousands of imperial agents involved in these activities (businessmen, engineers, soldiers, merchant mariners, missionaries, etc.) were at the same time spreading the British way of life around the globe. Naturally, this way of life included sports and games.

Roughly one-third of all the entries in this volume are of British sports and games. A handful of others were either heavily influenced by earlier British games (e.g., baseball), had significant origins in English sports culture (e.g., figure skating and swimming), or were adapted by the English from other cultures and formalized (e.g., polo).

While the ways of England are indelibly stamped on this volume, the effects of Western industry and imperialism are also evident by what is missing. Colonies were settled to further economic and political interests rather than the well-being of the native population. Beginning in the 16th century with the brutal occupation of Latin America by the Spanish, and continuing into the 17th century with the heightened slave trade in Africa, many indigenous cultures suffered at the hands of the technologically superior West. During the 18th and 19th centuries, various groups in native Australia, the Pacific Islands, India, China, Southeast Asia, and Africa came under the control of Britain and other European countries. As a form of socialization, many of these natives were encouraged to adopt European values and beliefs. As a result, several British games were adopted and mastered by formerly subject peoples (e.g., field hockey in India, badminton in Malaysia, table tennis in China, and cricket in the East Indies). However, many traditional sports and games that were definitive of native cultures were either discouraged, suppressed, or wiped out. Indigenous sports that continued to exist were often preserved by isolated cultures that were not touched by Western influence (see Chapters 1, 5, and 7).

SCOPE OF STUDY

This volume examines how sports and games reflected life around the world in the 18th and 19th centuries. It is divided geographically into seven chapters:

Africa (including northern Africa bordering on the Mediterranean);

Asia (extending from Saudi Arabia and Iran in the west to China and Southeast Asia);

The British Isles (including England, Scotland, Ireland, and Wales);

Europe (stretching from France, Spain, and the Baltic and Scandinavian countries in the west/northwest to the Ural Mountains in the east);

Latin America (Central and South America);

North America (Canada and the United States, including Alaska); and

Oceania (encompassing a region in the South Pacific that includes Australia, New Zealand, and the islands throughout Polynesia, Micronesia, and Melanesia).

Each chapter begins with an overview of sports and games in that region. The most popular sports and games of the era are then examined individually, with the focus on history (Where did the sport originate? How did it develop?), its cultural implications (Why was it played? How might it have symbolized a people's values and beliefs?), and some of the sport's basic rules to give readers an idea of how it is played. In many cases, the manner in which a sport's equipment and rules have changed since the 18th and 19th centuries is discussed as well.

As indicated above, England had a significant influence on the world economy and culture during this era. Accordingly, Britain is dealt with in a separate chapter. Because of political events in Africa and Latin America during the 18th and 19th centuries, there was very little traditional sport and game activity on these continents, at least none that was region-wide. Thus sports and games in Africa and Latin America are represented by chapter-long essays, which also discuss the social, political, and economic situations on these continents. It should also be noted that there is very little discussion of sports in the Middle East, which is included in the chapter on Asia. Later forms of Islam that had became prevalent in the Middle East and Northern Africa during the 18th and 19th centuries were antithetical to sports and games. Unlike the early Islam of Muhammad, which emphasized the attainment of wealth, power, and glory—thus justifying competitive sport and warfare—the latter-day Persian concept of Islam was fatalistic, resigned to the world's order, shrouded in a mysticism that considered the material world unimportant.

SELECTION CRITERIA

In choosing sports and games to highlight, the following questions have been considered: Did either a large or an important segment of the population play? Does a sport or game define or reflect certain aspects of a culture? How does it relate to sports or games today?

It is the intention of this volume to present a menu of sports and games that are representative of the times in which they originated or gained popularity, and that reflect the values and beliefs of those who played them.

METHODOLOGY

In researching the entries for this volume, I have attempted to examine at least three sources for each entry. In most cases, the sources include either histories or how-to books devoted entirely to a specific sport. General sports encyclopedias have not been used unless information sources on a sport are extremely rare and/or the encyclopedia entry is comprehensive and authored by an authority on the sport.

Many books dealing with sports history and culture are out of print, or available only in libraries or from rare-book dealers or used-book shops. The Internet proved to be an invaluable research source throughout this project. Many official sports associations maintain Web sites that reprint historical articles. This is also the best source for up-to-date rules. In citing Web sources, the author and date of the article are included when this information has been provided. If no author is cited, the material is either listed solely by title or, in the case of a sports association Web site, attributed to the association. In all cases, the Web address has been provided, along with the date that the information was accessed.

▦ AFRICA

INTRODUCTION

Though many of the traditional African sports and games discussed below date back to ancient times, their prevalence throughout the continent was diminished greatly during the 18th and 19th centuries. Traditional life and culture on the western Ivory Coast, in the south, and in the interior of Africa came under assault starting with the slave trade in the late 16th to early 17th centuries. Western European influence intensified during the age of imperialism, when, from the mid-19th century to the early 20th century, virtually every corner of Africa was seized by one or another European country for economic and political gain.

Today, traditional sport in Africa has survived in nomadic, hunter-gatherer, and pastoral societies least touched by European influence. As many of these sports and games are linked with work, religion, celebrations, family life, birth, coming of age, and death, they are central to the cultural experience of a people. Thus some traditional sports have also resurfaced in modern urban areas as an affirmation of African cultural heritage.

HISTORICAL AND CULTURAL PERSPECTIVE

Africa is a continent of contrasts, stretching from the arid sub-Saharan north through the dense, lush Congo in the interior to the Kalahari in the south, and bracketed by the grassy highlands in the east and the rich Gold Coast in the west. Not surprisingly, a continent diverse in geography, resources, and climate has also produced diverse peoples. Along the Nile in the north, Egypt thrived as one of the world's most advanced ancient civilization (1450 B.C.), and Carthage (located in the area of modern-day

Libya and Algeria) rivaled the Roman Republic for domination of the Mediterranean around 500 B.C. Between the 13th and 15th centuries, large city-states in the areas of Nigeria, Mali, and Ghana had built fairly sophisticated economies based on trade with Europe and Asia. Yet life for many Africans went unchanged for centuries. Pastoralists in East Africa (Kenya and Ethiopia) built societies that were based on subsistence agriculture and raising cattle. Hunter-gatherers in the south (South Africa, Namibia, Zimbabwe) and the interior (Zaire) had a much different relationship to land and animals. Given land that wouldn't produce crops, they relied upon their skills in hunting and foraging for food. Herdsmen in sub-Saharan northern Africa created highly mobile nomadic societies, constantly on the move for water and vegetation.

Given such diversity, it is difficult to make generalizations about African culture, though several events had profound impact either on the continent as a whole or on vast regions of Africa. The spread of Islam, first in the north between the 7th and 11th centuries, and then in the east between the 12th and 14th centuries, would serve to place the northern section of the continent in Middle Eastern society.

During the Middle Ages, the western coast of Africa, known as the Gold Coast, had furnished two-thirds of the world's gold supply. This lure of riches, and Africa's location en route to the West Indies, made the continent attractive to European mercantilists. By the 16th century, the Portuguese and Dutch had set up outposts in Africa, and the British soon followed. Starting in the mid-1500s and continuing to the mid-1800s, European agrarian and industrial needs would tear western and central African culture apart. During these three centuries, an estimated 10 million black Africans were sold into slavery, primarily to work on the sugar and cotton plantations in Brazil, Latin America, the American South, and the West Indies.

Though the slave trade ended in the mid-1800s, Africa's subservience to Europe continued. From the 1870s to 1914 and the start of World War I, many European nations competed among themselves in what has come to be known as the "Scramble for Africa." Intent on seizing the continent's rich natural resources, creating new markets for industrial goods, and, in many cases, grabbing land that was strategically significant vis-à-vis their rivals, a host of European countries claimed vast areas of Africa as their own. Britain, Germany, Italy, France, Portugal, and Belgium all established colonies where native Africans essentially became subjects of European-run colonial governments. In almost every case, political rule was accompanied by religious control. Christian missionaries established churches throughout Africa and tried to force the indigenous population to abandon its "heathen" culture in exchange for European concepts of God, family, thrift, industry, and so on. Since traditional sports were definitive of indigenous African culture, most were discouraged or banned by missionaries and colonial governments.

SPORTS IN MODERN AFRICA

Because of colonialism and a pervasive European influence, much of Africa has become urban and "modern," which is to say that large groups of people have accepted Western concepts of work, time, and the materialist culture. Families no longer live together in extended clan systems, as many young adults leave to go to work and school in the cities. Many work nine-to-five jobs in factories and offices. They have become part of the corporate culture. Education is based on the Western university system. Newspapers, magazines, and books are readily available, and computers and the Internet have become pervasive in urban Africa.

Within this cultural context, it is not surprising that European sports have become very popular. Soccer, track and field, and basketball are the most common sports played by African men and women today. For men, wrestling and boxing are also popular. Although wrestling has its roots in ancient African culture (see below), boxing was imported from Britain and as in that country, became popular in schools and clubs and as a professional spectator sport.

All of these sports are "organized," in the sense that

- a set of rules for each is written down and enforced;
- they are results-oriented rather than process-oriented, meaning that there are clear-cut winners and losers as a result of play; and
- they are engaged in outside of everyday life, during leisure or free time (e.g., schools or clubs have come together to form leagues and play a series of games which lead to a championship match or series).

These organized sports contrast with traditional African sports, which, as discussed below, are often

- process-oriented, meaning that the activity itself is more important than the end result;
- significant for the collective or group rather than the individual. That is, an individual may be recognized for his or her achievement, but accolades are in the context of role on the team rather than individual glory; and
- embedded in the culture, playing out action that is highly symbolic.

TRADITIONAL SPORTS IN AFRICA IN THE 18TH AND 19TH CENTURIES

During the 18th and 19th centuries, traditional sport in Africa survived and today continues to be played out in those societies that were least touched by European influence. As many of these sports and games are an intrinsic part of everyday life, they are definitive of a people's culture. The following are some of the most common traditional sports.

▦ Wrestling

Several cultures in Africa have rich wrestling traditions. In ancient Egypt, wrestling was a requisite undertaking for all young men. It was considered essential training for war. For the Nuba tribe (Sudan), wrestling was linked to the annual harvest and celebration. To wrestle was to curry the favor of the gods of nature, to give thanks, and to honor one's ancestors. Entire villages would gather to watch a series of matches, where competitors, their bodies smeared with white ash to symbolize the sacred powers derived from the strength of their ancestors, would attempt to throw opponents on their back. Dancing and music preceded the competition, and all those in attendance would be adorned in symbolic jewelry and headdresses. When the matches were over, the whole village would engage in a feast, celebrating the harvest and the continuation of health and prosperity for all.

The Ibo tribe (Nigeria) has a wrestling tradition similar to that of the Nuba. For three months during the harvest season, Ibo men would wrestle every eighth day to placate the harvest gods. An all-day tournament/feast marking the end of the harvest and honoring the corn deity would be staged. For the young Ibo male, wrestling was an initiation to adulthood. Boys became men when they wrestled in these ceremonial matches.

Interestingly, Nuba and Ibo women were allowed to wrestle once a year after the harvest, and their prowess earned them respect and attention from males. In some sections of Gambia, Gabon, and Cameroon, young women also wrestled—in some cultures the family of the best female wrestler would join the family of the champion male wrestler through marriage.

▦ Running

Ancient Egyptian artwork depicts runners, and we know that the Egyptians, like the Greeks and the Romans, engaged in running races. By running, young men developed speed, agility, and strength necessary for fighting. For many other cultures in Africa, running was a way of life. Today's dominance of the world long-distance running scene by Kenyan and Ethiopian athletes is rooted in those nations' cultures. For centuries, pre-teenage boys in the Masai (Kenya and Tanzania) and Kikuyu (Kenya and Ethiopia) tribes have been responsible for tending cattle. Even today, it is not uncommon for a young boy to run 10–20 miles per day roundtrip to the pasture. Once on the job, many boys engage in impromptu races. This high volume of daily running, coupled with East Africa's high altitude, has produced a society of extremely fit endurance runners. British track and field athletes visiting Kenya in the 1920s were shocked to discover the running ability of an average schoolboy. With no formal training and competing in bare feet, scores of Kenyans were running times over

1,500–5,000 meters that would have placed them in contention for British national championship medals.

▦ Jumping

For the Tutsi and Watusi (Rwanda and Burundi), height conveyed a sense of status. Men from these tribes are generally tall. Traditionally, young men in both cultures practiced high jumping as an initiation of sorts. Watusi males became men when they could jump higher than their own height.

▦ Stick Sports and Games

Many tribes fought and hunted with sticks. Similar to the tradition of cudgeling in Europe and Asia, tribes also fought among themselves with sticks to prepare for battle, or as training for the hunt. The Zulus (South Africa) are famous for their two-handed stick fighting, where the combatant uses one stick to fend off or direct an opponent, and the other to club him. We know much about the Zulus' stick-fighting prowess from the writings of the English army, which faced Shaka Zulu, the famous warrior king, in several colonial battles in the mid-19th century.

Other tribes threw sticks and spears. The Baganda tribe (Uganda) threw short 1½-foot sticks for distance. The Masai (Kenya) threw spears for accuracy. One game involved rolling a tree stump or small log down a hill, the object being to spear the log from a distance before it reached the bottom. Many young Masai males practiced this game and similar ones in preparation for their grand initiation rite: the killing of a lion. Because so many Africans hunted out of necessity, we do not consider their hunting to be sport. However, hunting becomes sport when it takes on symbolic significance. In the case of the Masai, young males are sent out in the wilds, armed with only a spear, netting, and their own guile. Similarly, the Nuer (southern Sudan and southwestern Ethiopia) proved their manhood by tracking and running down a gazelle, a process that could take as much as a week or more. Such initiation rites usually demonstrate the mastery of a skill or skill set (speed, endurance, strength, etc.) that will be important to the lifeblood of the community. They are also often respectful of nature and the place of humans within it. For example, to run down a gazelle or to kill a lion with a spear is not easy, and man's ability to do so reaffirms his place vis-à-vis the animal kingdom.

▦ Rowing

The ancient Egyptians were considered pioneer rowers, using galleys for warships and to transport goods up and down the Nile. However, other African cultures raced boats for competition. Such competition was rooted in the pattern and needs of day-to-day work. The Boloki (Congo), Luo (Kenya), and Malagasy (Madagascar) all used a round of racing to test out their boats. The Malagasy, who subsisted by fishing in coastal waters, would race new boats at least a month before the height of fishing season to ensure that they would have time to correct any problems or make repairs.

▦ Ball Games

Both western and eastern African tribes developed their own ball games, which usually involved large groups of players and took on a collective ethos. The Luhyas tribe (Kenya) played a game similar to dodge ball where the object was to keep the ball moving by kicking it back and forth. Success was marked by nonstop play and no one getting hit by or touching the ball without kicking it. The Masai also played a kick-for-distance game, where those men who could kick the ball the farthest were thought to be the wisest in questions involving planting, harvesting, and raising cattle. They used balls made by weaving dried reeds around a rock or a large oval-shaped root. Both the Ashanti and Ibo (Nigeria) were said to play a form of field hockey just before the planting season. The sticks symbolized hoes or similar farming tools, and a gourd or rounded root was used as a ball. Played out on the field that was soon to be sowed, the game enacted a fertility ceremony.

The San (South Africa) also played a cooperative ball game that used a hard rubbery ball made out of the hide of a hippopotamus. The game would begin when one player bounced the ball high off a hardened root or rock. A group of players gathered underneath would jockey for position, shoving each other out of the way to catch the ball. The object of the game was to not let the ball touch the ground.

Bibliography

Baker, William J. (1999). "Traditional Sports, Africa." In David Levinson and Karen Christensen (eds.), *Encyclopedia of World Sport*. New York: Oxford University Press.
Baker, William J., and James A. Mangan (eds.). (1987). *Sport in Africa: Essays in Social History*. New York: Africana.
Dorr, John F., Donald A. Jawger, David L. Moore, and Sherry Wolf. (1971). "Ethnolinguistic Map of the Peoples of Africa." Washington, DC: National Geographic Society.
Iliffe, John. (1995). *Africans: The History of the Continent*. Cambridge: Cambridge University Press.
Van Dalen, D., and B. L. Bennett. (1971). *A World History of Physical Education*. Englewood Cliffs, NJ: Prentice-Hall.
Wagner, Eric A. (ed.). (1989). *Sport in Asia and Africa: A Comparative Handbook*. Westport, CT: Greenwood Press.

▦ ASIA

HISTORICAL OVERVIEW

The 18th and 19th centuries were times of change for the people and institutions of Asia. Prior to this period, imperial dynasties in East Asia had given way to a fragmented system of regional government, in which powerful warlords and their gangs controlled cities and territories. But by the mid-19th century, England controlled the port city of Hong Kong and had opened up China to trade with Western Europe. Japan, too, was experiencing great change. Following the decline of the Shoguns, a growing segment of the population interested in Western democracy, education, and the capitalist economy began to gain influence in the latter half of the 19th century. India, Asia's other vast territory, had also come under British influence. England's East India Tea Company had established a strong presence in India by the mid-18th century. Besides the trade in tea, spice, and textiles, India was strategically positioned at the head of the Indian Ocean—a key base en route to the East Indies and China. Following the disintegration of Muhgal rule in India, the British government enacted legislation that in effect made England—in cooperation with India's princely class—the political and economic ruler of India.

THE LEGACY OF 18TH- AND 19TH-CENTURY SPORTS AND GAMES

Sports and games in Asia during this time reflected traditional culture and the change that was under way on the continent. Martial arts were central to much of Asian culture at the time, and many forms continue to be practiced throughout the world today. Much more than methods of self-defense or survival, martial arts were a way of life for those who practiced them. Grounded in ancient Eastern religion and philosophy, many martial arts required followers to turn inward to assess themselves before acting on the material world, and to balance the strength of mind and body. In general, martial arts not only improved one's physical ability and health, but also created willpower and provided an ongoing spiritual experience or connection. Many people from all classes practiced martial arts in Asia. There were and remain today literally hundreds of different martial arts. This volume describes one of the major forms from which many lesser martial arts have been derived—**Tai Chi**—along with three forms that have become quite popular in the West. **Karate** and **judo** were both developed in Japan during the 18th and 19th centuries, respectively. **Tae kwon do,** a Korean martial art, was formalized in the early 20th century. It is interesting to note that both karate and judo, though practiced by many as simply a form of recreation, exercise, and self-defense, also developed formal rules to govern competition, thus reflecting a Western influence or direction. **Silambam,** a common form of traditional Indian stick fighting, or cudgeling, is also included.

China, Thailand, and Japan also have strong traditions of wrestling and boxing, with most forms of these sports linked to the martial arts as well. Thai boxing, or kick boxing, is one of only two professional sports in modern-day Thailand. **Sumo wrestling,** which is included in this volume, is extremely popular in Japan and has ardent followers throughout the world. Originally part of an annual harvest ritual, sumo wrestling, with its hierarchical ranking system, ritual, and pageantry, grew to define Japanese culture and to link traditional Japan with the modern country. Though there have never been great numbers of sumo wrestlers, sumo became a mass cultural event with the professionalization of the sport in the 18th century. Thousands of Japanese—from commoners to royalty—became paying spectators at a rate that rivaled boxing and soccer in England and baseball in America.

Aerial and water sports were also quite common in Asia—the latter in coastal areas, where communities and economies were built around fishing. Boat sailing and racing throughout the region were linked with fertility rituals in ancient times, and some of these traditional practices continued, particularly in southwestern Asia, where boat racing in the spring still has connections to prospective rainfall necessary for a strong rice crop. **Kite flying** is another ancient Asian rite. Kites were related to national and military myth, were a practical means of fishing, and were symbols of fertility, growth, adulthood, and even courtship.

Raising animals, racing or performing animals, and pitting animals against one another for sport have also been traditional Asian pastimes. Cockfighting, bullfighting (bull vs. bull), goat fighting, and even fish fighting have been popular throughout Southeast Asia among all classes, particularly the working class and the rural and urban poor. Today, these fights are sanctioned and held in special arenas or buildings. Most spectators bet heavily on the outcome. For several centuries, Thai royalty, their descendants, and the country's well-to-do have bred doves for selected characteristics. Recently, this sport has become competitive with the staging of dove-cooing contests. Doves are judged on the quality of voice, singing technique, and duration of song.

While organized horse racing in Asia began only in the 20th century, a tradition of horsemanship in Asian culture dates back many centuries to the influence of the Mongol hordes that invaded much of the continent during the Middle Ages. Nomadic warriors, the Mongols were great horsemen and left their mark on the inner-Asian peoples, particularly in India, Mongolia, Tibet, and northern China, where many traditional sports involved horsemanship and hunting. **Polo,** though formalized and popularized by the British, is derived from the Asian nomadic tradition. England's first contact with the sport came from watching natives of Manipur (India) play. In India, the game was far from a "rich" game—any commoner who owned a horse could play, and most games were held on a town's main street.

By the close of the 19th century, the British and European influence in Asia was being felt throughout the culture, including sports. Western businessmen, professional engineers and builders, commercial sailors, and missionaries all had a hand in introducing such organized sports as hockey, soccer, cricket, badminton, and table tennis to Asian natives. While several former colonial or Third World nations came to dominate one or another Western sport (e.g., India in field hockey, China in table tennis, Malaysia in badminton), others created organized Western-style sports out of traditional Asian games. Such is the case with **sepak takraw,** a game with roots in ancient Southeast Asia which was created in the late 19th and early 20th centuries by adapting rules of badminton and volleyball. Today, the sport is known as "the international ball game of Southeast Asia."

Though barely a century old, the United States also had a significant impact on East Asia. The Philippines, which came under American influence at the end of the 19th century, began playing baseball, softball, basketball, and volleyball—due largely to the establishment of a system of YMCAs in the country.

Bibliography

Trevitheck, Alan. (1999). "Traditional Sports, Asia." In David Levinson and Karen Christensen (eds.), *Encyclopedia of World Sport*. New York: Oxford University Press.

Wagner, Eric A. (ed.). (1989). *Sport in Asia and Africa: A Comparative Handbook*. Westport, CT: Greenwood Press.

▦ Judo

Definition

Judo is an Oriental form of wrestling in which two competitors use movement, balance, and leverage to gain advantage over each other. Originally developed from jujitsu, the Japanese martial arts, judo is regarded as a sport, as a method of self-defense, and as a discipline through which an individual strives to develop his or her abilities and character to achieve self-actualization and ultimately benefit the whole of society.

History

Judo has its roots in the ancient art of combat known as jujitsu, which dates back to before 1000 B.C. Unarmed lama monks in China were said to have developed an early form of jujitsu to protect themselves from robbers as they traveled between villages. We have accounts of the Japanese practicing jujitsu well over 2,000 years ago. In the third century B.C., a jujitsu contest was staged before the Emperor of Japan. The practice thrived among commoners, who, under the empire's old feudal system, were denied the right to bear arms. These poor folk used the techniques of jujitsu to ward off swordsmen by hand. Jujitsu became so popular that by the 16th century several martial arts schools had opened in Japan, and chroniclers, or historians, began to record jujitsu techniques and teachings.

Though jujitsu declined in Japan with the breakdown of the old feudal order in the mid- to late 19th century, judo at the same time began to develop and gain adherents who regarded the sport as symbolic of welcomed Western rationalism and culture. Dr. Jigoro Kano, president of the University of Education in Tokyo, is credited with codifying the rules and techniques of judo in 1882. Having studied jujitsu, Kano was interested in using the ancient practice to create a system for physical culture and moral training. Taking what he considered to be the best jujitsu techniques, Kano adapted and integrated these ancient forms into a sport that could be used to educate people spiritually, mentally, and physically.

Judo, which is translated as the "gentle way," teaches the efficient use of balance, leverage, and economy of movement. Kano's school of judo was known as *Kodokan*, a word which is made up of three characters: *ko* (meaning lecture, study, or method), *do* (way or path), and *kan* (place). Thus *Kodokan* can be translated as "a place to study the way." Such judo principles as "maximum efficiency" and "mutual welfare and benefit" are not only central to the sport but are also applicable in one's dealings with others and society in general. In judo, as in life, one must learn how to give way, rather than use force, and to draw on skill, technique, and timing to overcome a stronger opponent, a difficult force, or a hardship. Judo, therefore, is very different from many other popular martial arts like karate (*see* Karate) or tae kwon do, which use force to overcome an opponent.

Originally judo had no weight classes, as Kano theorized that a judo specialist should be able to use an opponent's weight to his advantage. By mastering an array of throwing, holding, and grappling techniques, the judoist bests his opponent and demonstrates mastery of basic skills. Kano also created a "belt" system to rank competitors by knowledge and ability. Novices begin with a white belt and advance up the ladder, eventually earning a black belt, which is awarded in ten *dans*, or gradations. The eighth *dan* in black belts is the highest competitive degree.

Kano initially had only nine students who trained in a small hall in Eishoji Temple in Tokyo. Yet he gave his sport a boost when 15 of his experts were paired against 15 jujitsu specialists in an exhibition judo tournament in 1886. The judoists won 12 matches and drew 3. Thereafter, judo's prominence as a sport gained rapidly in Japan, and throughout the early 20th century it spread to England and Western Europe. Later United States soldiers stationed in the Far East during World War II were trained in judo techniques, and they brought the sport home to America. Judo was introduced as a demonstration sport for women at the Olympic Games in Tokyo in 1964 and became a regularly contested medal sport in 1972 at Munich. Judo was introduced as a demonstration sport for women at the 1988 Summer Games and as a medal sport in 1992.

The sport retains a strong following in Japan, where the International Judo Center in Tokyo houses a 500-mat practice and competition hall, a judo hall of fame, conference and exhibition facilities, and a 500-seat viewing area. Over a million people visit the center each year.

Equipment

Judo is an inexpensive activity. The only equipment needed is a simple uniform, called a *judogi*, which consists of a white jacket and loose-fitting white trousers, secured by a colored belt signifying the judoist's skill level. (In 2000 major international competitions began using a dress code in which one competitor wears a white *judogi* and the other a blue *judogi*.)

Rules

Judo competitors are typically paired by skill level, with separate weight divisions and age groups for men, women, boys, and girls. Matches are contested on a mat that ranges in size from 14 to 16 meters square, including a red border 3 meters wide, called the danger zone, that marks the boundary of the contest area. Judo contests are officiated by one referee and two judges. International contests last four minutes for women and five minutes for men, though a match ends immediately when a contestant scores an *ippon*. An *ippon*, or a full point, is the equivalent of a pin in wrestling or a knockout in boxing. An *ippon* is scored when a contestant with control throws an opponent on his/her back with considerable force and speed, or when an opponent is held on his/her back, with one or both shoulders pinned to the mat, for a period of 25 seconds. An *ippon* may also be scored when a contestant gives up by tapping twice or more on the mat with his/her hand or foot, generally as a result of an opponent's successful stranglehold or armlock.

If an *ippon* is not scored, the winner is determined by a point system. Points are scored in the following ways:

Waza-ari is scored when a contestant throws his/her opponent, but the technique is lacking one of the elements necessary for an *ippon*, or when a contestant holds his/her opponent for 20 seconds or more, but less than 25 seconds.

Yuko is scored when a contestant throws his/her opponent, but the technique is lacking in two of the three elements necessary for an *ippon*, or when a contestant holds his/her opponent for 15 seconds or more, but less than 20 seconds.

Koka is scored when a contestant throws his/her opponent onto his/her thighs or buttocks with force, or when a contestant holds his/her opponent for 10 seconds or more, but less than 15 seconds.

The winner of the contest is not determined by total points, but rather by who scores the most moves which hold the highest value. For example, a *yuko* has a higher value than a *koka*. If one contestant scores two *yukos* and one *koka*, and the other scores one *yuko* and seven *koka*, the judoist who earned two *yukos* would be declared the winner. If the score is tied at the end of competition, the referee and judges determine the winner based on technique.

Bibliography

"Judo: The Basic Techniques and Competition." (2000). Judo Info.com Web site, *www.judoinfo.com* (January 2, 2001).

Tegner, Bruce. (1967). *The Complete Book of Judo*. New York: Bantam Books.

▥ Juggling

Definition

Juggling is the art of tossing and catching or manipulating objects, keeping them in constant motion. Though juggling has roots in ancient Egypt and medieval Europe, the pastime as we know it today was heavily influenced by 19th-century Asian performing arts, and, subsequently, vaudeville and circus shows in Europe and America at the turn of the century. Today, there are thousands of expert jugglers around the world.

History

The earliest known depiction of a juggler is from the tomb of an unknown ancient Egyptian prince dating back to about 2000 B.C. The earliest written reference to juggling is from the Chinese *Book of Lie Zi*, written during the Warring States Period (475–221 B.C.) and attributed to Lie Yukou, describing a figure from an earlier period who juggled seven swords. Other accounts of early juggling indicate that the activity was practiced in ancient times in Japan, Southeast Asia, Persia (modern-day Iran), and Tibet. Juggling in these early cultures seems to have been linked to religious ceremonies or primitive rituals.

Juggling was enjoyed by Greeks and Romans as well, who lumped jugglers under an umbrella that also included knife-throwers (*ventilatores*) and ball players in general (*pilarii*). During the Middle Ages, juggling in Europe was often combined with other forms of entertainment like magic and acrobatics. The French used the term *jongleurs*, which included singers. In England, the traveling minstrel and juggler were for a time interchangeable.

The earliest reference to juggling as a specialized art didn't occur until 1832, when a Chinese juggler, Lau Laura, performed at Drury Lane in England. The early Oriental jugglers were said to have been extremely influential in the development of juggling in Europe. However, very little was written about them, probably because they were a minority group in Europe, considered outsiders by the common citizen. Their skill seems to have been underestimated, perhaps because, as foreigners, they were thought to have natural talent or inbred ability to perform what was clearly not a natural activity.

The brand of juggling the Chinese brought to the West had much to do with performing arts. Chinese juggling consisted largely of balancing feats. In one trick, a large trident was rolled on the body in a variety of ways. Most Chinese juggling was paired with contortions and acrobatic feats. Another routine involved the manipulation and handling of large balls of twine or yarn.

Whereas the Asian way of juggling was subtle and artistic, the European forms that grew out of it in the mid- to late 19th century tended to be showy and more suited to the circus. One common form of juggling included *jongleurs de force*, or "weight juggling," where practitioners would work with heavy objects like cannonballs. One performer, known as Spadoni, entered the ring dressed as a Roman on a chariot. After dismissing the horses, Spadoni would proceed to balance the chariot on his head. "Salon juggling" was also popular. In this form, the juggler, who would stage his act in a restaurant or inn, would work with common objects often found in a drawing room, like hats, canes, bouquets, books, and so on. Several other forms of juggling were directly related to the circus: equestrian juggling, where a juggler would perform while standing on the back of a moving horse; antipodism, in which a juggler lies on his back and juggles objects with his feet; and group juggling, where teams of jugglers—often family members in a circus company—juggle objects back and forth.

In the United States, juggling grew to be an essential component of vaudeville, a form of variety entertainment that dominated popular culture in the late 19th and early 20th centuries. Prior to motion pictures, every city and most towns in the United States had a vaudeville house or auditorium that hosted a regular schedule of shows. These shows included comedy or drama, music, dancing, and always a "dumb act," such as juggling, acrobatics, or magic. These acts—called "dumb" because they used no speech—were visual, requiring the audience's full attention. As such, they were almost always scheduled at the start of the show to help quiet the crowd. The best jugglers on the vaudeville circuit could work for years perfecting the same 10-minute act.

With the decline of circuses and vaudeville in the United States and Europe, juggling too suffered a decline in the 20th century. The International Jugglers Association (IJA) was created out of concern for preserving the art of juggling. Today, the IJA has over 4,000 members in more than 50 countries.

Equipment

The most basic juggling objects include balls, rings, and clubs. Other cultures, particularly the Chinese and Japanese, use very different objects. The Japanese roll objects around the rim of a parasol. These objects are often uneven in shape, and the performer delights in rolling them as slowly as possible along the edge of the parasol. The Japanese have also perfected the art of *ken dama*, which essentially involves the catching of a ball with a hole in it on a pointed stick. A short string connects the ball and the stick. This act can appear highly choreographed, as the juggler executes unexpected tosses and catches.

The Chinese are famous for ceramic vase tossing, a difficult and dangerous feat where heavy vases are tossed and caught, usually on the forehead. The Chinese have also introduced the devil stick and the diabolo to the juggling world. The devil stick, a long, thin wooden stick, is spun, tossed, and caught by manipulating it with two other sticks held in each hand. The diabolo is cylindrical, thin in the middle, and rolls along a string attached at each end to sticks held in both hands. By whipping the string from side to side, the diabolo is spun around and can be rolled, tossed, or caught on the string. Accomplished practitioners can manipulate three diabolos on one string simultaneously.

Rules

In an activity like juggling, there are no rules per se, although competitors at the annual IJA Championships must observe some basic guidelines regarding the manipulation of objects. The principal goal of most competitions involves trying to juggle as many objects as possible. Competitors have to juggle a certain number of objects before attempting a higher number.

In general, there are three basic paths, or patterns, that jugglers follow in manipulating props:

Cascade Pattern: The cascade is the commonest pattern. Balls or other props follow a horizontal figure-eight pattern above the hands.

Fountain Pattern: In the fountain pattern, each hand throws balls straight up into the air and each ball is caught in the same hand that throws it.

Shower Pattern: For any number of props greater than two, the shower pattern is the most difficult. In the shower pattern, every ball is thrown in a high arc from the right hand to the left (or vice versa) and then quickly passed off with a low throw from the left to the right hand (or vice versa).

Bibliography

Dingman, Richard. (1996). *The Ultimate Juggling Book*. Philadelphia: Running Press.
Lewbel, Arthur. (1995). "Research in Juggling History." Juggling Information Service Web site, *www.juggling.org/papers/history-1/* (April 25, 2001).
"A Primer on the History of Juggling in America." (1987). *Juggler's World* Vol. 39, No. 2, Juggling Information Service Web site, *www.juggling.org/jw/87/2/vaudeville.html* (April 25, 2001).
Truzzi, Marcello, with Massimiliano Truzzi. (1974). "Notes Toward a History of Juggling." *Bandwaggon* (Vol. 18, No. 2, March–April 1974).

▦ Karate

Definition

Karate is a martial art of unarmed self-defense in which directed blows of the hands and feet are dealt to an opponent's head, face, neck, abdomen, chest, back, and side. Developed in Japan during the 17th century, karate today is practiced all around the world as a method of self-defense, as a competitive sport, and as a fitness exercise.

History

"Karate" means "empty hand" in Japanese. Though historians speculate that karate has much the same Chinese roots as many of the other "self-defense" martial arts, meaning that it is over 1,000 years old, there is little evidence that the sport was practiced on a large scale in Japan until the 17th and 18th centuries. By that time it had become highly developed as almost an art form on the island of Okinawa, Japan.

Karate is similar to judo, except that there is an emphasis on striking an opponent with kicks and punches rather than relying on balance and wrestling-like technique to throw an opponent (*see* Judo). Good karate technique is dependent on intense concentration on one's opponent, as well as speed, strength, and timing. The ability to anticipate an opponent's move and preempt it and to incorporate the element of surprise in an attack are vital karate skills.

In Japan, karate has for many years been a national practice of sorts. By the late 19th century, the Japanese military was using karate as a form of basic training for all soldiers and officers. In 1922 Funakoshi Gichin, a karate specialist from Okinawa, introduced the sport to the Japanese public. Beginning in the 1920s, karate was taught in high school physical education classes throughout the country, and in 1936 Funakoshi opened the first karate training hall, or *dojo*, in Tokyo. Yet during Japan's war with China (1937–1945), government officials frowned on the sport for its Chinese roots and stopped teaching karate to military recruits.

The sport did not make a comeback until after World War II, and in a much different form. Funakoshi's sons devised a form of karate in which punches and kicks were no longer delivered but rather "pulled" back. This noncontact form of karate has become quite popular, both within Japan and throughout the Western world. Though a counter-movement began in the 1980s to revive full-contact karate, this has for the most part been resisted by officials, clubs, and the majority of competitors, who consider lethal techniques to be in strict opposition to the foundations of the sport. In 1957 the Japanese Karate Association standardized the rules of karate. Today, karate is commonly taught in schools or clubs run by specialists. In the United States, karate is practiced as a competitive sport and as a popular method of self-defense. Each year, hundreds of tournaments are held throughout America. Among the most prestigious are the American Championships of the Japan Karate Association, which are usually held in California or Hawaii, and the All-American Open Karate Championships, held annually at Madison Square Garden in New York.

Since the early 1970s, karate has been the most popular and widespread of the Asian martial arts. Today, an estimated 15 million people worldwide practice some form of karate.

Equipment

Competitors wear a white *gi*, or uniform, which consists of a jacket worn over loose-fitting cotton pants. Either a red or white belt must be worn over the jacket to distinguish between the two competitors. Thin gloves and mouthpieces are mandatory. Many contestants also wear soft shin pads. Plastic shin guards or any other hard-shelled guards used for protection are forbidden.

Rules

All matches occur on a square mat measuring at least 10 × 10 meters, with the competition area actually constituted by an 8 × 8 meter border. A referee administers the match, with assistance from a scorekeeper and a timekeeper.

Matches last three minutes for senior men (age 20 and over) and two minutes for women and juniors. The first competitor to receive three full points, or *ippons*, is the winner. Half-points, or *waza-ari*, are also scored. Though two *waza-ari* equal one *ippon*, in technical terms a *waza-ari* is equal to 90 percent of an *ippon*. An *ippon* may be awarded in one of two ways:

1. A move is performed with "good form," "correct attitude," "vigorous application," "perfect finish," "proper timing," and "correct distance"; or
2. A move is deficient in one of the above criteria but conforms to one or more of the following:
   - exhibits a technically difficult technique;
   - deflects an attack and scores to the unguarded back of an opponent;
   - exhibits a sweeping or throwing move followed by a scoring technique;
   - delivers a combination technique, the components of which each score in their own right; or
   - successfully scores at the same moment the opponent attacks.

A *waza-ari* is awarded for a commendable technique that rates slightly lower than an *ippon*.

In general, if neither competitor has scored three *ippons*, the total number of *ippons* and *waza-ari* is considered, along with such intangibles as attitude, spirit, and strength, as well as overall display of tactics and techniques. In some cases, a draw is declared; in others, the judge declares a winner, referred to as *hantei*. When two teams have won the same number of bouts, a competitor from each team must contest a sudden-death extension bout, or *encho-sen*, where the first to score an *ippon* or *waza-ari* is declared the winner.

More than 200 terms are used to describe specific blows, blocking and kicking techniques, and combinations of moves. Competitors spend time studying the human body and gaining expertise regarding the points above the waist that are most vulnerable. In competition, attacks are limited to the head, face, neck, abdomen, chest, back (excluding the shoulders), and side.

Competitors also spend a good deal of time performing stretching and strengthening exercises. Stretching keeps the body supple and able to perform kicks that are vital for attack and defense. The hands, legs, and feet also need to be strong, and many specialists regularly practice with sand-filled kick bags, heavy bags, and striking boards. Focus is also placed on concentration techniques, centering oneself, and marshalling strength for precise, explosive bursts of energy and movement.

Bibliography

Frederic, Louis. (1991). *A Dictionary of the Martial Arts*. Rutland, VT: Charles Tuttle Press.

Peiser, Benny Joseph. (1996). "Western Theories About the Origins of Sport in Ancient China." *Sports Historian* Vol. 16, pp. 136–162.

United States Olympic Committee. (2001). "Karate Online." USOC Olympics Online, *www.usoc.org/* (March 2, 2001).

▦ Kite Flying

Definition

Kite flying is the practice of using the power of wind to lift and keep aloft an object called a kite. Most kites are made of light wood framing and paper or light fabric and attached to a long string held by a person on the ground. Kites originated in China over 2,000 years ago and were adapted by many cultures throughout Asia. In the United States, kites have been popular with scientists, meteorologists, and millions of children.

History

Kite flying predates written history in China. Folklore tells a story about a famous Chinese general who in 200 B.C. was in command of a rebel army attempting to overthrow a corrupt emperor. By flying a kite over the emperor's palace, the general was able to mark on the kite string the distance to the palace courtyard. This information enabled the rebel forces to dig a tunnel into the palace, through which they entered at night and defeated the evil emperor's men. A more fantastic version of this story has the general's men strapping him to the kite and flying him over the enemy fortress at night. By speaking to the enemy forces as if he were a wise spirit, the general was able to convince his opponents to lay down their weapons and flee.

Kites were also common among the people of the South Sea Islands, who used them in fishing. Bait was attached to the tail of the kite, along with a net in which to catch fish. Similar practices are followed today by fishermen in the Solomon Islands in the Pacific. Kites have also been invested with religious significance. The Maori, indigenous peoples to what today is New Zealand, believed that birds could carry messages to the gods. They would make kites in the shape of birds and fly them to placate or entreat the gods. In some instances, the kites represented gods themselves.

During the 6th to 8th centuries A.D., it is believed that kite flying was brought from China and Korea to Japan. It is speculated that Buddhists priests introduced the kite at religious festivals. Certainly, early kite flying in Japan carried much religious symbolism. Kites were designed in a variety of shapes and colors, often depicting lucky or fortuitous birds and animals that were said to bring good luck, ensure prosperity, or frighten away evil spirits. In the 18th century, kites were flown throughout Japan as part of an annual harvest ritual. The Japanese believed that the flight of a kite could predict the success or failure of crops, and kites were flown in the fall as a gesture of thanksgiving for a plentiful harvest. Kites were also sold at Shinto temples and shrines for use as charms against illness or bad luck.

Though kites began to lose their religious significance in the 19th century, they continued to be part and parcel of many festivals and religious holidays throughout Asia. In Korea, it is a tradition to write the names and birthdates of male children on kites and then to fly them. The kite line is then cut to guarantee a good year, as the kite is presumed to take all the bad spirits away with it. Throughout the 19th century, a boys' festival was celebrated in many parts of Japan on May 5. If a male child had been born to a household in the preceding year, a kite was flown to celebrate. All households with male children would also fly windsocks (a small, narrow type of kite shaped in the design of a sock). These windsocks would often carry an insignia of a carp, known as a hardy fish, able to battle upstream against the current. The carp symbolized courage and strength—important traits for a young boy to have as he learned how to cope with the challenges of life. Today this festival includes girls and is called Children's Day.

Kites have also had many uses—both pleasurable and practical—in the Western world. Kites were employed by engineers in Europe to move materials and take measurements over difficult or inaccessible terrain such as river gorges. During the mid-18th century, scientists began conducting experiments to measure temperatures at varying altitudes. To do this, they would fly several kites in a train, with thermometers attached to each kite. Benjamin Franklin's experiment with electricity is perhaps the most famous American kite story. In 1752 Franklin sought to illustrate the electrical properties of lightning by attaching a key with a strand of silk ribbon to the end of the kite's line. During an electrical storm, Franklin stood in the doorway of his laboratory and watched as lightning struck the kite and shot an electrical current down the line. Later in the 19th century, scientists and engineers used kites to gain a better understanding of aerodynamic principles that eventually led to the development of the airplane.

Though kite flying in the contemporary world has been hindered by the proliferation of utility lines and high-rise buildings, the sport has made a comeback in America since the 1960s and 1970s. Lightweight synthetic materials have made kites cheaper and, in many cases, easier to fly; and kite flying has grown to be regarded as an ideal activity to be shared by parents and their children.

Equipment

Kites have a sturdy, lightweight framing, usually made of wood or fiberglass and covered with light, durable cloth or paper to catch the wind. Most kites also have a tail, often made of various pieces of material, to increase drag. This lends stability to the kite, helping to keep it aloft. Kites are usually brightly colored with lively drawings—the art on a kite is at times as interesting as the act of flying it.

There are a number of different types of kites:

Flat Kite: the most popular and traditional kite design, usually in the shape of a diamond or square.

Bow Kite: similar to the flat kite, but with bowed or slightly bent cross-sticks that give it more stability. The bow kite may be indigenous to Malaysian fishermen.

Box Kite: a three-dimensional framework—usually square or rectangular—with paper wrapping. The box kite is popular in traditional China and Korea.

Soft Kite: a kite lacking a framework, or possessing extremely flexible framing.

Stunt Kite: a kite with two or more lines, which provide maximum control for trick flying.

How to Fly a Kite

A kite flies as a result of the interaction between wind and thermal air currents that hit its surface and are divided into areas of high and low pressure. These differences in pressure cause the kite to rise. Kite fliers talk about the opposing forces of "lift" and "drag," which must be kept in balance in order to keep the kite aloft. Many kites, particularly the lighter designs, need a tail (often made of pieces of material), which is attached to the bottom of the kite to increase drag.

Kite Fighting

Kite fighting is a variation of kite flying and is popular throughout India, China, and Japan. Kite strings are coated with shards of glass or pottery, sharp sand, or even tiny knife blades, and the kites are flown in an attempt to cross and cut an opponent's kite line. Though seemingly violent to the Western observer, kite fighting is actually regarded as wholesome sport by the cultures in which it is practiced. It is surmised that kite fighters regard the sport as an escape from formal society and a respite from the harsh living conditions common to rural Asia.

Bibliography

Hart, Clive. (1967). *Kites: An Historical Survey*. Mt. Vernon, NY: Paul P. Appel.
Hosking, Wayne. (1990). *Flights of Imagination: An Introduction to Aerodynamics*. Washington, DC: National Science Teachers Association.

————. (1992). *Kites*. New York: Mallard Press.

Pelham, David. (1976). *The Penguin Book of Kites*. New York: St. Martin's Press.

▦ Polo

Definition

Polo is a game played on horseback between two teams of four players each, using long-handled mallets to drive a small wooden ball downfield and into the opponent's goal for a score. Polo originated in ancient Persia (modern-day Iran) as far back as 2,500 years ago, before spreading across the central plains of Asia to India, Tibet, and China. Today the game is played professionally and on amateur levels and has gained acceptance throughout the world. Polo is now played in about 40 nations.

History

Polo is perhaps one of the world's oldest team sports, with some version of the game being played by nomadic warriors in Asia over two thousand years ago. Polo was considered excellent training for soldiers on horseback, and it was through war that the sport spread across Asia during ancient times through the Middle Ages. Touted in the East as the "Game of Kings," polo was a symbol of power and the ultimate test of cavalry prowess. Alexander the Great, upon his ascendancy to the throne as the king of Macedonia (336 B.C.), was presented with a polo mallet and ball by the emperor of Persia, Darius III. Darius included a message with his gift that counseled Alexander to stick to sport, and leave the business of war to those who could handle it. Alexander replied by invoking the polo mallet as a symbol of himself and the ball as representative of the earth that he planned to conquer.

Timur Lang (Tamerlane), the 14th-century Mongol emperor, kept ornate polo grounds. Their remains may still be seen in Samarkand. In India, Babar, the founder of the Mughal dynasty in the 15th century, made polo into a national game of sorts. Polo was regularly played at the royal court, and noblemen patronized the game throughout the kingdom. The name "polo" was derived from the Tibetan word *pulu*, meaning "ball." Though polo suffered a setback with the decline of the Mughal dynasty in the 18th century, the game continued to be played in the mountainous regions of India, particularly in the remote northeastern states of Manipur and Gilgit (in present-day Pakistan).

In Manipur, the game was played in most villages, with few rules and the number of players limited only by the number of horses available (see illustration). A long, narrow village main street was usually used for a field. Play was extremely fast and rough. Players protected their legs by attaching leather shields to their saddles and girths. Still, death was a com-

Figure 1. Natives of Manipur, India, playing a game of polo. (© Bettmann/COR-BIS)

mon occurrence in a game that was considered by this nomadic culture as the supreme test of courage and horsemanship.

The British were introduced to polo in the mid-19th century when military officers and tea planters in India witnessed the game being played by Manipuri tribesmen. Military officers imported the game to England in the 1860s. These cavalrymen drew up the sport's first rules. Soon polo clubs were established by the elite throughout south England and western Europe.

It should be noted that "Europeanized" polo played in the late 19th century was very different from that which was played in Manipur. The game was slow and methodical, with little passing between players and few set plays that required specific movements by participants without the ball. Neither players nor horses were trained to play a fast, nonstop game. In fact, the concept of a good polo horse at that time was one that could stop on a dime to allow its mount to get a clean hit. This brand of polo was no match for those with superlative equestrian skills and aggressive methods of play. From the 1880s to the 1910s, a host of teams representing Indian principalities dominated the international polo scene. Indian maharajas (descendants of royalty) were said to have "polo in their blood," and it was their success and skill that the British emulated.

Three segments of the British population are generally credited with spreading organized polo worldwide in the late 19th and early 20th century. While the aristocracy introduced polo to royalty and the elite classes in Europe, it was Britain's army and naval officers who brought the game to Australia, New Zealand, and South Africa. British ranchers exported the game to South America, where it became extremely popular in Argentina. With an endless supply of horses and miles of flat pampas land on which to play, Argentina was ideally suited for the game, and, in fact, Argentines have dominated world play since the mid-20th century.

Polo also became popular in the United States. In 1876 James Gordon Bennett, publisher of the *New York Herald* and a noted adventurer (at the time, he held several long-distance ballooning records), brought the sport to New York, where it was embraced by the old and new moneyed classes alike. By the 1890s, there were major polo clubs all along the East Coast, including such affluent communities as Newport, Rhode Island, and the Hamptons on Long Island.

Though British players dominated the international polo scene starting in the early 20th century, it might be said that the proverbial "death and taxes" did them in. First, England lost most of its prominent players as a result of World War I. Then, with the advent of World War II and the bombing of London, the government levied higher progressive taxes to sustain and rebuild the nation, thus cutting the discretionary spending of the upper classes. Many could no longer afford to spend a fortune on breeding and caring for a stable of polo ponies.

It was during this time that polo enjoyed its "Golden Age" in America. Throughout the 1930s and 1940s, crowds in excess of 30,000 regularly attended international matches at Meadowbrook Polo Club on Long Island, and such stars as Cecil Smith, a Texas cowboy, and Tommy Hitchcock, a war hero, attained perfect 10 goal handicaps (see page 29).

Today, India, Argentina, the United States, and Britain field the best international polo teams, and the sport's oldest, preeminent events are held in these countries, including the Argentine Open, the U.S. Open, and the Coronation Cup in England. While polo is still popular among the country club set, all of the sport's best players are professionals. Each year, a pro circuit of 30 to 40 teams, made up of players from North and South America, Europe, Oceania, and North and South Africa, plays a series of matches leading up to seasonal championships. Play takes place during the winter in Palm Beach, Florida; during the summer at Hurlingham, England; and in the fall in Buenos Aires, Argentina.

Equipment

In the Western world, polo has always been a game of the affluent. Horses are extremely important in polo, and most of the sport's expense involves breeding and training fast, maneuverable thoroughbred horses. Because of the large size of the playing field and the general speed of play, all competitors change horses after each period of play. It is not uncommon for a championship player to bring several horses to a match.

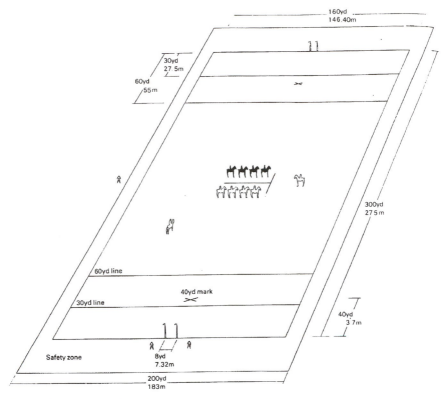

Figure 2. Modern polo field. (Reproduced from *Rules of the Game,* by the Diagram Group [New York: St. Martin's Press, 1990], p. 274.)

Basic polo equipment includes a mallet, ball, and protective gear. The ball, which was formerly made of wood, is now constructed of hard plastic, measuring about 3–3½ inches in diameter and weighing between 3½ and 4½ ounces. The mallet has a wooden head and a thin, flexible bamboo or graphite handle, measuring 47–54 inches long. Players wear helmets and knee pads, while all horses wear leg bandages for protection.

Rules

The standard polo field measures 160 yards wide and 300 yards long (see illustration). Polo goals consist of two uprights, eight yards wide and placed at the end of each field on the center of the end line. Play is divided into eight seven-minute periods, or "chukkas." There is a three-minute rest interval between each period and a five-minute halftime. Play is continuous, with stoppage occurring only in the event of an injury or penalty. The object of the game is to score goals by hitting the ball between the goalposts, no matter how high in the air. The basic pattern of play, which is fast and fluid, is similar to soccer, though there are few set plays. Players take forward and backward strokes, sending the ball from beneath the horse's neck or belly, and from behind its tail. Teams have four players, each with a different function related to defending or sweeping the field, passing or moving the ball upfield, and shooting and scoring.

A central concept of polo is the right-of-way rule, which establishes a path ahead of the player and in the direction in which he is riding. The right-of-way allows players to hit the ball on the offside (right side) of the horse, and there is a short list of dos and don'ts regarding accessing or crossing the right-of-way. Within limitations, a player can hook an opponent's mallet, push him off the right-of-way, bump him with his horse, and steal the ball from him.

Polo games are played with or without handicapping. All registered players are given a skill rating of between (-2) and 10. When two teams meet, the sum total ratings of the players on each team are compared and subtracted from one another. The difference is awarded to the lower-rated team, which then begins the game with an advantage in goals.

Bibliography

"The Evolution of Polo." (2000). IndiaPolo.com Web site, *www.indiapolo.com/* (March 11, 2001).

"The Mists of Time: Origins of Polo." (2000). IndiaPolo.com Web site, *www.india polo.com/* (March 11, 2001).

"Polo Facts and Figures." United States Polo Association Web site, *www.uspolo.org/* (January 20, 2001).

Worth, Sylvia (ed.). (1990). *The rules of the Game*. New York: St. Martin's Press.

"Princely India." (2000). IndiaPolo.com Web site, *www.indiapolo.com/* (March 11, 2001). United States Polo Association.

"Outdoor Rules of Play." United States Polo Association Web site, *www.uspolo.org/* (January 20, 2001).

▥ Sepak Takraw

Definition

Sepak takraw is Thai for "kick" and "woven ball," which defines the gist of this team sport that is known today as the international ball game of Southeast Asia. Two teams of three players each use their feet and head to volley a rattan or plastic ball back and forth over a net and on a court that is regulation size for badminton. Though the sport, in general, follows volleyball rules, it is derived from a centuries-old folk practice.

History

Games resembling sepak takraw were played as early as the 11th century throughout much of Southeast Asia, including areas that today are

Thailand, the Philippines, Malaysia, Singapore, Brunei, Myanmar, Indonesia, and Laos. Marco Polo is even said to have brought back a game from China in which individuals or groups kicked a round object into the air. The traditional game was played by villagers, with the object being to dribble the ball back and forth in the air between one another and count the number of dribbles or kicks. Similar to modern-day hackey sack, the goal of early sepak takraw play was to build a sense of teamwork and shared community. Historically, the sport's cultural importance is underscored by the frequency with which sepak takraw was played at festivals and celebrations. The sport's popularity was noted in the Philippines during Spanish colonization in the 18th century and later during American occupation of the islands during the late 19th and early 20th centuries. Sepak takraw (referred to as *sipa* in the Philippines) continued to be a popular pastime at weddings, harvest festivals, and village fiestas. Today this traditional circle game is still played throughout Southeast Asia—by schoolchildren and adults, by rural residents and city dwellers—and is fittingly regarded as a sport for all.

The modern game really didn't take shape until the late 19th century. Various areas of Southeast Asia claim credit for introducing the net to the game, with dates ranging from the 1880s to the 1920s. For example, the state of Negeri Sembilan in Malaysia is said to have introduced the net game in 1915 at an exhibition in honor of England's King George V during his Silver Jubilee Celebration. Though Malaysians claim that this was the first time that the game was played using a badminton net and badminton rules, with players on both sides of the net, it is unlikely that so many changes to the game could have occurred simultaneously in one place. The net game continued to grow in popularity during the 1930s and 1940s—particularly in high schools—until 1945, when a trio of players from Penang, Malaysia, wrote down the rules of sepak jaring ("kick the net") and played the first exhibition game. These rules were standardized in 1960 when a group of takraw organizations from Singapore, Malaysia, and Thailand came together to agree on uniform regulations for the sport and a common name—sepak takraw. This marked the birth of the Southeast Asian Games Federation, which began sanctioning international championship competition in 1965.

Though sepak takraw has gained little popularity in the United States (a smattering of colleges have students who play the game on an intramural and club level), it is wildly popular in Southeast Asia. There millions of boys and girls and men and women play the game at various levels all the way up to world class at the Asian Games.

Equipment

Sepak takraw balls were originally woven from rattan. Woven synthetic balls were introduced in Thailand in 1982, and this mass production has revolutionized the sport by making sepak takraw accessible to many more

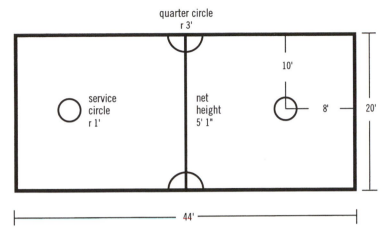

Figure 3. Sepak takraw court.

players. Like soccer balls in this country, sepak takraw balls are manufactured in different sizes and weights to suit the maturity of all players; a beginning player uses a ball weighing 140 grams, and a ball for advanced play weighs 175 grams. A women's sepak takraw ball is slightly smaller than a men's regulation-size ball. In general, the tightness of the ball's weave determines its responsiveness. A soft ball has less bounce, whereas a tight ball will have maximum bounce, or spring. Uniforms are similar to those worn in volleyball. Footwear is extremely important. Most players wear shoes with a flat instep, such as low-cut tennis or basketball shoes.

Rules

Sepak takraw courts are standard in size, measuring 44 feet long by 20 feet wide (see illustration). A net is strung across center court at a height of 5 feet, 1 inch from the top of the net to the floor. Each half of the court has a service circle, measuring 2 feet in diameter, which is located about 8 feet from the back line and 10 feet from the side boundary.

Teams consist of three players, with the object of the game being to spike the ball into the opponent's court. Rules are essentially the same as for volleyball, with the following exceptions:

- Players are prohibited from using their hands.
- A player is allowed to touch the ball three consecutive times.
- Player positions on the defensive team are not rotated.
- A served ball that hits the net is considered in play.

A sepak takraw match consists of three sets. The first team to score 15 points wins a set. The first team to win two sets wins a match. If a set is tied at 13, the first team to reach 13 points may choose to decide the set through a 5-point match; if the teams are tied at 14, the first team to reach 14 points may choose to decide the set by playing a 3-point match.

Much of the game's terminology is identical to volleyball's. In sepak takraw one serves and blocks; there are digs and dinks; set-up specialists are called "feeders," while players who spike the ball are known as "killers."

The game demands a high level of hand-eye coordination, balance, and flexibility. Just imagine playing volleyball without your hands and you'll realize the high degree of kicking skill developed by the top players. Though a spike may be executed by hitting the ball with either the foot or the head, two of the game's most exciting moves involve kick spikes. In a roll spike, the player jumps with his back to the net, rotates in the air, and kicks the ball over the shoulder opposite from the kicking foot. In a sun-back spike, the player jumps with his back to the net and kicks the ball over the shoulder on the same side as the kicking foot. The latter move is known as a bicycle kick in soccer.

Bibliography

"A Brief History of Sepak Raga." (2000). Gaja Takraw Industries Web site, *www* *.gajahmas.com/* (February 8, 2001).

Douglas, Stephen A. (1989). "Sport in Malaysia." In Eric A. Wagner (ed.), *Sport in Asia and Africa: A Comparative Handbook.* Westport, CT: Greenwood Press.

International Sepak Takraw Federation. (1996). "The Rules of Sepak Takraw." International Sepak Takraw Web site, *www.sepaktakraw.com/* (February 8, 2001).

———. (2000). "Takraw: A Game of Yesterday, Today and the Future" and "A Glossary of Terminology." International Sepak Takraw Web site, *www.sepak-takraw.com/* (February 8, 2001).

▓ Silambam

Definition

Silambam, promoted as a method of self-defense, is believed to be the oldest form of scientific staff fencing in the world, with origins dating back to ancient India. Practitioners coordinate swift foot movement with the use of a long staff, or stave, which is swung, thrust, or used in a reflexive defensive action. As with many of the other Eastern martial arts, practicing silambam also has quasi-spiritual implications related to the fusion of meditation, or concentration, and physical movement.

History

The state of Tamil Nadu in southern India is believed to be the birthplace of silambam. According to literature dating back to the 1st or 2nd century A.D., royalty in Tamil Nadu promoted silambam. Fighting with long staffs was a highly organized sport in the royal court, and seems to have been considered a divine practice. Tamil mythology cites staff fencing as a creation of the gods, and silambam seems to have been practiced for ritualistic purposes. The staves of the very best fencers were given names. Young men of all classes were also trained to defend themselves with staves, both as a ritual and in the event of an emergency.

The ancient trading center of Maduri City in southern India served as a focal point for the spread of silambam. There, Romans, Greeks, and Egyptians obtained the prized silambam staff and took it back to Europe, the Middle East, and throughout northern Africa. The Tamil Kingdom, which encompassed southern India and Sri Lanka, also spread silambam throughout Southeast Asia. Today, people in Malaysia, Thailand, Indonesia, and the Philippines practice silambam for recreation and self-defense. During the 18th and 19th centuries, the sport was much more prevalent in Southeast Asia than in India, where the British banned martial arts during colonial rule.

Silambam's popularity—first in India and then throughout Southeast Asia—has much to do with its spiritual links to Hinduism and Buddhism. Physical perfection or self-realization through an understanding and control of the body and its functions is an integral part of Hinduism. Both Indian yoga and silambam encompass techniques associated with breathing control, correct body posture, and meditation. These very same techniques were espoused by the Buddhist pilgrims in the Far East and have much in common with the Eastern martial arts (*see* Tai Chi; Karate; Judo).

Equipment

As discussed above, the staves are central to the sport of silambam and, in a classic sense, have ritual significance. Made of wood, most measure about four feet. Some staves are adorned with balls of cloth at one end.

Practitioners generally wear loose clothing that allows for movement. Silambam competitors wear long pants, sleeveless vests, turbans, tennis or court shoes, and a light chest guard. Competitors also use a wicker shield, which is usually affixed to the back of the forearm/wrist.

Rules

Though many people practice the movements of silambam as a form of recreation, silambam is also a competitive sport in India and Southeast Asia. In general, competitors use both their hands and feet. Fast foot movement either to create a large sphere of control or to establish a defensive posture is crucial. Competitors may use both hands to wield the stave. The object is to master the ability to create momentum, while directing the stave with precision. Typical movements involve cutting, chopping, thrusting, and sweeping. Competitors must also concentrate on and anticipate an opponent's movements in order to impose a series of defensive postures and fake strokes.

There are generally three types of contests: a duel to the finish, when one competitor loses his stave; a contest in which a competitor must guard an object placed at his feet; and a competition involving the touches one opponent leaves on another during a set period of time. The latter contest is the most common today. The ends of the staves are coated with a sticky powder that leaves a mark on an opponent. Generally, one mark counts one point, though in some variations a mark above the waist counts two points. In some areas, the winner is the one who makes a mark on his opponent's back, whereas other versions of this competition award the win to the first competitor who scores three touches. Play usually lasts 6 to 10 minutes and is divided into four equal quarters.

Silambam is contested on a flat, hard surface that provides good footing. The area of play is usually circular, typically measuring between 40 and 50 feet in diameter.

Bibliography

Hick, Steve. (1999). "Cudgeling." In David Levinson and Karen Christensen (eds.), *The Encyclopedia of World Sport*. New York: Oxford University Press.

"Martial Arts: Silambam." (1997). India Past and Present Web site, *http:// library.thinkquest.org/11372* (February 9, 2001).

"Traditional Games: Sports in Ancient India." (1997). India Past and Present Web site, *http://library.thinkquest.org/11372* (February 9, 2001).

▦ Sumo Wrestling

Definition

Sumo is a traditional form of Japanese wrestling marked by pageantry and ritual. In competition, heavy wrestlers attempt to knock each other either down or out of a small ring by pushing, tripping, slapping, or resorting to various body throws. Today, the professional sport of sumo is second only to baseball in terms of popularity as a spectator sport in Japan.

History

The earliest written reference to sumo is found in the *Kojiki* (The Record of Ancient Matters), a book dated A.D. 712. The book recounts a legend about how the possession of the Japanese islands was determined by a sumo match between two gods. Prehistoric cave paintings have been found in Japan that depict sumo-like wrestling matches that seem to have been conducted in relation to agricultural rituals. The Japanese adopted the Chinese writing system in the 7th century, and it is from this time that the first historically authenticated sumo matches took place. Beginning in the mid-7th century, sumo appears to have been connected with the imperial court. During the reign of Emperor Shomu (724–749), the Imperial Palace hosted an annual festival called Sechie, where *sumotori* were recruited from throughout the country to perform. Sechie also involved the intelligentsia and cultured classes, whose members gathered to write poetry and discuss spiritual and political issues facing the Japanese realm. These people probably represented the first large grouping of sumo spectators, who regarded the sumo demonstration as a large-scale rite to pray for peace and prosperity for Japanese society. Referred to as *sechie-zumo*, sumo in this context began to take on some of the spiritual ritual that marks the sport to this day. Sumo continued to be popular at the imperial court; an annual tournament was instituted in 821, where the wrestlers were drawn from the imperial bodyguard. The tourney was held in the Shishinden (Hall for State Ceremonies), where the sumo entered to the accompaniment of gongs and drums. The wrestlers were followed by government officials, musicians, dancers, and, at the rear, the emperor and his attendants. Matches were decided by falls, or when an opponent could no longer continue and had to be dragged to his tent. (This is similar to sumo today, where the match ends when one wrestler is either thrown to the floor or forced out of the ring.) These imperial tournaments were largely annual events until the late 12th century, when the shoguns (warrior rulers) began to grow more powerful than the emperor.

Sumo continued to be sponsored by a handful of *daimyo*, or feudal lords, who sometimes staged tourneys in conjunction with martial arts competitions. Oda Nobunaga, a major feudal lord, held a tournament at his castle in 1578 where over 1,500 *sumotori* from throughout Japan competed. Beginning in the 17th century and continuing into the mid-19th century, several of the most powerful *daimyo* acted as patrons to the strongest *sumotori*. In a sense these *sumotori* were sumo's first professionals. One-part bodyguard, one-part walking billboard, the *sumotori* were paid a generous stipend and wore ceremonial aprons, embroidered with the feudal lord's name.

The roots of modern organized professional sumo wrestling are found in the 18th century. A group of *toshiyori*, or elders, began staging regular matches for the pleasure of the shogun. Again, these matches had spiritual and political significance. Rules and rituals surrounding matches were codified for the first time. Initially referred to as *kanjin-zumo*, *toshiyori* collected donations from spectators and ongoing supporters, ostensibly to go toward the construction or preservation of shrines, temples, bridges, and other public works throughout Japan. But a portion of the money went to support the *sumotori*. Soon, a number of *toshiyori* were maintaining their own *heya* (meaning room or barracks in Japanese, though, in this context, connoting team or stable of wrestlers, like a stable of racehorses). The largest and most famous *heya* were sanctioned by the shogun and based in Tokyo during the mid to late 18th century. By the late 19th century, there were over 100 elders running *heya* throughout Japan. Though the sport had an elaborate ranking system for *sumotori* (see below), sumo had no national organization until 1927, when associations of *toshiyori* from Tokyo and Osaka came together.

Today, the Nihon Sumo Kyokai, or Japanese Sumo Association, administers sumo through Japan's Ministry of Education. There are currently 28 *heya* in Japan. *Sumotori* enter a *heya* at age 15 and follow a strict training regimen in hopes of rising through the professional ranks. Each year there are many minor and intermediate tournaments throughout Japan, and six grand tournaments, or *basho*, where the top professionals vie. Each *basho* lasts 15 days, and *sumotori* wrestle as many as 15 different opponents.

During the 1980s, sumo began to be followed by significant numbers of people outside of Japan. Today, the sport boasts fans from Britain, Western Europe, and the United States.

Equipment

Sumotori compete barefoot and naked to the waist, with a loincloth and thick belt, or *mawashi*, wrapped around their waist. Competitors wear their hair in a topknot, with the style dependent upon their ranking. Matches take place in a square ring, called a *dohyo*, measuring 12 feet on a side. The *dohyo* has a playing surface made of earth, and its surrounding pillars and roof overhead reflect the sport's ritualistic underpinnings. The pillars, which are positioned at each corner of the ring, signify the gods of spring, summer, fall, and winter. The roof is much like that of a Shinto temple.

Rules

The object of sumo is quite simple: a competitor tries to force his opponent out of the *dohyo*, or to make any part of his opponent's body (except the soles of the feet) touch the playing surface. Matches are extremely short—some last only a few seconds; few last longer than several minutes. Competitors cannot pull hair, gouge eyes, or strike with a closed fist. Pushing, tripping, and slapping are allowed, though, and the very best wrestlers are able to use their weight and balance to throw an opponent. Though *sumotori* weigh between 130 and 200 kilograms (about 285–440 pounds), there is more to the sport than simple brute strength or body mass. Some of the basic sumo techniques include:

Tsuppari: a series of rapid hand slaps intended to drive an opponent out of the ring
Hataki-komi: stepping aside and pushing the opponent past and out of the ring
Ketaguri: pulling an opponent's legs out from under him as he advances
Ashi-tori: holding an opponent's leg until he loses his balance and falls
Vorikiri: grabbing an opponent's belt and pulling him past and out of the ring

The prelude to the wrestling is at times as interesting as the bouts themselves. An elaborate processional marks the start of a grand tournament, with the *sumotori* marching around the ring and performing a series of rit- ualistic movements. Before the start of a match, *sumotori* throw handfuls of salt over their shoulders to purify the *dohyo*. Competitors then stomp around, pound their fists on the playing surface, and glare at one another in an attempt to psyche out or intimidate their opponents.

Sumo is a hierarchical sport where *sumotori* start at the bottom and work their way up through the ranks, gaining better pay and social status as they win more bouts. A complicated ranking system is followed, with sev- eral divisions and many gradations or levels within each division. About 1 in every 60 *sumotori* makes it to the *juryo* division, and from there an elite 30 go on to the *makunouchi* division—comparable to an all-star team in a pro league like the National Basketball Association or the Major Leagues. *Yokozuna* is the highest ranking a wrestler can achieve. Only 65 men have ever held this ranking. The status accorded to a *yokozuna* is such that de- motion to a lower ranking is impossible; should a *yokozuna* begin to lose his abilities with age, he is expected to retire. Though the rank of *yokozuna* has, for the most part, been reserved for Japanese wrestlers only, a Hawai- ian, Jesse Kuhaulua, achieved *yokozuna* status in the 1970s, and, more recently, another American, Chad Rowan, rose to this status in the mid- 1990s.

The culture of sumo—much like Japanese culture as a whole—is a mer- itocracy, and this aspect, in addition to the sport's traditional trappings, makes it a tremendously popular spectator sport, followed by millions of men and women throughout Japan.

Bibliography

Coller, Ken. (1996). "The History of Sumo." Sumo FAQ Web site, *www.scgroup.com /sumo/faq* (February 2, 2001).

Cuyler, P. L. (1979). *Sumo: From Rite to Sport*. New York: Weatherhill Press.

Sharnoff, Lora. (1996). "Grand Sumo: The Living Sport and Tradition." Sumo FAQ Web site, *www.scgroup.com/sumo/faq* (February 2, 2001).

"Sumo Rules and Techniques." (2000). Sumo Web home page, *www.sumoweb.com/* (February 1, 2001).

▦ Tae Kwon Do

Definition

The literal meaning of tae kwon do (Korean) is "a method of defending yourself with your hands and feet." A Korean martial art, tae kwon do fo- cuses on the individual, striving to develop the character, personality, and positive moral and ethical traits in each practitioner. As a means of self-de- fense, exercise, and recreation, tae kwon do is practiced today by more than 20 million students throughout the world.

History

It is not certain whether tae kwon do is indigenous to Korea. Certainly, the sport's emphasis on spiritual and moral development is emblematic of Eastern religion and philosophy. Tae kwon do's use of the hands and feet also places it within the Asian martial arts. Given Japan's historic influence over Korea (Japan occupied Korea between 1910 and 1945), the sport may have roots in Japanese or Okinawan karate. Still, some accounts trace tae kwon do's origins to Korea's Three Kingdom era (1st century B.C.), when Silla dynasty warriors, known as *hwarang*, practiced a traditional martial art, tae kyon ("foot-hand"), throughout Korea.

Modern-day tae kwon do originated in the early 20th century, and appears to have been a reaction or form of resistance to Japanese control. General Choi Hong Fi, who is generally regarded as the father of modern tae kwon do, was a leader of the resistance movement against Japan. Choi had studied tae kyon as a child. As an adolescent, Choi also learned karate, in which he attained a rank of first degree black belt. Later, while interned as a political prisoner during World War II, Choi began developing an amalgam of the two sports and teaching it to his fellow prisoners. Throughout the 1950s, Choi would move up the ladder of command in the South Korean military, placing him in an advantageous position to spread the sport of tae kwon do, particularly to the United States, an ally of South Korea. In 1955 Choi and a panel of distinguished South Korean citizens formalized the sport and officially named it tae kwon do. In 1966 the International Tae Kwon Do Federation (ITF) was formed, with national associations in nine countries, including the United States. Though tae kwon do was a demonstration sport at the Seoul Olympic Games in 1988, it has yet to be accorded official medal status. At the close of the 20th century, not enough countries worldwide were conducting championship competition to merit representation in the Olympic Games.

Rather, tae kwon do has gained popularity throughout the world because its practitioners are intent on training for individual self-improvement and personal fitness. In the United States, tens of thousands of students take lessons at private martial arts schools.

Equipment

Practitioners wear loose-fitting white pants and a white smock, fastened with a belt around the waist. A padded mat is used as a surface. Shoes are not worn.

Rules

Tae kwon do uses both quick linear movements, as in karate, and circular, flowing movements similar to Tai Chi. Tae kwon do's emphasis on powerful kicking movements is unique among the Asian martial arts. Students are taught to defend themselves from attack from all sides using arms and legs. There are four basic techniques or movements: blocks, kicks, stances, and strikes. Mastery of the sport is attained through constant repetition of these techniques. Ultimately, the student of tae kwon do is expected to marshal an immediate physical reaction to counter an opponent's force.

Like many Asian martial arts, tae kwon do is a philosophy or way of life. The "Trinity of Tae Kwon Do" consists of three major aspects: the body, mind, and spirit. One must develop each to be a well-rounded person. It should be noted that the ultimate goal of tae kwon do is a more peaceful world. In this manner, tae kwon do strives to develop the positive aspects of an individual's personality for the well-being of society and mankind. The tenets of tae kwon do are the very characteristics that a practitioner must possess if he/she is to become a total individual and a true student of the art. These tenets, which are recited at the beginning and end of every class, are as follows:

courtesy (*ye ui*)

integrity (*yom chi*)

perseverance (*in nae*)

self-control (*guk gi*)

indomitable spirit (*baekjul boolgool*)

Bibliography

Benko, James S. (1974). "The Philosophy of Tae Kwon Do." International Tae Kwon Do Association Web site, *www.itatkd.com/* (April 24, 2001).

International Taekwon-Do Federation/United States Taekwon-Do Federation. (2001). "History of the International Taekwon-Do Federation." USTF Web site, *http://ucsu.colorado.edu/~tkd/USTF/USTF_home.html* (April 24, 2001).

Soon, Man Lee, and Gaetane Ricke. (1999). *Modern Taekwondo: The Official Training Manual.* London: Sterling Publications.

▦ Tai Chi

Definition

Tai Chi Chuan, which can be translated as "Supreme Ultimate Force," is a Chinese martial arts form that uses soft, slow, flowing movement to redirect an opponent's force. The sense of "supreme ultimate" is often associated with the Chinese concept of yin-yang, which posits a dynamic duality in all things. "Force," or, in a literal sense, "fist," can be regarded as a means of achieving yin-yang, or balance, harmony. With roots dating back to the 6th century B.C., Tai Chi today is practiced by millions of people in the East and West as a form of "moving" yoga and meditation.

History

The origins of Tai Chi are associated with ancient Chinese philosophy and health, which are both founded on movement systems. Lao Tsu, the 6th century B.C. scholar and philosopher (he was a contemporary of Confucius), wrote the seminal work of Taoism, the *Tao Te Ching*. One of Taoism's fundamental principles involves the concept of yin-yang. Though yin and yang are regarded as opposite forces, each is meant to merge into the other, creating a dynamic duality which is representative of the world's natural balance. Taoism urges its followers to maintain a calm, reflective view of the world, and to live in harmony with oneself and nature. The following couplets from the *Tao Te Ching* summarize this philosophy: "Yield and Overcome; / Bend and be straight," and "He who stands on tiptoe is not steady. / He who strides cannot maintain the pace."

Tai Chi also has a strong connection with the *I Ching*, a Chinese system of divination. There are associations between the eight basic *I Ching* trigrams plus the five elements of Chinese alchemy (metal, wood, fire, water, and earth), and the 13 basic postures of Tai Chi created by Chang San-feng, the storied founder of Tai Chi.

Though some scholars question the very existence of Chang San-feng, arguing that he is little more than a historical construct posited by later generations to explain and advance accepted views about Tai Chi, Chang is believed to have lived around the first half of the 15th century. Chang, a monk of the Wu Tang Monastery in Hunan Province, linked some earlier teachings about the importance of regular exercise and movement in aiding digestion and circulation, and the Taoist notion of yin-yang, with the *I Ching* in creating the fundamental "Thirteen Postures" of Tai Chi. These postures, which emphasize the soft, or internal, aspects of exercise, are actually divided into eight postures and five attitudes. The eight postures are:

1. ward off
2. rollback
3. press
4. push
5. pull
6. split
7. elbow strike
8. shoulder strike

The five attitudes are:

1. advance
2. retreat

3. look left
4. gaze right
5. central equilibrium

Chang's exercises stress flexibility as opposed to hardness and force. They incorporate philosophy, physiology, psychology, and the basic laws of dynamics, or movement; collectively they symbolize and advance a way of life.

Chang's postures were expanded upon in the late 18th century by Wang Tsung Yueh, a schoolteacher, and his student, Jiang Fa. Wang and Jiang are credited with developing continuous sequences of movements that link together the 13 postures and that serve as a basis of contemporary Tai Chi. Jiang taught his brand of Tai Chi to villagers who lived in Honan Township (most of whom were named Chen), and this marks the creation of the first family school of Tai Chi, known as the Chen style. During the 19th century, various forms of Tai Chi were developed from the Chen style, the most prominent being the Yang style.

Yang Luchan, who taught in Beijing during the early to mid-19th century, was known as Yang the Invincible, having accepted many challenges from the leading martial arts masters of Beijing and apparently never lost. Yang was appointed martial arts instructor to the imperial court, and it was from this position of prominence that he popularized Tai Chi. The form publicly taught by Yang and his followers stressed the meditative and health-related sides of Tai Chi over the movement's martial aspects. Although there are thousands who continue to practice styles of Tai Chi that are more martial and physically strenuous, many more engage in Yang style Tai Chi to enhance the body's circulation, to build muscle tone, and to engender a calm, relaxed state of mind.

Though Tai Chi came under attack for its spiritual and apolitical antecedents during Mao's Cultural Revolution in the 1960s, it was reinstated by Communist leaders in the 1980s as a uniquely Chinese form of art and sport. Basic Tai Chi is now taught in parks and public buildings throughout China, and special schools have been created to offer advanced instruction and sponsor form competitions. Chinese emigrants have spread Tai Chi to London, Paris, and the northeastern cities in the United States.

Tai Chi Today

If you were to take up Tai Chi, what types of activities would you engage in? Tai Chi consists of a sequence of postures, or exercises, which, if done properly, are said to enhance one's balance, alignment, fine motor skill, and overall rhythm of movement. The key to executing these movements is the cultivation of a calm, relaxed mind that is able to focus within to foster the circulation of *chi*, a vital life force that animates and enriches the body. The more in tune one is with one's inner self, the greater awareness one has of nature and other forces that are generated from outside the self. This is the basis of all meditative practice, and its mastery is central to Tai Chi.

Tai Chi's movements also have martial applications. In a two-person exercise called "push hands," Tai Chi principles are developed to help one become sensitive to and responsive of a partner's *chi*, or vital energy. A number of paired practice routines actually simulate martial encounters. These exercises range from duo form sequences to freestyle sparring. The emphasis in Tai Chi is on the ability to channel potentially destructive energy (e.g., a kick, punch, or assault) away from one in a manner that will either dissipate the energy or send it in a direction where it is no longer threatening.

Bibliography

Henning, Stanley. (1994). "Ignorance, Legend and Taijiquan." *Journal of Chen Style Taijiquan Research Association of Hawaii* Vol. 2, No. 3, pp. 1–7.

"The History of Tai Chi." (2000). Yang Style Tai Chi Web site, *www.chebucto.ns.ca/* (January 30, 2001).

Lim, Peter. "The Historical Development of Tai Chi Chuan: The Origins Theory." Peter Lim Web page, *http://web.singnet.com.sg/~limttk/* (January 30, 2001).

"What Is Tai Chi?" (2000). Yang Style Tai Chi Web site, *www.chebucto.ns.ca/* (January 30, 2001).

▦ BRITISH ISLES

HISTORICAL OVERVIEW

Britain during the 18th and 19th centuries was the most powerful country in the world. Having achieved national unification far earlier than its Western European neighbors, Britain was able to place political and economic power in the hands of mercantile interests—men involved in manufacturing, finance, and trade. Given its geography, Britain had been a maritime power since the 16th century. As the country industrialized, its strength at sea was crucial in advancing Britain's commercial objectives and, ultimately, in structuring what came to be known as the British Empire, a federation of colonies, protectorates, and settlements with political and economic ties to Britain. During the period covered by this volume, Britain held colonies in Africa, Asia, the South Pacific, and North and South America. It also settled Australia and New Zealand, and established a controlling commercial interest in the Far East. Wherever British business went, its civil servants, soldiers, builders, engineers, teachers, and missionaries were sure to either precede or follow. Collectively they advanced British culture; in some cases (as with religion and education) this culture was imposed on native subjects; in others indigenous peoples copied British mannerisms, developed British interests, and engaged in British pastimes, including sports and games.

LEGACY OF BRITAIN'S
18TH- AND 19TH-CENTURY SPORTS AND GAMES

Britain put its stamp on the sports world during this time. Over a third of all entries in this volume relate to sports that were either created or developed by Britain. Given the origin of the United States, it is not surprising that many of these sports have either become popular in our culture or have characteristics that have influenced the development of similar sports and games in North America. The British Empire provided a network by means of which sport was spread throughout the world. Methods of dissemination varied. In some cases, civil servants in the colonies consciously created allegiance to Britain by teaching a sport to the local elite (e.g., cricket and field hockey in India and Southeast Asia, polo in South America). In other instances, a sport was transmitted directly to the masses (e.g., soccer and track and field).

There are several important concepts and trends to distinguish in English sport. First and foremost, the British refined the concept of sport as organized competition where there are winners and losers. This ideal has strong underpinnings in Protestant moral teachings and in the ethics of capitalism and market competition. Just as the British enacted laws to govern commerce and wrote guidelines to spell out particular trading agreements, so too did they create uniform sets of rules to govern play in their sports. It seems that the British may have originated the ideal of fair play, or at least the perception that all must be done to facilitate a level playing field in sports. Ironically, this ideal was clearly related to the British penchant for gambling. Both cricket in England and hurling in Ireland had rules specifically written at the urging of the gentry, who bet heavily on these sports. Thoroughbred racing's detailed records on breeding and the creation of a strong sanctioning body for the sport were directly related to the need to protect the investment of horse owners and to regulate gambling.

Though gambling has of course been prevalent since ancient times and present in many different cultures, one can get a sense of how pervasive it was in British society in the 18th and 19th centuries by reading about the country's sports and games. At one time or another, boxing, rowing, and pedestrianism in Britain largely existed to provide the citizenry with opportunities to make bets. These professional sports attracted as participants working-class men, who could often win much more in prize money from one event than they could earn in an entire year working a factory job. While rich and poor betted on almost every sport, promoters and investors also made money by owning sports teams and charging admission to competition. Britain during the latter half of the 19th century witnessed the birth of the spectator sport, with soccer, rugby, horse racing, and boxing attracting thousands of paying fans.

Though many organized sports either originated in the British public school or university system (e.g., soccer, rugby, cross country, field hockey, rowing, and squash) or flourished in amateur clubs throughout the country (e.g., cycling, cricket, and track and field), most developed professional forms that the amateurs were direct in distinguishing themselves from. In some cases, as in boxing and the Queensberry Rules, or with Rugby Union and Rugby League football, separate sets of rules were written to set the amateur pursuit off from the professional. In others, like tennis, golf, and track and field, an amateur was defined as anyone who did not accept payment of any kind related to sport. This practice not only banned the factory hand who was hired for his sporting prowess, but also barred coaches who provided sport and physical education instruction and anyone who was given money or gifts by an advertiser to use a certain product.

In other cases, such as with soccer and cricket, professionals and amateurs would play side by side, particularly when the nation's honor was at stake in international play. For many British, sport was considered a test of national worth and character. Britain was *the* world power, and sport was considered both an extension and a symbol of the country's geopolitical and economic position during the 18th and 19th centuries.

Taken in this context, the processes followed and the lessons mastered in engaging in school sports like soccer, rugby, cross country, and track and field played an important role in educating the leaders of tomorrow. Though boys of all classes played sports, it was the upper- and upper-middle-class boys in the public schools who played them in an organized fashion.

Victorian England frowned upon women engaging in sports, finding the proposition part immoral and part unnatural (e.g., women as the weaker sex, with body and mind not up to the rigors of sport). However, a number of sports are included in this chapter in which women either took part or in some cases were urged to do so. Field hockey was conceived as a school sport and recommended for young women, particularly those from the aristocracy and upper middle class who needed to be in good shape to bear healthy children (presumably boys—the leaders of tomorrow). Sports and games like croquet, badminton, and table tennis were also favorites with women, who, in most cases, didn't need to modify their dress or even mannerisms to play these rather undemanding activities. Cycling was a different story. Though thousands of women took part in cycling, to pursue the sport with any seriousness meant shedding long dresses and hoop skirts and wearing clothing like vests and bloomers that permitted freedom of movement. This caused quite a stir among the establishment and made cycling an uphill battle for many women in the late 19th century.

Organized golf and tennis originated in Scotland and England, respectively. During the late 19th century, both sports were adopted by the elite as exclusive club activities. In order to play, one had to have a membership (i.e., gain acceptance among a circle of elites), and, in the case of golf, invest a fair amount of money in purchasing equipment. Though both sports have spread throughout the world, they remain in many areas largely upper-class pursuits.

▦ Badminton

Definition

Badminton is a court game, played as a singles or doubles contest, where participants use light, long-handled rackets to volley a small cork-and-feather object, called a shuttlecock, over a net. The object is to keep the shuttlecock from hitting the ground. With origins in ancient Asia, the competitive game developed in Britain during the 19th century. Today the sport's governing body, the International Badminton Federation (IBF), claims over 130 member nations.

History

Badminton seems to have evolved from a 1st century B.C. Chinese game called Ti Juan Zu, in which competitors kicked, rather than hit, the shuttlecock. This game was also popular in Japan and India and later spread to parts of the Middle East and Greece. A later version of Ti Juan Zu was played in ancient Greece using a racket. A game more similar to badminton, called shuttlecock, developed in Europe in the 15th and 16th centuries. With no net or playing court boundaries, players simply tested their skill at keeping the shuttlecock in the air. The game seems to have had mass appeal, played by children and royalty alike. In Adam Manyoki's portrait *Young Prince Sulkowski*, a member of the Polish royal family who lived around the turn of the 18th century, the subject is shown holding a shuttlecock and a racket.

Reportedly British army officers brought a version of badminton back from India in the 1870s. Since there is some mention of a badminton-like game (called "battledore") as far back as the 12th century in the royal court records of England, we can assume that badminton, or a version of the sport, had already been imported to England from the East.

When the Duke of Beaufort introduced the game to royalty at his country estate in 1873, players used a net, boundaries to the field of play were set, and there were rules regarding serving, volleying, and so on. Shortly thereafter, private badminton clubs began to be formed by the nation's aristocracy. In 1893 the Badminton Association of England was established to further organize and govern the sport. By 1899 the association had conducted its first national championship, and by the early 20th century, it had embarked on a mission to promote the sport in other countries. Following several international exhibition tours, badminton soon became popular in Europe, East Asia, and North America.

Badminton's roots as a club sport among the elite classes in Britain are still apparent. Though the game is played in over 2,500 clubs across the country, it has never caught on among members of the working class, who generally do not have access to club memberships or indoor courts. By contrast, badminton has been embraced by a broader stratum of society in

East Asia, where many badminton players are among their country's best athletes. Since the late 1980s, players from China, Indonesia, South Korea, and now Denmark have dominated the world championships and the Olympic Games.

Since 1979 badminton has been a professional sport. Several hundred players, predominantly from Asia and Western Europe, compete for several million dollars in prize money on a year-round grand prix tour.

Equipment

Badminton rackets weigh between 3½ and 5 ounces and consist of a leather handle, a long, thin shaft, and a stringed area called the head. Rules limit the length of a racket to 26¾ inches, while the dimensions of the head of the racket are 11 inches long and 8½ inches wide. The head is usually strung at between 25 and 35 pounds of tension with synthetic nylon or thin-gauge gut. Earlier rackets were made of light wood like ash, beech, or hickory. Today, most rackets are made of aluminum, boron, graphite, or titanium—all light yet responsive materials.

A tournament shuttlecock weighs just two-tenths of an ounce and is made of a small round cork base with 16 goose feathers protruding from one side of the ball. Recreation-model shuttlecocks are usually made of plastic. Shuttlecocks are 2½ inches long.

Rules

The game has developed as one of speed, power, and agility. When hit at top speed, the shuttlecock can travel up to 160 miles per hour; tapped gently, the shuttlecock floats slower than most objects hit in other sports. This variation in pace makes the game exciting to watch and keeps participants on their toes. Like tennis, badminton demands a good deal of stamina, and players constantly move from side to side and back and forth.

A badminton court is 20 feet wide by 40 feet long (see illustration). There is a designated short service area for singles play and a long service area for doubles play. Play is initiated by one player or side serving to the other side, with the shuttlecock volleyed over the net until one side fails to make a good return. Only the serving side is allowed to score points. If the serving side fails to make a good return, the serve goes to the other side. Men's singles and doubles games are played until one side scores 15 points; women's singles games are played to 11 points. There is a method of extending the game called "setting the score," which may be followed if the game is tied at 14–14 (or 10–10 in women's singles). The first side to have reached 14 (or 10) elects either to "play through," meaning that the next side to win a point wins the game, or to "set the game" to 3 additional points, meaning that the first side to reach 17 points (or 13 in women's singles play) wins the game. Each badminton match is a best-of-three-games series.

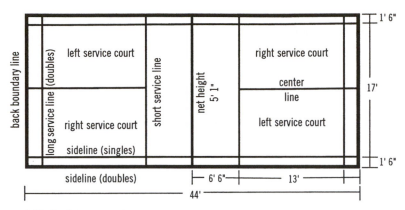

Figure 4. Badminton court.

An umpire keeps score and rules on faults during match play. A service judge and two or more side judges aid the umpire.

Bibliography

Bloss, Margaret Varner, and R. Stanton Hales. (1994). *Badminton*. Dubuque, IA: Brown and Benchmark.

Boga, Steven. (1996). *Badminton*. Harrisburg, PA: Stackpole Books.

Davidson, Kenneth R., and Lealand R. Gustavson. (1953). *Winning Badminton*, New York: A. S. Barnes and Co.

Kings, William. (2000). "Badminton." Microsoft Encarta Online Encyclopedia 2000, *http://encarta.msn.com* (December 16, 2000).

▦ Bandy

Definition

Bandy is a stick-and-ball game played on ice between two teams of 11 players. Bandy is sometimes referred to as "winter soccer," in that the playing field is the size of a soccer field and many of the game's rules are similar to soccer. Bandy became an organized sport in Britain during the 19th century, and soon spread throughout Europe. Today, the sport is particularly popular in Sweden and Russia, which, between them, have won all the World Championships back to the inaugural game in 1957.

History

Games similar to bandy have been played since ancient times. Egyptian tombs contain drawings of figures hitting a ball or ring with curved sticks. Both the Greeks and Romans (*Paganica*) played stick-and-ball games. Similarly, a game called Knattlekr in Iceland is described in 9th-century sagas, and we can assume that either the Romans directly, or by way of the British Isles (e.g., hurling or shinty), influenced this game.

Bandy seems to have direct roots in the British Isles. The term "bandy," or *bando* (Welsh), is derived from the Teutonic word *bandja*, meaning "curved stick." A 13th-century painted glass window in Canterbury Cathedral shows a boy holding a curved stick in one hand and a ball in the other very similar to a bandy stick and ball. There are other literary and pictorial references to bandy in 14th- and 15th-century prayer books. Even Shakespeare, in *Romeo and Juliet*, mentions bandy. ("The Prince expressly hath forbidden bandying in the Verona steets.")

As an organized sport, bandy bears striking similarities to field hockey (*see* Field Hockey), and the two sports were actually referred to interchangeably in Britain in the 18th and 19th centuries. Early variations of bandy used either balls or pucks as in ice hockey, and were played on frozen fens. The early sport was organized around the village common, and can be thought of as a pastime engaged in mostly by rural folk. The Fen District in England, particularly around Lincolnshire and Cambridgeshire, was a hotbed of bandy play. Records dating back to the early 19th century indicate that the village of Bury-on-Fen in England had a bandy team that hadn't lost for over a century.

The sport never really gained popularity in Britain on a national level, probably because of the unpredictability of ice during the generally temperate winters there. Also, increasing urbanization in the south of the country left rural areas like the Fen District somewhat isolated. Still, the National Bandy Association was formed in Britain in 1891, and the first international match was played the same year with a Dutch team. Before the turn of the century, the sport was introduced to Scandinavia, Switzerland, and Germany.

Bandy as a competitive sport owes much to the Swedes and Russians. In Sweden, the sport took off, with nearly 200 local clubs by 1926 and almost 500 today. In Russia, and formerly the Soviet Union, bandy has at times challenged soccer as the country's most popular team sport. There are accounts of thousands of spectators drawn to bandy games during World War II, when the sport was a welcome diversion from the horrors of the war with Germany. Both Sweden and the USSR/Russia have dominated international play—between them the two countries have won every World Championship and World Cup title that has been contested.

Due to the popularity of ice hockey in the United States, bandy has been virtually nonexistent in America. A dry-ground variation of the game, popular in scholastic physical education classes or out in the urban streets, is known as street hockey. Players use a hockey stick with a hard plastic blade to hit a round plastic ball into a goal. The game is played either wearing sneakers or on "wheels," with players using in-line skates.

Equipment

A bandy stick is four feet long with a curved U-shaped blade. It is smaller than a hockey stick, and players typically hold it in one hand. The ball is plastic with a cork center, painted orange for visibility, and roughly the size of a tennis ball. Players wear ice hockey skates for maneuverability. They also wear padding similar to that worn in ice hockey (*see* Ice Hockey). Though a bandy goalie wears a face mask and has large leg and arm pads like his hockey counterpart, he is not allowed to use a stick.

Rules

Bandy is played on an ice surface the size of a soccer field (120 yards long and 70 yards wide). There is a half-foot-high strip surrounding the ice to keep the ball in play. Though a bandy player is allowed to "shoulder" an opponent, there is no checking in bandy, hence no need for high boards around the ice.

Games consist of two 45-minute periods with a 10-minute break at the half. Each team fields 11 players, including the goalie, and substitutions are made "on the fly," as in hockey. At 7 feet high and 11 feet wide, bandy goals are larger than in hockey. Though the goalie must be quite adept at fielding the ball—this position has more in common with a soccer goalie or perhaps an acrobatic shortstop in baseball than it does with a goaltender in ice hockey—goals in bandy are more common than in hockey or soccer. A typical bandy score might be 10–7.

In general, the rules of bandy are very similar to those of soccer. There are rules governing offsides, goal throws (as opposed to goal kicks), corners (i.e., corner kicks), free strokes (i.e., free kicks), and penalty strokes (i.e., penalty kicks).

Players are not allowed to hit an opponent with a stick. Though contact is allowed when challenging an opponent for the ball, there is no tackling. Kicking, pushing, tripping, holding, or interference in general is forbidden. Though there are penalties of between 5 and 10 minutes, incidents of repeated dangerous infractions are dealt with by expulsion from the game. Both the severity of the penalty and perhaps stricter enforcement of the rules have made bandy a safer game than ice hockey. A recent medical study found the incidence of injury in bandy to be less than half of that experienced in ice hockey.

Bibliography

Edelman, Robert. (1993). *Serious Fun: A History of Spectator Sports in the USSR.* London: Oxford University Press.

Harste, Ann K. (1990). "Bandy: Soccer on Ice." *The Physician and Sports Medicine* (November 1990).

"How Bandy is Played." (2001). Bandy Tipset Web site, *http://www.geocities.com /bandytips/* (March 22, 2001).

Olsson, Per G. (2001). "A Short History of Bandy." Bandy Tipset Web site, *http://www.geocities.com/bandytips/* (March 22, 2001).

▦ Boxing

Definition

Boxing is the art of gloved fist fighting between two opponents inside an elevated ring—typically a square, canvas-covered mat surrounded by ropes. A contestant attempts to win by either knocking out his opponent or scoring more points after an agreed-upon number of rounds, or periods. Today, professional and amateur boxing is popular throughout the world.

History

"Boxing" is an old English term, originating in the 16th century and meaning "fighting with the fists." Boxing's roots can be traced back to ancient Greece, where a form of the sport was practiced in the original Olympic Games (7th century B.C.). Grecian boxers bound their hands and forearms with soft leather wrapping for protection. Later, during the Roman Empire, fighters wore *cesti*, or gloves studded with metal. Boxing became, in effect, a blood sport, with gladiators pitted against one another in a fight to the death.

Following the fall of the Roman Empire, boxing disappeared from history, failing to return until the 1500s, when accounts from Elizabethan England tell of the "rabble" cheering on two fighters engaged in what might today be termed a brawl. Boxing didn't begin to take the form of organized sport until the early 18th century, when the first rules of prizefighting (a term synonymous with boxing) were set forth. Jack Broughton, who was the heavyweight champion of England from 1734 to 1750, first introduced rules in which a round lasted until a man went down, and if, after 30 seconds, a fighter could not continue, then the match was over. Broughton's rules forbade grabbing an opponent below the waist and hitting a fighter who had fallen. Prior to this time, a fighter would often clasp, hold, or wrestle an opponent, and there was no provision against hitting after he went down. Broughton's guidelines not only helped to civilize the sport, but also gave competitors room in which to develop movements and strategy that would come to distinguish boxing from simply fighting. Daniel Mendoza, another British heavyweight who fought in the late 1780s, is generally regarded as the first boxer to take a scientific approach to the sport. Mendoza developed the left jab and emphasized balance and footwork over stationary fighting. Mendoza's successor, John

"Gentleman" Jackson, further developed the essential concepts of movement and advance-retreat.

By the early 1800s, boxing was beginning to be regarded as an art that demanded both offensive and defensive strategies. Increasingly, boxers and the public began to link skill, rather than pure muscle, to manliness, and this perception led to the development of rules and guidelines to enhance competition. In 1839 the London Prize Ring Rules were promulgated. These rules, which were revised in 1853, determined the size of the ring, that it would be surrounded by ropes for safety, and that biting, kicking, gouging, head-butting, and blows below the belt were forbidden.

Soon the educated classes in Britain tried to do to boxing what they attempted to do to so many other sports in the late 19th century, including rugby, soccer, cricket, and pedestrianism—they moved to exclude working-class elements from "their" sports. In 1867 a Cambridge University athlete, John Graham Chambers, created a canon of boxing rules for both amateurs and professionals that was published by Sir John Sholto Douglas, the eighth Marquis of Queensberry. Known as the Marquis of Queensberry Rules, they distinguished between boxing competitions and contests. Competitions were for amateurs. Bouts lasted three rounds and were decided by points. Contests were tests of endurance, strictly professional events where two men fought until one could no longer continue. Amateurs "sparred," and it was regarded as unsporting to try to score a knockout in an amateur competition. Common to both competitions and contests was the concept of rounds lasting a set amount of time, with opponents taking a one-minute rest interval between each round. Revisions to these rules in the 1880s stipulated the use of "gloves of fair size and best quality."

For a time, professionals continued to fight bare-knuckled under the old London Prize Ring Rules. It wasn't until Gentleman Jim Corbett defeated the American champion, John L. Sullivan, to win the World Heavyweight Championship in 1892 that a professional championship bout was fought under Marquess of Queensberry Rules. From then on, both the amateur and professional boxing worlds embraced the same set of rules.

Ironically, it was because of these rules that the professional sport began to flourish in the late 19th and early 20th centuries. All bouts had to take place in a standard-size ring, usually indoors, and this led promoters to rent public halls and charge admission at the door. With Britain at the height of its industrial boom, even the factory hand and the common laborer had money to spend on entertainment. This scene was repeated across the Atlantic in America, where waves of European immigrants supplied boxing with an endless pool of poor, struggling fighters, intent on making it big in what to many appeared to be a rags-to-riches sport. Irish, Italian, and Jewish boxers all figured prominently in the U.S. tradition of developing world championship prizefighters. Though African Ameri-

WORLD'S CHAMPIONSHIP BATTLE, JULY 4, 1910
ROUND 2

Figure 5. Second round action of a July 4, 1910, world heavyweight title bout between Jack Johnson (right), the reigning world heavyweight champion (1908–1915), and James Jeffries in Reno, Nevada. Johnson, the first African American sports hero to gain national acclaim, knocked out Jeffries in the 15th round. (Reproduced from the Collections of the Library of Congress)

cans faced racism in boxing as in almost every other walk of life, prizefighters like Jack Johnson (see illustration) and Joe Louis (world heavyweight champion, 1937–1949) competed against white athletes and attained professional world champion status long before black athletes in other major sports.

In the 19th and 20th centuries, the Americans and British spread boxing throughout much of the world. First England brought the sport to the British Isles and to its Commonwealth countries, New Zealand, Australia, and Canada. In the early 20th century, the United States introduced the sport to territories and countries within its own political sphere, including the Philippines, Puerto Rico, Cuba, and Latin America. After World War II, the sport spread to East Asia and to Africa's newly independent nations.

Professional boxing—by its very nature—has gained much more acclaim with the public than the amateur sport. Corporate sponsorship drives lucrative television and broadcasting deals, and creates incredibly rich purses for championship fights. By 2000 a heavyweight fighter could earn as much as $35 million in one heavyweight bout. Yet amateur boxing still has a strong following in the United States and around the world. Both the Amateur Boxing Association in England and the Amateur Athletic Union in America began sanctioning national championships in 1880 and 1888, respectively. The Golden Gloves Tournament, which was initiated by the *Chicago Tribune* in 1926, has proven to be the ultimate testing ground for American youth intent on developing basic boxing skills while getting a taste of competition. A series of elimination tournaments is held annually on local and regional levels, culminating in the championships each spring in Chicago.

Boxing has been staged as a medal sport in the Olympics since 1904 (except in Stockholm, Sweden, in 1912, where boxing was illegal at the time). Following World War II, participation from African, Asian, Middle Eastern, and Oceanic countries made boxing a truly worldwide amateur pastime. Before the fall of communism in Eastern Europe, most of the Eastern bloc countries supported their athletes to train and compete nationally, and it was during the 1970s and 1980s that amateur boxers from the Soviet Union and East Germany did particularly well in the Olympic Games. Similarly, boxers from Castro's Cuba have dominated competition over the past few Olympiads.

Equipment

All fighters wear protective, molded mouthpieces over their upper teeth. Boxing gloves are heavily padded, and fighters tape their hands and wrists for protection. As boxers are forbidden to hit below the belt, most wear large, long-legged shorts, drawn well above their waist. Boxers wear special high-top shoes that are light, yet provide support for quick lateral movement. Since the 1980s, amateur boxers have worn headguards, which offer some protection to the front and side of the head, including the ears and eyes.

Rules

In general, a boxer is not permitted to use any part of his body other than his fists in attacking an opponent, or his arms and hands in blocking an opponent's punches. All blows must land above the waist and to the front and sides of the head. A referee in the ring ensures that the sport's rules are followed. Should a boxer go down, the referee administers a 10-second count. If the boxer cannot rise after 10 seconds, his opponent is declared the winner. The referee may stop the fight at any time if he judges one boxer to be unable to continue or at risk of incurring severe or permanent injury. Should a bout stop for the latter purpose, the winner is awarded a technical knockout. While all amateur fights last 3 rounds of three minutes each in duration, professional fights now last anywhere from 4 to 12 rounds, and, because of this, professional boxers usually must pace themselves. If the boxers reach the end of the bout and neither has been knocked out, a decision is rendered based on the aggregate total of points scored per round for each fighter by a panel of three to five judges who are seated at ringside.

Prior to the mid-19th century, most boxers were classified as either lightweights (i.e., less than 175 pounds) or heavyweights (more than 175 pounds). It wasn't until the 1860s in Britain that a range of weight divisions began to appear to open up the sport to many more competitors. Even though there are a number of national and international governing bodies in professional and amateur boxing, there is general agreement upon the weight classes, particularly around a tournament or championship event. The Olympic Games contest medals in the following 12 divisions:

Light Flyweight—not more than 106 pounds

Flyweight—not more than 112 pounds

Bantamweight—not more than 119 pounds

Featherweight—not more than 126 pounds

Lightweight—not more than 132 pounds

Light Welterweight—not more than 140 pounds

Welterweight—not more than 148 pounds

Light Middleweight—not more than 156 pounds

Middleweight—not more than 165 pounds

Light Heavyweight—not more than 179 pounds

Heavyweight—not more than 200.5 pounds

Super Heavyweight—more than 200.5 pounds

Bibliography

Fleischer, Nat, and Sam Andre. (1980). *A Pictorial History of Boxing*. London: Hamlyn Press.

Gorn, Elliot J. (1986). *The Manly Art*. Ithaca, NY: Cornell University Press.

Sammons, Jeffrey T. (1990). *Beyond the Ring: The Role of Boxing in American Society*. Champaign: University of Illinois Press.

Sugden, John Peter. (1997). *Boxing and Society: An International Analysis*. Manchester, England: Manchester University Press.

▦ Cricket

Definition

Cricket is a bat-and-ball game between two teams of 11 players each, who take turns batting a ball which is bowled to them. Batting and bowling take place on a 22-yard-long rectangular pitch in the center of a large elliptically shaped field. Regarded as a thoroughly British game, cricket has become popular in almost every Commonwealth country—particularly in Australia, New Zealand, and South Africa, where only rugby rivals cricket as a national pastime.

History

Fans of American baseball can relate to cricket's murky, ill-defined origins. The term "cricket" may refer to the wickets (three shafts or stumps of wood at both ends of the pitch) that the bowler targets. Some cricket historians argue that the word is related to the Flemish *krick-stoel*, meaning a low stool, which would resemble the earliest types of wickets. But the term may describe the bat that defends the wickets as well. The Old English word *crycc* means a staff for leaning on, and the Middle Flemish *crick* also refers to a stick or staff. The game itself bears similarities to various stick-and-ball games like cat-and-dog, stool-ball, rounders, shinty, bandy, and even golf. The earliest reference to a game that may have been a precursor of cricket is contained in the Wardrobe Accounts of the Royal Household for the year 1300, which notes a total of 100 shillings and 6 pounds spent on *creag* and other sports played by Prince Edward. During the 16th century, there are references to boys playing *creckett*, and during the 17th century there is mention of the warrior statesman Oliver Cromwell having played cricket in his youth.

The sport seems to have entered England's popular culture sometime around the late 17th to early 18th centuries. Stories about cricket began to appear in English newspapers about this time. Interestingly, there is very little description of play in these accounts; most of the subject matter centers on scheduling and the betting action on games. The wealthy gentry in England were patrons of cricket. They bet heavily on the sport, and because of this demanded a set of consistent, fair rules. Starting in 1744, a series of "laws" were incorporated that defined the sport of cricket, including regulations for equipment and methods of play. By 1864, when overarm bowling was legalized, essential rules of modern cricket were more or less complete.

Throughout the 18th century, cricket was transformed from a quaint village game to a serious national pastime of sorts. To understand this transformation—particularly why cricket has been so appealing to the English, while other cultures have shown little interest in the game—one must understand the historical socioeconomic class differences in England. The relationship between wealthy landowner and estate laborer was rapidly changing in England as the country industrialized during the 18th century. Though the landed aristocrats were never really dependent on the economic relationships they developed with the commoners who worked their land, these rich gentry felt a sense of paternalism and responsibility for their well-being. When the poor began to be crowded off the land by manufacturers, the new businessman farmer, and a pro-industry government, the old-money landowners—who were themselves left behind in the new economic and social order—felt a sense of loss and social dislocation. In this context, cricket was a nostalgic game that celebrated and defined the old order. The aristocrat could captain his local team and take a turn at bat, leaving the more arduous task of bowling to the farm laborer. The game was leisurely, usually beginning in late morning and breaking at midday for tea, with standard matches lasting several days. Cricket took place on the village green, out in the countryside. Action unfolded slowly; time, in a sense, passed at a more manageable pace.

By the mid-18th century, cricket was flourishing in England, with an estimated 1,000 or more clubs in the country. London became the site for important interregional and "All-England" matches. At a match between Kent and England at London's Artillery Grounds in 1744, the poet James Love immortalized cricket with a 316-line poem of praise to the sport (*Cricket: An Heroic Poem*). Love's poem includes the famous couplet "Hail, cricket! Glorious manly, British Game! / First of all Sports! Be first alike in Fame." Far from being only a "manly game," cricket also appealed to women, and intervillage games between ladies' teams became common in the mid-1700s. These games, too, involved gambling. They were advertised in the press, and admission was charged at the gate. However, women's cricket seems to have been little more than a novelty. Though women play cricket today at the highest levels of international play, the popularity of the women's game waned throughout the 19th and early 20th centuries.

The mid to late 19th century saw the rise of the working-class professional cricketer. But in cricket, unlike other sports, professionals played side by side with amateurs. Most of the best teams were dominated by professional players, who typically distinguished themselves as the best batsmen and bowlers. But the amateur players would assume the leadership roles, preserving age-old standings of class. In fact, amateurs would have dining and hotel accommodations that were separate from those of the professionals. Amateurs would enter the playing field from a different gate, and, when play was done, their name and initials would be recorded in the results, whereas the professionals' accomplishments would be denoted by surname only. This tradition lasted many years. It wasn't until 1953 that a nonamateur was appointed to lead England's national team.

While cricket became a profitable spectator sport in England, the game began to catch on in other parts of the world as well—particularly throughout the British Commonwealth, which was toured by England's national team in the 1860s. By 1878 Australia had a side that rivaled England's, and New Zealand's select team wasn't far behind.

Yet it would take cricket several decades to span the racial divide. The British were initially reticent about inviting the indigenous peoples of

Africa and Asia to partake in the game. In India, only British officers played cricket until well into the mid- to late 19th century, and cricket was solely a white man's sport throughout the West Indies. It wasn't until the late 19th and early 20th centuries that many of these Third World countries developed native cricket clubs. Ultimately, England's will to be the best motivated behavior that strengthened relationships with its colonial subjects. England began to invite native aristocrats to play for its national team. Many of these subjects invariably longed for the power held by their British rulers; to them, cricket conveyed a sense of status and entitlement and provided an opportunity to better themselves. K. S. Ranjitsinhji, an Indian prince picked for Team England in 1890, rewarded the English by referring to cricket as "one of the greatest contributions which the British people have made to the cause of humanity." Many formerly subject people came to embrace cricket as their own, adapting it to their own culture, or transporting it to other countries themselves (e.g., Indians and Pakistanis playing cricket in Paris and New York).

Throughout the 20th century, cricket has grown in international stature. Five-day test matches define international play, and those countries that have been accorded test status by the British (denoting "world-class" play) include Australia, New Zealand, South Africa, India, the West Indies, Pakistan, Zimbabwe, and Sri Lanka. Advertising, corporate sponsorship, and television coverage in the 1970s popularized cricket even further, making it a big-money sport, particularly in England and Australia. Today, cricket stages lucrative World Cup play for both men's and women's teams.

Cricket has never caught on in America. Though it was introduced during colonial times, it didn't stick—perhaps because it failed to appeal to the new society in America, perhaps, later on, because town ball and then baseball became much more popular stick-and-ball games.

Equipment

A cricket field is elliptically shaped, ranging in size from about 100 to 160 yards across, and usually bounded by a fence or hedge. At the center of the field is a rectangular pitch, measuring 22 yards long and 12 yards wide, with a wicket placed at each end (see illustration). The length of the pitch—22 yards—is actually the breadth of a Saxon strip-acre, an Old English agricultural measurement constituting an area 220 yards (one furlong, or a furrow—a ploughed strip of land) by 22 yards. When cricket fields began to be laid out in the 1700s, workers used surveying tools with units of measurement based on "chains." One chain was defined as 1/100th of the breadth of a furrow, or 7.92 inches. Thus, through the use of surveying chains, the English cricket field became standardized.

Wickets are made of wood and consist of three vertical stumps, measuring 29 inches high, with the outer stumps set 9 inches apart. Two

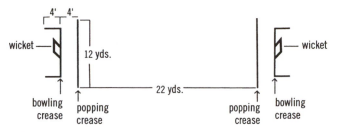

Figure 6. Cricket pitch.

wooden crosspieces set atop the stumps are referred to as bails. Cricket bats are made of wood, with rounded handles like baseball bats. One side of the head of the bat is flat, while the other side is curved. A bat's maximum width is 4¼ inches and the maximum length is 38 inches. Regulations guard against the bat head covering the width of the wickets, as several did prior to the Code of 1774, though there are no limitations on bat weight. (Some 18th-century accounts tell of bats weighing as much as 5 pounds.)

Balls are made of cork and string and covered with leather. Though the cricket ball is as hard as a baseball, the leather covering is thicker and the seam is similar to that of a tennis ball. A cricket ball weighs between 5½ and 5¾ ounces, with a circumference of between 8 ¹³/₁₆ and 9 inches. Traditionally, balls have been dyed red, although white-colored balls have begun to be used in nighttime play.

Rules

The area around each wicket, behind a white line four feet in front of each wicket and at the edge of the back of the pitch, serves as a base for the batsman (see illustration). This area is known as the popping crease; as long as the batsman is behind the popping crease, he or she can be put out. The team at bat has a batsman at each popping crease. A bowler, who is analogous to the pitcher in baseball, bowls the ball overhand (with elbow straightened) to the opposing batsman. An over (six balls) is bowled to the batsman on one end, and then an over is bowled to the batsman at the other end of the pitch. If the ball knocks the bails off the wicket or hits the batsman in front of the wicket, the batsman is out. The batsman tries to strike the ball in any direction away from the opposing team's fielders so that he or she can change places with his or her teammate in the opposite crease and score a run. If the ball reaches the boundary of the field, four runs are scored. If it clears the boundary, six runs are scored. Though a batsman needn't run after striking the ball, he or she can be put out by a fielder's catch, or by a throw that strikes the bail off the wicket while the batsman is between two creases. As one batsman is put out, another takes his place, until all 11 have been put out, which ends the inning.

Great players have been known to bat all day. Australia's Donald Bradman (1908–2001) has the highest career average of any cricketer with 99.94 runs per inning. In his prime in the 1930s, it was not uncommon for Bradman to score 400 runs in an afternoon.

The highest level of cricket, known as first-class cricket, is constituted by test match play. Test matches typically occur over five days and consist of six hours of play each day. Each team plays a total of two innings, which at times are not completed even at the end of five days. An alternate version of cricket, called one-day cricket, is limited to only one inning for each team, and there are also restrictions on the number of overs.

Bibliography

Littlewood, A. R. (June 13, 2000). "The History of Cricket Literature." CricInfo Web site, *http://www.cricket.org* (February 20, 2001).

———. (June 14, 2000). "The Measurements of Cricket." CricInfo Web site, *http://www.cricket.org* (February 20, 2001).

Mar, David. (November 27, 1998). "An Explanation of Cricket." CricInfo Web site, *http://www.cricket.org* (February 20, 2001).

Rundell, Michael. (1985). *The Dictionary of Cricket*. London: Allen and Unwin.

Stoddard, Brian, and Keith A.P. Saniford (eds.). (1998). *The Imperial Game: Cricket, Culture and Society*. Manchester, England: Manchester University Press.

▦ Croquet

Definition

Croquet is a lawn game in which players use long-handled mallets to drive wooden balls from one stake to another and back again through a series of nine wire wickets. The term "croquet" is derived from the French word *crochet*, meaning hook. Games similar to croquet developed in both France and Britain during the 17th century. Today, the game is enjoyed around the world on both the recreational and competitive tournament levels.

History

Croquet is believed to have its origins in pall mall, a British ball-and-mallet game that was popular among the British aristocracy in the 17th century. As noted above, the French had developed a similar game about the same time. Later on, in the mid-1800s, another croquet-like game called roque developed a following in America. In roque, players used short-handled mallets to knock a pair of balls through a series of 10 wickets. But the court was much smaller and made of clay, and the system of scoring and the manner in which roque was played were more similar to billiards than croquet.

Lawn croquet reached the height of its popularity during the 1860s in Britain, where an aristocrat, Walter James Whitmore, did much to promote and publicize the sport among the upper classes. Whitmore won the Moreton-on-Marsh Croquet Open Championship in 1867, then presided over the formation of the All England Croquet Club in 1868. Yet, just as croquet was becoming wildly popular, it was eclipsed in the mid-1870s by a new sport, lawn tennis (*see* Tennis). Tennis became the "in" sport—a tennis racquet became somewhat of a fashion accessory for many young well-to-do women—and because tennis courts required much more lawn space than croquet, the new craze ended up literally crowding out the older game. By 1875 the All England Croquet Club had added the words "and Lawn Tennis Club" to its name. By 1880, its name was shortened to the All England Lawn Tennis Club.

In the late 19th century, croquet seems to have spread from Britain and France to those parts of the world in which the two countries had colonial holdings. Thus the game became popular in Northern Africa, particularly Egypt, and in New Zealand and especially Australia, where today there are more registered championship players (over 6,000) than anywhere else in the world.

Croquet also gained prominence in Canada and the United States. In 1880 the American National Croquet League was established, and a series of sanctioned clubs and tournaments could be found in most northeastern United States cities. Croquet, along with bicycling, became one of the first sports in America in which women were competitive, though Victorian mores at the time led many to question whether women should exert themselves in such a manner, partly out of concern for the "weaker sex," and, perhaps more importantly, out of fear for the potentially shameful, immoral consequences of aggressive, competitive play. As a result, many women were encouraged to play more appropriate and less challenging indoor variations on the outdoor game, like parlor croquet, table croquet, and carpet croquet.

Today three types of croquet are played throughout the world. In North America, the United States Croquet Association endorses lawn croquet: in Britain, Australia, New Zealand, and throughout Europe a version called association croquet is favored; while in Egypt the game golf croquet is most popular.

Today, the MacRobertson International Shield is considered to be croquet's top honor, awarded annually to the player who wins the "world championship" tournament. The Croquet Association in Britain organizes all of the most important tournaments. Though the United States Croquet Association governs organized play in America, croquet as a competitive sport is not very popular in this country, probably because of its elitist status. Lawn croquet is much more popular in the United States as a recreation activity. For as little as $30–$50, a suburban family can buy a croquet set and stake out the back lawn for play.

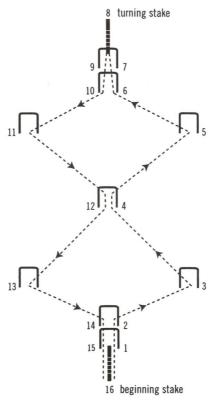

Figure 7. Layout for lawn croquet: Arrows denote the direction of play. Note that five of the nine wickets must be passed through twice, and both stakes must be hit to complete a circuit and win the game.

Equipment

The lawn croquet court is a flat, grassy area, measuring 35 by 28 yards and laid out as shown in the illustration. The beginning and turning stakes are 18 inches tall. Wickets are made of metal and are bent to form a 12-inch-high hoop with a flat top. Wickets are about 3¾ inches wide, or about one-eighth inch wider than the diameter of a croquet ball. The balls are colored blue, black, red, and yellow and weigh one pound each. Mallets must have parallel and identical end faces made of wood or a similar nonmetallic material.

Rules

As noted above, the object of the game is for each player to make the quickest complete circuit of a set of wickets. In lawn croquet, nine wickets are used, five of which must be passed through twice. A player receives bonus strokes when he or she hits a stake, passes through a wicket, or strikes an opponent's ball. The striking of another ball (known as a "roquet") gives the player the option of either playing two strokes after placing his or her ball a mallet-length away from the other ball or of driving the other ball away and playing one additional stroke. A player may accumulate no more than two additional strokes at one time. Given a series of successful wickets and roquets, a player may complete the entire croquet course in a single turn. Golf croquet is similar to association croquet. However, the wickets are referred to as hoops, and scoring is different. A match is the best of one, three or five games of seven, 13, or 19 points. One point is awarded for each hoop that the ball passes through.

Association croquet is also played between two sides of one or two players. The court has six wickets and a stake, or peg. In general, the object of the game is for each side to drive its two balls in turn through each of the six wickets, first in one direction and then in the other, and finally hit the peg placed in the middle of the court. One point is scored for each wicket made and for hitting the peg. The first team to score 26 points (13 for each player) is the winner.

Bibliography

Crawford, Scott A.G.M. (1999). "Croquet." In David Levinson and Karen Christensen (eds.), *The Encyclopedia of World Sport*. New York: Oxford University Press.

Croquet Association. (March 1999). "Introduction to the Games of Croquet." Croquet Association Web site, *http://www.croquet.org.uk/* (December 18, 2000).

Lamb, W. E. (1997). *Croquet (Know the Sport)*. Harrisburg, PA: Stackpole Books.

Lidz, F. (1995). "Mallets Aforethought." *Sports Illustrated* (September 14, 1995).

United States Croquet Assocation (USCA) Web site, *http://www.croquetamerica.com* (December 20, 2000).

■ Cross-Country Running

Definition

Cross-country running is a sport where individuals and/or teams compete over courses of varying distance and terrain. Most layouts feature hills; many courses go through streams and over wood or log barriers. Cross-country originated in the English public school and club system in the 19th century. Today, the sport is popular throughout the world, including in the United States, where thousands of boys and girls run on high school teams each fall.

History

Like many running-related sports, cross-country can point to roots in many different ancient cultures from the East African highlands to the

Middle East, Greece, Asia, and Roman-influenced Western Europe. For many cultures, running "cross-country" was a way of life—typically a means of transportation and often essential to hunting. The Greeks and Romans also used running as a means of training for combat. And the Greeks considered running to be an important component of a young man's education.

The concept of long-distance running as a character builder resurfaced in the 19th century when public schools in England began conducting cross-country races. Referred to as "paper chases" or "hare and hounds," these contests usually involved sending out a pair of "hares," armed with sacks of shredded paper procured from bookbinders, to lay a trail of paper for the following pack of "hounds." Races varied in distance, typically from 5 to 10 miles. As a prime objective of the event was to try to deceive the hounds, most trails had numerous false scents—offshoots that went up a hill or around a hedge and led nowhere. The winner of such a race had to possess a fair amount of cunning in addition to endurance.

Although the first formal paper chase competition is reputed to be the "Crick Run," held at Rugby School in 1837, it seems likely that there were earlier competitions, for the sport was quite popular in schools throughout England by the mid-19th century. Schoolboys also raced over predetermined courses. According to F.A.M. Webster's *Athletics of Today* (1929), an overview and history of sports in England, many of these courses approached 10–12 miles, with extremely difficult hills and all manner of natural hazards, including water jumps, "stiff-set hedges," and "running through 15 feet of deep water in a trout pool." Considering that most schools contested cross-country in the late fall and winter as a conditioner for soccer, rowing, or cricket, one can imagine the degree of difficulty inherent in most events. Indeed, within a modern context, these traditional races would border on child abuse.

Early cross-country races were also referred to as "steeplechases," after the practice of racing horses over hill and dale to the nearest church steeple. In 1867 the Thames Rowing Club held the first nonscholastic cross-country steeplechase at the Wimbledon Common. Twelve runners slogged their way through a bog and "up and around some of the nastiest terrain."

While cross-country became a popular off-season conditioner for amateur sportsmen, its very nature discouraged professionalism. Courses, as a rule, were located in remote wooded sites, eliminating the possibility of cordoning off an area for spectators and charging admission. Neither did the sport lend itself to gambling, as events were difficult to police. In fact, cross-country lent itself to the unexpected. At the sport's inaugural English National Championships, held at Epping Forrest in 1876, all of the runners reportedly got lost.

Nevertheless, cross-country caught on throughout Western Europe. England and France met in the first international race in 1898, and soon thereafter England inaugurated an "international" championship in 1903 between England, Ireland, Scotland, and Wales. The event became truly international in stature when France joined the competition in 1907.

Cross-country was briefly an Olympic sport in 1912, 1920, and 1924. However, the latter event, held in Paris, met with adversity when only 15 of 40 starters were able to finish a race that was contested in 97-degree heat. Thereafter, cross-country was considered ill-suited for summertime and summarily dropped from the Olympic slate of events.

Cross-country in the United States followed a different trail of development. In the 1880s and 1890s, the sport first became popular with collegiates training for track and field and with amateur club athletes. As early as 1890, the Amateur Athletic Union (AAU) was contesting championship cross-country events, and several athletic associations regulated the college sport. Though it's difficult to imagine today, the best college teams in the early 20th century were from Ivy League schools. Beginning in 1908, Cornell won four straight national cross-country titles and would claim nine championships in a 16-year period. Harvard and the University of Pennsylvania also had powerhouse teams. Cross-country was popular in the Midwest as well, particularly among Big Ten schools like Wisconsin and Illinois. It wasn't until the 1950s and 1960s that western schools like the University of Oregon, Stanford, and UCLA began to field national-class teams.

Cross-country became a popular scholastic sport in America in the early 20th century. Each weekend in the fall, all over the country, "invitational" meets are contested, where groups of boys' and girls' teams compete according to school size, ability, and/or age. Many of these meets are huge undertakings; the Manhattan Invitational, held each October at Van Cortlandt Park in New York City, usually draws over 5,000 runners from some 250 schools. Unlike other sports in America, high school cross-country also contests a true national championship. Each November, boys and girls compete in four regional qualifying races (Northeast/Mid-Atlantic, West, South, and Midwest). The top eight finishers in each race go to the national championships, held in early December in Orlando, Florida.

Though cross-country remains a non-Olympic sport, the International Amateur Athletic Federation (IAAF) contests a World Championship event for men and women each March. Since the late 1980s, runners from East Africa—specifically Kenya and Ethiopia—have dominated the race. (The two nations claimed 11 of the top 13 places in the 1991 Championship—a race with 230 finishers.) Sports physiologists have performed experiments that suggest that runners who live and train in high altitude (such as the East African highlands) have adapted their bodies to use oxygen more efficiently. As African governments began to encourage their women to train and compete in the 1990s, runners from Kenya and Ethiopia have also begun to finish high in the women's race as well.

The American women have done comparatively better at the World Championships than have the U.S. men, perhaps because the development of women's athletics in the United States was more advanced than in many other countries in the late 1960s and 1970s. The American Doris Brown Heritage won a record-tying four individual world titles, in 1967, 1968, 1969, and 1971. The U.S. women finished first in 1983, 1984, 1985, and 1987, while Lynn Jennings won back-to-back gold medals in 1990 and 1991. The U.S. men have never won the team championship. Craig Virgin is the only U.S. male ever to win individually, placing first in 1980 and 1981.

Equipment

One of the advantages of cross-country running is the low cost. Besides shorts and a T-shirt (and, of course, tights, sweatpants, sweatshirt, hat, gloves, etc., for cold-weather wear), the most money a runner invests in the sport is to buy a good pair of running shoes. Shoes that provide good support and shock absorption are essential, as young runners usually train between 5 and 10 miles a day on varying terrain, while collegiate and open runners may run as many as 10 to 15 miles a day. For competition, runners wear shoes that are lighter and more flexible. Many cross-country competitors wear spiked shoes in races. Spikes have a hard plastic plate in the forefoot that holds screw-in metal spikes. Spikes vary in length, usually between ¼ inch and ⅝ inch, depending on the terrain and ground conditions.

Rules

No two cross-country courses are the same. Most high school runners compete over 5 kilometers (3.1 miles), while collegiate men race between 8 and 10 kilometers (5 to 6.2 miles) and women run 5 kilometers. International races are usually about 12 kilometers (7.4 miles) for men and 6 to 7 kilometers (3.7 to 4.3 miles) for women.

Most team events allow between seven and nine runners per team to compete, though only the first five runners count toward the team score. Runners score by placement (e.g., 1st-3rd-5th-10th-15th yields a team score of 34). The lowest score wins.

Bibliography

Anderson, Bob, and Joe Henderson (eds.) (1977). *Guide to Distance Running*. Mountain View, CA: World Publications.

Bloom, Marc. (1978). *Cross Country Running*. Mountain View, CA: World Publications.

Lunzenfichter, Alain. (1992). *International Amateur Athletic Federation World and International Cross Country Championships*. London: IAAF Press.

▦ Cycling

Definition

Cycling is the sport of racing or riding a bicycle. Common forms of bicycle racing include road racing and track racing. The concept of riding a bicycle for competition and recreation originated in Europe, where the history of the sport closely follows the development and improvements made to the bicycle throughout the 19th century.

History

Baron Von Drais, a German nobleman, is generally credited with inventing the first rudimentary bicycle. Dubbed a "Draisine" in 1816, the machine was little more than a saddle atop a bar connecting two wheels. The rider moved the Draisine by pushing his feet along the ground. At about the same time in England the "Hobby Horse" appeared. Also known as the "Dandy Horse" (so named because its riders were mostly "dandies," or aristocratic gentlemen), the Hobby Horse added little more than a crude steering mechanism to the Draisine's bare-bones design.

But these machines were ill suited for transportation. It wasn't until the 1840s that a two-wheeled vehicle was developed that could carry a rider forward by its own propulsion. Kirkpatrick Macmillan, a Scottish blacksmith, redesigned the Hobby Horse, adding pedals and levers to provide a continuous drive to the back wheel. Equipped with a wooden frame and wooden wheels with iron-band tires, Macmillan's vehicle became the first bicycle-like contraption to cover a significant distance when the inventor rode it 70 miles to Glasgow in 1844.

However, no actual model or plans for Macmillan's cycle exist today. During the 1850s and 1860s, the French velocipede emerged as the next and perhaps greatest step toward modern bicycle design. Its name was derived from the Latin prefix *veloc*, meaning quickness, and *ped*, meaning foot. The velocipede sported pedals connected to the hub of the front of the wheel, which was slightly larger than the back wheel, a lever shoe brake on the back wheel, and framing and tires made of iron. Pierre Michaux, a Parisian manufacturer of baby carriages, is regarded as the father of the velocipede. In 1861 Michaux's shop made two velocipedes. In 1865 it filled 400 orders. Pierre Lallement, an associate of Michaux, immigrated to the United States in 1863–64, where he patented the velocipede and began manufacturing cycles in New York.

The velocipede's popularity grew in both America and France, where young men began to join velocipede clubs. St. Cloud, France, was the site of the first velocipede race, a 1200-meter sprint in 1868. One year later, over 100 riders took part in the inaugural Paris-Rouen road race, a 123-kilometer affair won by James Moore in a reported 10¾ hours.

Though the further development of the velocipede was curtailed in France by the start of the Franco-Prussian War in 1870, the machine actually received a boost on the other side of the Channel. Entrepreneurs in Britain began to mass-produce the velocipede, which became known as the "boneshaker" because of the discomfort it caused the rider over a bumpy road.

James Starley, a British inventor, relegated the boneshaker to the museum with his "Ordinary" or "High" bicycle, which he introduced in 1870. The Ordinary's basic design sported a front wheel which was roughly three times larger in diameter than the back wheel. This feature made the bicycle go much farther and faster in just one pedal stroke. Solid rubber tires, a spring-cushioned seat, and a slim all-metal frame made the Ordinary lighter and more comfortable. Between 1870 and 1878, the Ordinary underwent continual, rapid improvement as scores of patents were filed for new designs, parts, and accessories. These changes made the bicycle more popular and created the need for increased production to meet greater demand. By 1874 there were 20 firms in Britain making bicycles. By 1878 there were 64 cycling clubs in London and 189 throughout Britain. The larger clubs had over 100 members.

However, cycling was not accessible to everyone. In the early 1870s, the price of an Ordinary was about eight pounds—equivalent to eight times the average man's weekly wage. Most riders were well-to-do upper-middle-class professionals and aristocrats who had the disposable income, athletic ability, and adventuresome nature to handle the Ordinary. For older riders, children, women, and the less physically fit, the Ordinary's high center of gravity was too challenging and potentially dangerous. Even the most adept riders had to walk their bicycles down most hills, and given the condition of many of rural England's roads during the 1870s, all cyclists had to be prepared to take an occasional fall.

Though Starley also patented a tricycle design in 1878, which provided stability and ease of handling, the machine lacked the lure and excitement of a two-wheeled cycle. Enter the revolutionary "Safety" bicycle. Introduced in the 1880s, the Safety was just that—a safe, comfortable bike with equal-sized wheels, coaster brakes, and adjustable handlebars and seat. The Safety was also lighter and faster, featuring hollow steel-tube framing, a chain-driven back wheel, and inflated pneumatic tires, which were introduced by the Michelin Company in 1888.

Figure 8. (opposite) Stylized advertisements from cycling manufacturers in the late 19th century are prized artwork today. This poster was issued by Keating Cycles, a bicycle manufacturer in Holyoke, Massachusetts. (Reproduced from the Collections of the Library of Congress)

SEE THAT CUR[VE]

KEATING CYCLES

365 DAYS AHEAD OF THEM ALL

The Safety became the choice of racers and recreation cyclists alike. The Cyclist Touring Club of Great Britain, a national organization which mapped cycling routes throughout the country and lobbied for better roads and more signage, could count over 21,000 members by the late 1880s. During the 1890s, it seemed that every aristocrat and royal family in Europe was staging bicycle parties. The well-to-do regarded cycling as chic. To be seen biking in the posh parks of Western Europe was a symbol of social status. Cycling became the premiere outdoor amusement in France, with Paris established as the seat of the cycle trade. In 1890 the Avenue de la Grande Armée sported 20 bike show rooms on one street alone. Those who wanted to learn how to ride a bike could visit a bicycle rink, a large, smooth, open surface sheltered from the sun and rain. Men paid 12 francs for a lesson; women (considered more of a challenge to teach) paid 15 francs. The general public paid daily, monthly, or yearly fees to either ride inside (off the rough roads), or to simply be seen engaging in what was regarded as the fashionable social event of the day. Several large velodromes were built in Paris around the rinks. These velodromes staged races on Sunday, rented space to bike dealers, and even had restaurants on the premises.

People throughout Europe, regardless of class, were taking up cycling, as many found it easy to combine the sport with other activities. Painters, photographers, and sightseers became avid cyclists. Bike frames were designed especially for women, whose fashion went through historic changes to accommodate cycling. Cumbersome dresses and hoop skirts gave way to light jackets and matching knickerbockers or bloomers.

Mass production also made bicycles cheaper and affordable to the working classes, which used them for transportation. By the mid-1890s, bicycle manufacturing was a major consumer industry. The Palace of Industry in Paris staged twice-yearly bike shows featuring new machines and accessories. In 1895 the annual Stanley Bicycle Show in London featured 3,000 different models from over 200 manufacturers. Bike companies were pioneers in consumer marketing. To advertise their products, they produced attractive posters, many of which are considered works of art today (see illustration).

In America, over 2 million bikes were produced in 1897, driving the price of a Safety down to about $100—a marked difference from the Ordinary, which sold for around $300 in 1880 (when an average factory worker in the United States was making about $30 a month).

Bicycle racing also became popular, with point-to-point road races, multiday stage races, sprint races, and track races, conducted on an indoor, banked track called a velodrome. (See discussion of racing, following.) With so many firms invested in the business of cycling, competition was fierce for sponsored riders. The Raleigh was advertised throughout France as "La Meilleure Bicyclette du Monde" (The World's Best Bicycle), and

Raleigh paid cycling great Arthur-Auguste Zimmerman to ride its bikes. Zimmerman, a renowned sprinter, won over 1,400 races, including the British National Championships at 1, 5, and 50 miles in 1892. In America, bicycle companies like Monarch, Imperial, and Columbia paid competitive cyclists to use their products and wear jerseys sporting the company name and logo.

Though these cyclists were professionals, they didn't make a lot of money—cash prizes for road and sprint races were small. Most events also staged concurrent amateur contests. Grueling six-day races were the exception. In these events, large halls were rented and cash purses were raised to be awarded to the cyclist who could cover the most miles in six days. Such events drew thousands of spectators to the Crystal Palace in London and Madison Square Garden in New York, where followers bet on one or another of the cyclists to win, place, or show. While gambling led to rampant cheating and race fixing, as it did in many other sports, religious leaders and the medical profession also raised objections over the morality of the event. As a result, indoor endurance cycling events enjoyed only sporadic support after the turn of the century.

While the sport of cycling suffered a precipitous decline in popularity throughout the early 20th century, as the automobile became a more fashionable and exciting mode of transportation, the bicycle would stage a comeback in Europe and throughout the world in the 1920s and 1930s. Today a wide range of bicycle models makes the sport appealing and affordable to the majority of the population.

Equipment

Today there are essentially three types of bicycles: the touring/road racing model, the track racing bike, and the mountain bike. Road racing bikes have light frames typically built of aluminum, titanium, or carbon fiber. Accessories are streamlined to limit the bike's overall weight. Drop handlebars and saddles are sleek, and each pedal provides little more than a fixture onto which a cycling shoe is attached. Gearing consists of a front derailleur, which moves the chain between two or three chain rings, and a rear derailleur, which shifts the chain between as many as nine cranks. Tires are extremely thin—as narrow as 20 millimeters—and inflated to 120 pounds of pressure. Some bikes weigh as little as 20 pounds.

Track racing bikes typically have shorter frames than road bikes, are equipped with a single gear ratio, and have no brakes. Track bikes have no free wheel so that a cyclist can pedal forward or backward and at times remain stationary by applying slight pressure to the pedals in the forward and backward motion.

Mountain bikes have smaller frames, straight handlebars, front and sometimes rear shocks, and low-pressure knobby tires—all for rugged riding on variable surfaces and terrain. Though mountain bikes may have the same number of gears as a road bike, the ratios are usually much lower due to smaller chain rings in the front and larger cranks in the back.

Rules

The three types of bicycles described earlier are generally used for three different kinds of races, of which there are several variants.

Road racing is the oldest and most common form of bike racing. Road races include one-day events, stage races, criteriums, and time trials.

One-day events are usually conducted on point-to-point courses varying in distance from 100 to 300 kilometers (62 to 186 miles). Strategy and finishing speed are keys to success, as most national-class cyclists can ride for hours on end at speeds of up to 25–30 miles per hour.

Stage racing is a form of cycling that is most popular in Europe. Cyclists race each day over courses of varying distance, with the winner determined by the lowest cumulative time. Cyclists in the Tour de France, held annually throughout the first three weeks in July, circle France in a series of races totaling over 2,000 miles. Endurance, strength, and speed are the attributes of a successful stage racer.

Criterium racing consists of a series of laps held over a short closed course. Riders are typically bunched in a pack for the entire competition, with the winner decided by a sprint finish. Balance, positioning, speed, and tactical acumen are the hallmarks of the criterium specialist.

Time trialing involves racing against the clock. This form of road racing is unlike any other because the cyclist is not allowed to draft an opponent.

Track racing is conducted in a velodrome. Similar to an indoor sports arena, a velodrome has a short, banked track, usually made of wood or concrete, which is conducive to high-speed cycling. Olympic track cycling contests match sprint and 1,000-meter time trials, as well as individual and team tactical races called pursuits.

Since the late 1980s, mountain bike racing has been gaining popularity. The 2000 Olympics in Sydney, Australia, staged men's and women's cross-country and short-track races, as well as downhill and slalom events similar to those held in skiing.

Bibliography

Beeley, Serena. (1992). *A History of Bicycles*. Secaucus, NJ: Wellfleet Books.

Hammond, Richard. (1971). "Progress and Flight: An Interpretation of the American Cycle Craze of the 1890s." *American Journal of Social History* Vol. 5, pp. 235–257.

Kita, Joe. (2000). "Cycling." Microsoft Encarta Online Encyclopedia 2000, *http://encarta.msn.com* (December 28, 2000).

Rennert, Jack. (1973). *One Hundred Years of Bicycle Posters*. New York: Harper & Row.

St. Pierre, Roger. (1973). *The Book of the Bicycle*. London: Triune Books.

▦ Field Hockey

Definition

Field hockey is a game played on a wide rectangular field between two teams of 11 players who use hooked sticks to hit, push, and pass a small, hard ball downfield and into the opponent's goal. Though the origins of the sport date back thousands of years, field hockey today is played by over 4 million men and women worldwide.

History

Images from within ancient Egyptian tombs dating back to 2000 B.C. depict figures using hooked sticks to play what must have been a crude form of field hockey. History also indicates that a similar sport was played in Ethiopia before the birth of Christ, and classical Greece, Imperial Rome, and the ancient Persians, Arabs, and Aztecs in Central America can all claim hockey-like stick-and-ball games as part of their sports cultures. Similar games were played throughout Europe during the Middle Ages (A.D. 500–1500).

Hockey became a common game played among English schoolboys in the 18th century. The word "hockey" is probably derived from the French term *hocquet*, meaning shepherd's crook, perhaps by way of the English slang "hookey," meaning bent stick. It should be noted that we refer to the sport as field hockey to distinguish it from ice hockey; today, in most other parts of the world, the sport is still known as hockey.

Early accounts of hockey games in Britain point to the sport's disorganization and violence—the winning team more often than not was the side that either had more players or proved more skilled in striking the opponent with their sticks. Like so many sports and games in Britain, hockey's rules were not codified and standardized until the mid- to late 19th century, when the sport began to be considered as something more than a cold-weather alternative to cricket. By the late 19th century, British businessmen, professionals, and military officers who had played hockey as schoolboys were spreading the sport throughout the British Empire. In New Zealand, Australia, and southern Africa, hockey clubs flourished, and in India the game became more popular than it ever was in Britain. The first Indian hockey club was formed in Calcutta in 1885. By 1895 men's and women's national teams from England toured the European continent, and soon hockey was popular in France, Germany, and Spain.

Three waves of international expansion followed: in Western and Central Europe, where the sport developed regional and national organizations prior to World War I; in Latin America during the 1920s and 1930s, where hockey became popular on the club level, particularly in Brazil and Argentina; and in Eastern Europe after World War II, when hockey was embraced by a number of Eastern bloc countries as a means to demonstrate systemic political and social accomplishments.

With the formation of the International Hockey Federation (FIH) for men in 1924, the sport gained the international governing body it needed to become accepted as a team championship event in the Olympics. Beginning in 1928, India's national team has dominated Olympic competition, winning seven gold medals. Pakistan, which separated from India after the former gained its independence from Britain in 1947, has won three gold medals. Today, FIH has five affiliated continental associations—Africa, Pan America, Asia, Europe, and Oceania—and 119 member countries.

Hockey is like few other sports that were organized in the 19th century in that the popularity and competitive aspect of the women's game developed almost as quickly as did the men's. In England, women's hockey was a national campaign of sorts to preserve the country's social fabric. British scientists and social engineers argued that the country needed to create and promote health, nutrition, and exercise programs for its young upper-class women to ensure the development of healthy, productive mothers. This was during the height of Britain's world power, and the country's ruling elite wanted to maintain their standing at home and abroad. The All England Women's Hockey Association was established in 1895. The men's rules of play were immediately adopted, and the women played their first "international" game against Ireland later that year. By 1939 England had 2,100 women's hockey clubs.

The women's international game also developed along similar lines, starting with the formation of the International Federation of Women's Hockey Associations (IFWHA) in 1927. Though women's field hockey wasn't accepted as an Olympic sport until 1980, international championships have been conducted since the 1930s. In 1982 the IFWHA and the FIH merged into one organization known as the International Hockey Federation.

Hockey in the United States has been played primarily by women since its introduction in the country in the early 1920s. In 1922 the U.S. Field Hockey Association was founded, and the organization has largely promoted interscholastic and intercollegiate competition. By the 1990s, over 20,000 young women were playing hockey in the United States.

Equipment

A hockey field is 100 yards long and between 50 and 60 yards wide (see illustration). Goals are situated at the center of each goal line, and measure 12 feet wide and 7 feet high. The ball has a circumference of 9¼ inches, and has a cork center wound with twine and covered with seamless white leather. Hockey sticks have grown shorter since the 19th century, due largely to the innovation of Indian players, who found in the 1930s that a

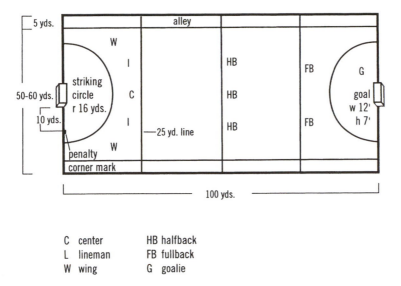

C center   HB halfback
L lineman   FB fullback
W wing   G goalie

Figure 9. A diagram of a hockey field, with a typical team formation indicated by position.

shorter stick generated more power. Sticks are made of wood and measure about 1 yard long. The stick is curved at one end on the right side and flattened on the left side. Players normally wear a shirt and shorts, or skirts, and mouth and shin guards are standard protective gear. Goalkeepers wear padding similar to that worn by an ice hockey goalie, along with a face guard and helmet.

Rules

A hockey game lasts 70 minutes—two halves of 35 minutes each. Play is resumed after each goal and at the start of each half with a bully, a ritual between two opposing players that is analogous to the face-off in ice hockey. The players tap the ground three times and the opponent's stick three times, alternately, before hitting the ball that is placed on the ground between them.

There are 11 players on each team, with positions and roles similar to those in soccer (see illustration). A general formation includes five forwards, whose main role it is to attack, three halfbacks, who patrol the midfield, two fullbacks, who play defense, and the goalkeeper.

Success in hockey depends upon stick-handling skill. All players need to be able to control, push, pass, stop, and shoot the ball. Players are permitted to shoot the ball with the flat side of the stick only. Scoring can only be done from a field goal, from a penalty corner, or from a penalty stroke.

A field goal is scored during continuous play. A field goal attempt can only be taken from within the shooting circle, a 16-yard semicircle surrounding the opponent's goal.

A penalty corner is the result of a foul committed by the defending team—usually from within the shooting circle. A member of the attacking team places the ball at the corner where the goal line bisects the sideline and passes it back to a teammate. In general, the ball must first be pushed outside the shooting circle and then pushed back in before an attacker may take a shot on goal.

A penalty stroke is a shot taken on goal by a selected player and defended only by the goalkeeper. The shot is taken from a spot 7 yards in front of the goal, and all players besides the shooter and the goalkeeper must stand outside the circle. Penalty strokes are usually the result of a foul committed by the defending team that prevented a shot from going in the goal.

Though hockey is not a contact sport—players are not permitted to hit, shove, or trip an opponent, nor are they allowed to strike, hook, or hold down an opponent's stick—the flow of action is nonstop and demands stamina and endurance similar to soccer and cross-country running.

Bibliography

Anders, Elizabeth, and Sue Myers. (1998). *Field Hockey: Steps to Success*. Champaign, IL: Human Kinetics.

"India's Olympic History: Golden Moments (1928–1980)." (2001). Indian Field Hockey Home Page, *http://www.bharatiyahockey.org/* (April 26, 2001).

Miloy, Neville. *The History of Hockey*. Laleham on Thames, England: Lifeline Books.

U.S. Field Hockey Association. (2001). "About Field Hockey Rules." U.S. Field Hockey Association Web site, *http://www.usfieldhockey.com/* (February 8, 2001).

▦ Gaelic Football

Definition

Gaelic football is a game played between two teams of 15 players on a large rectangular field with an H-shaped goal at each end. The object of the game is to kick or punch the ball either through the uprights or past the goalkeeper into the net. Though the game appears to have elements of rugby and soccer, it originated in the Middle Ages in Ireland. During the late 19th and early 20th century, Gaelic football became a very popular spectator sport in Ireland, symbolizing the importance of a distinct Irish culture and the Irish nationalist movement itself.

History

Gaelic football has roots very similar to those of hurling (*see* Hurling). There are accounts of football games in Ireland dating back to the 8th century. During medieval times, entire villages would engage in a folk version of Gaelic football. The men from each village would gather at a point equidistant from each settlement. As many as 100 or more men a side would attempt to advance the ball to the opposing town, where the game would end when the ball was driven over a predetermined boundary.

It wasn't until the 19th century that Gaelic football was formalized as a competitive sport. Ireland, which had come under British control, was interested in preserving its traditional culture. In 1884 the Gaelic Athletic Association (GAA) was founded in Dublin to keep traditional Gaelic sports from dying out. The next year, the first rules for Gaelic football were written, and the GAA began contesting a national championship in 1887. Like hurling, Gaelic football's national tournament brought together teams representing each county in Ireland. As a result, the game had a unifying influence on a country that had been devastated culturally and economically by British rule. For much of the 20th century, Gaelic football has been connected with the Irish nationalist movement. Political leaders often speak at games, and, in some cases, games have been held to raise funds for the nationalist cause. Gaelic football is linked with the infamous "Bloody Sunday," when, on November 21, 1920, violence erupted between Irish nationalists and British troops. After a group led by the Irish nationalist leader Michael Collins killed 12 British soldiers in retaliation for British intelligence's infiltration of the nationalist movement, the British "Black and Tans" and the Dublin police entered Croke Park in Dublin during a Gaelic football match. The troops and police began firing at the field and into the crowd of 10,000 spectators. Two players and at least 12 spectators were killed.

Today, the GAA still conducts the All-Ireland championships each summer, while professional league play is contested in the winter. Gaelic football is Ireland's most popular participatory sport, with an estimated 250,000–275,000 men and women playing the game at various competitive levels. Though the sport has little following outside of Ireland, Irish immigrants to America, Canada, and Australia have brought the game on a club level to urban areas in these countries. Australian Rules football is played by similar rules, and many players have excelled at both Aussie Rules and Gaelic football (*see* Australian Rules Football).

Equipment

Players wear jerseys, shorts, and soccer cleats for traction. The ball that is used is round and slightly smaller than a soccer ball.

Rules

Gaelic football is played on a field approximately 140 yards long and 90 yards wide. The goalposts are the same as those used in hurling. Two vertical posts are set 14 yards apart, with a crossbar set 8 feet off the ground between them. The bottom section of the goal is strung with netting.

A point is scored by playing the ball over the crossbar. A goal, worth three points, is scored by playing the ball between the goalposts and under the crossbar.

The ball is advanced by either kicking or "hand-passing"—a striking motion with the hand or fist. A player may also carry the ball a distance of four steps, at which time the ball must be either bounced or "soloed"—an action of dropping the ball onto the foot and kicking it back into the hand. Players are not allowed to bounce the ball more than twice in a row. Players are also not allowed to lift the ball directly from the ground.

A defensive player can use either of two methods to try to take the ball from an attacking player. A defender can tackle an opponent "shoulder-to-shoulder," where contact is made with the shoulder in an attempt to throw the opponent off balance. The hips or elbows cannot be used in this maneuver, and at least one foot of the tackling player needs to be on the ground. Players are also allowed to knock the ball from the attacker's hands with an open palm.

Teams consist of 15 players. A goalkeeper, fullback, two corner backs, and three halfbacks are defensive players. There are two midfielders and eight forwards, who are chiefly attacking, or offensive, players. Each team is allowed three substitutes throughout the game. Games consist of two 45-minute halves.

As indicated above, there are two methods of scoring. Players may score by using either the hand or foot. However, a goal may not be scored by hand-passing. A goal scored by the hand only counts if a player in possession of the ball drops it and then punches the ball into the goal.

Bibliography

Gaelic Athletic Association. (2001). "The Early Years of the GAA: 1884–1922." Gaelic Athletic Association Web site, *www.gaa.ie/* (April 20, 2001).

———. (2001). "An Introduction to Gaelic Football." Gaelic Athletic Association Web site, *www.gaa.ie/* (April 20, 2001).

International Australian Football Championship. (2001). "Early History of Australian Football." International Australian Football Championship Web site, *www.iafc.org.au/origins.html* (April 20, 2001).

▦ Golf

Definition

Golf is a ball-and-stick game in which a player attempts to drive a small, hard ball into a series of 18 holes on a specially designed course in as few strokes as possible. Originating in Scotland, the game has spread to virtually all corners of the globe. By the end of the 20th century, golf in America was more popular as recreation than at any other time in history, as an estimated 20-plus million Americans were playing at least one round of golf each year.

History

Golf's beginnings are ill defined. Some historians date the start of the sport from the late 13th century in Belgium, where a game called *chole* consisted of players using clubs with iron heads to hit egg-shaped wooden balls toward a target. A similar sport in northern France involved knocking feather-stuffed balls at posts and tree stumps. Sixteenth-century illustrations depict both the Dutch (*het kolven*) and the French (*jeu de mail*) playing golf-like games, though these pastimes were confined to much smaller spaces. Dutch writings and artwork of the 16th and 17th centuries also suggest a diversion played in the countryside and on frozen canals: *spel metten colve*, which translates to "game played with a club."

Residents of St. Andrews in Scotland also claim golf as their own, suggesting that the locals played a crude version of golf as early as the 12th century. It is not altogether clear whether this game was closer to shinny or hurling. However, a mid-14th-century stained glass window at Gloucester Cathedral in Scotland depicts a figure swinging a club at a ball, and by the mid-15th century the term "golfe" began to appear in the decrees of the Parliament of King James II. The king issued several proclamations in the mid- to late 15th century that effectively banned golf in Scotland, setting fines and imprisonment not only for those who played the game, but also for subjects who permitted their land to be used for golf.

During this time, archery was still the chief method of warfare, and the king was worried that too many knights and noblemen were devoting too much attention to golf, and not enough time to practicing with bow and arrow. It wasn't until the early 16th century that gunpowder made cannons and guns the principal means of national defense. And it was then, not surprisingly, that Scottish noblemen and gentry were able to persuade the then king, James IV, to rescind the anti-golf legislation and to take up the game himself. From that time on, golf in Scotland was considered a royal game of sorts. Though Scottish nobility spread the game to England and throughout the British Isles during the 17th century, the sport lacked formal structure until the formation in 1754 of the St. Andrews Society of Golfers (which in 1834 would become the Royal and Ancient Golf Club, the name by which it is known today, when King William IV joined its ranks). The society issued the first rules for golf in 1754—an initial attempt to standardize what must have been a very imprecise game.

Early courses in Scotland and England were little more than rough stretches of pastureland that were often shared with livestock, schoolchildren, horse racers, cricketers, and even companies of soldiers on maneuvers. Often a player would employ a "fore-caddie," whose job it was to run ahead and clear the course of people and debris. The fore-caddie would also mark each hole with a stake, which would be carried from hole to hole around the course. As late as 1856, the famed St. Andrews course—which is still used for the prestigious British Open—consisted of just nine holes. One played the course forward then backward to complete a round of eighteen. Given the presence of stone walls, gouges in the ground left by carts and livestock, and the random stream or bog that might appear in the middle of the fairway, there was no need to design hazards or sand traps. In fact, the idea of hiring a course architect and laying out 18 holes with man-made obstacles is a late 19th–early 20th-century development.

Golf has always been a sport of the upper classes. In the 18th and 19th centuries, the majority of the players in the British Isles were aristocrats and gentry. These were men who had the means and leisure to pursue a game that took several hours to play, and that required equipment that could cost as much as a laborer's annual wage. (A set consisted of 8–10 clubs, and even the balls were handmade.) Golf players also lived on estates, or had access to large rural tracts of land, a good way from crowded villages and cities.

Though most players were termed amateurs—they didn't make a living from golf—there was a growing class of professionals beginning in the early 19th century in Scotland. But unlike today's club professional, who spends time giving golf lessons and recommending equipment for club members, the 19th-century golf pro was more like a prizefighter—someone club members could bet on in competition with the rival club pro. A popular form of play was single or doubles match play. Two sides would play an agreed-upon number of holes, with the side recording the lowest number of strokes declared the winner. Some of these matches were extremely lucrative for both player and backers. An 1849 match between St. Andrews' resident pros, Tom Morris and Allan Robertson, and the Dunn brothers of Musselburgh Club awarded a purse of 400 pounds. In contrast, the 1899 British Open, the most prestigious championship of its time for professional golfers, offered a purse of just 50 pounds to the winner.

Prior to the late 19th century, there was no such concept as par (the average, or accepted standard, for each hole)—players simply counted total strokes, and scores were extremely high compared to today's standards. Tom Morris, Jr., a Tiger Woods–like phenom of the 1860s and 1870s, had won four British Opens by the age of 21 (see illustration). Young Tom's 1868 score of 157 over 36 holes was a record by 13 strokes, and many considered his 149 in 1870 to be an "untouchable mark."

Rough course conditions and primitive equipment explain the high scores. Before the mid-1800s, players used "featheries," or balls which were stuffed with goosefeathers. Ball makers would stitch three pieces of horsehide together in the shape of an orb, then turn it inside out, leaving a tiny opening. The ball would then be stuffed with feathers, sewn up tight,

Figure 10. Scotland's top professional golfers gathered at St. Andrews in 1867. Young Tom Morris is second from the right; his father, Tom Morris, is third from right. Willie Dunn is fifth from right. (PGA Golf Hall of Fame)

and soaked in water to shrink the casing. When the feathers on the inside dried, they expanded, producing a hard ball. Unfortunately, the ball did not hold its shape well, and was prone to flattening or going lopsided when it got wet. Golf ball technology didn't advance until the 1850s and 1860s, when balls began to be made out of gutta-percha, a rubber-like resin from Singapore. These balls were known as "gutties," and were immediately preferred over featheries because they flew farther and held their shape much longer. Though gutties were initially smooth-surfaced, golfers soon began to notice that balls that were nicked or dented actually played straighter. This led manufacturers to fashion pocked molds, which produced balls that look much like those in use today.

The advent of the guttie also revolutionized the golf club. Prior to the 1870s, most clubs had wooden heads. The guttie—which could take a pounding and maintain its shape—made the iron-faced club a reality. Clubs actually improved markedly over the 18th and 19th centuries. A famous verse of 1721 refers to a golf club as a "weighty engine," and a poem from 1743 describes a golfer who "strain'd his stout arm the mighty club to wield." Early clubs measured as long as 4½ feet from the head to the end of the shaft. Most shafts were made of hickory, with apple, ash, or beechwood used for the head. A piece of lead was inserted into the back of the head to give the club weight and power. These old clubs were closer in design to a hockey stick than a modern golf club, as the face of the club was set at a 90-degree angle to the ground. Early in the 18th century, club makers began to produce a club with a concave head that could scoop or lift the ball up out of sand, dirt, and gravel. These clubs came to be known as spoons, and by the 19th century a well-equipped golfer had a long, middle, and short spoon. The driver—a club used exclusively to hit for distance—began to resemble its modern namesake in the mid-19th century, when players discovered that a convex-shaped head—though perhaps more difficult to control—would hit a ball much farther than a flat-shaped head.

Perhaps it was golf's "noble" beginnings that explain its lack of popularity in America until the late 19th century. It wasn't until the 1880s and 1890s that the United States, a new industrial giant, had developed a significant class of wealthy families, many of whom had amassed their riches through finance, railroads, oil, mining, and manufacturing. Games like golf and tennis were embraced by the rich—not so much as sport, but as a context for and symbol of social status. Exclusive clubs were founded in posh northeastern neighborhoods like Southampton (New York), Brookline (Boston), and Newport (Rhode Island), where the upper classes could display their wealth and fashion far from the working classes. The late 19th century was also a time of violent labor strife in America, as millions of uneducated low-wage factory workers, many of them recent immigrants from Europe and virtually all of them uprooted from rural life, struggled to improve wages and working conditions. Taken in this context, it is not difficult to understand the traditional criticism of golf in the United States as a classist and racist game.

Though golf today still can't be classified as a popular "working-class" sport like baseball or football, it is being played by more and more people as the country's booming economy in the 1990s made the game affordable to a greater portion of the population. Changing patterns of work have perhaps created more leisure time in which to enjoy golf. Golf is also a "life sport." Men and women play golf well into their 70s and 80s, and the proliferation of new golf courses in the warm-weather retirement states of Arizona and Florida attests to the game's popularity among senior citizens. Golf has also become more popular among teenagers, with many schools throughout the country either fielding boys' and girls' interscholastic golf teams or funding intramural programs at local clubs.

Rules

To win a game of golf a player must complete a certain number of holes with the least amount of strokes. While a game of golf generally consists of 18 holes, most tournaments score 36–72 holes. Par is the theoretical score that the best golfer would record over each hole and is based on the length of the hole and any relevant course factors such as water hazards, roughs, trees, and so on. Par is higher for women than men, and most holes rate between three and five strokes. One stroke under par is known as a birdie, two strokes under is an eagle, and one stroke over par is a bogie.

While most tournaments are scored by stroke play—the number of strokes for each hole is counted—a common form of recreational play is known as match play. In match play, golfers play an agreed-upon number of holes. Each hole is won by the side with the fewest strokes; the game is won by the side that has won the most holes. In best-ball play, typically contested between two pairs of golfers, one side plays its better ball against the better ball of its opponents.

Bibliography

Astor, Gerald. (1991). *The PGA World Golf Hall of Fame Book*. New York: Prentice-Hall.

Cotton, Henry. (1975). *A History of Golf*. Philadelphia: J. B. Lippincott.

Grimsley, Will. (1966). *Golf: Its History, People and Events*. Englewood Cliffs, NJ: Prentice-Hall.

▦ Handball

Definition

Handball is a singles or doubles game played on a one-, three-, or four-wall court in which opposing players alternately hit a small rubber ball to the front wall. The object of the game is to make a shot that the opposition cannot return. Though the ancient Egyptians played a handball-like game, the modern sport of organized handball began in the late 19th century in Ireland. Today the game is played worldwide for recreation and exercise.

History

The first recorded history of a ball game played with the hand is from Egypt and North and South America. Ancient Egyptian priests (2000 B.C.) of the temple of Osiris in Thebes are depicted, on tombs, striking a ball with the hand. Over 700 ball courts have been identified at sites stretching from modern-day Arizona to Nicaragua, with the oldest dating back to about 1500 B.C. in the Mexican plateau area. In Europe, the Greeks, too, had a handball-like game. Alexander the Great (450 B.C.) of Macedonia is credited with spreading the game to the Greek colonies in Italy. We can surmise that handball was then disseminated throughout Europe by the Roman Empire.

In more recent times, the development of handball has been linked to racket sports. Fourteenth-century accounts of the French *jeu de paume* tell of a tennis-like game in which participants struck a ball back and forth with a hand bound with cord or rattan. But this game didn't use a wall to rebound the ball. Ball play with the hand against a wall is first mentioned in Scotland in 1427, when King James I, an ardent handball player, had his men block up a cellar window in the palace courtyard that was interfering with his game. Unfortunately, this move contributed to his downfall when, shortly thereafter, assassins came to murder him and his only escape route, the cellar window, was blocked.

Though such handball games seem to have been popular in alleyways and courtyards throughout Europe in the 16th century, the game came under fire from the church in the 17th century. Concerned with preserving their stained glass windows, many churches forbade the play of handball in their precincts.

There are many accounts of one-wall handball being played in Ireland in the 18th century, and Irish immigrants to England, Australia, and the United States spread the game to a much wider audience. In the early 19th century, handball in England began to be played with two sidewalls (the English referred to this game as "fives"), and this feature was brought back to Ireland. During this time, the game was supported by the aristocracy in England, who built expensive courts at their country estates, and by the military and landowning classes in the Dublin area. Commoners continued to play a one-walled version of the game, often against the wall of a house or church.

It wasn't until the mid- to late 19th century that the sport began to take shape as a competitive, organized game. Itinerant Irish professionals began to travel throughout the country, taking on all comers and earning a living from wagering and prize money. Many professionals were also accomplished athletes in other sports. David Browning of Limerick, the top handball player of the 1880s, was also a champion rower, weight thrower, and boxer. During the 1880s, self-proclaimed Irish and American champions played each other in Ireland and New York. These matches drew thousands of spectators. Yet by the late 19th century, the sport was suffering from disorganization. No two courts were the same, rules varied according to region, and the machinations of promoters and gamblers jeopardized the legitimacy of play.

The Gaelic Athletic Association in Ireland (organized, 1884) wrote the first rules for the game. The Amateur Athletic Union (AAU) in America held the first official tournament in 1897. During the early 20th century, the sport introduced several major changes, chief among them the introduction of a back wall. During the latter half of the 20th century, the game became more accessible as a form of exercise to a greater portion of the population in Europe and America. In the United States, handball was promoted by the YMCA, which built courts and conducted regional and national tournaments from the 1930s through the 1960s. The game also became a favorite at colleges, with many recreation centers constructing handball and squash courts. The U.S. Handball Association regulates tournament play and makes periodic revisions to the sport's rules.

Equipment

Besides a basic uniform of shorts, T-shirt, and court shoes, handball players need little else beyond a glove and a ball. Soft leather gloves are worn on both hands. The ball is made of rubber, weighing about 2.3 ounces and measuring approximately 1⅞ inches in diameter. Balls have a good deal of rebound. Rules stipulate that a ball dropped on a hardwood floor from a height of 70 inches must have a rebound of between 48 and 52 inches.

Rules

Today, virtually all courts are indoor and made of wood. Dimensions are 20 feet high, 20 feet wide, and 40 feet long, with a back wall measuring at least 14 feet. Five lines are marked on the court:

Short line: The short line is parallel to the front and back wall and is 20 feet from the front wall.

Service line: The service line is parallel to the short line and five feet in front of it.

Service zone: The service zone is the area between the short line and service line.

Service box: Two service boxes are located at each end of the service zone, measuring 18 inches from each side wall.

Receiver's restraining lines: These lines are located five feet behind the short line and extend six feet from each side wall.

The basic rules of handball are as follows:

- A game consists of 21 points. If one side reaches 21 with a less than 2-point lead, the game continues until one side has gained a 2-point margin. A match consists of three games, with the first side to win two games winning the match.
- Handball is most commonly a singles or doubles game.
- Only the serving side can score points.
- The front wall, back wall, side wall, and ceiling may be used for shots.
- A serve must hit the front wall and rebound to the floor beyond the service zone before an opponent can return it.
- Opponents must return the ball to the front wall before it hits the floor a second time. The ball may rebound off side walls or the ceiling before it hits the front wall.

Bibliography

McElligott, Thomas. (1984). *The Story of Handball: The Game, the Players, the History.* Dublin: Wolfhound Press.

O'Connor, Tom. (2001). "History of Handball." U.S. Handball Association Web site, *http://ushandball.org/* (April 20, 2001).

U.S. Handball Association. (1990). *The Official United States Handball Association Handball Rules.*

U.S. Handball Association Web site, *http://ushandball.org/* (April 20, 2001).

▦ Horse Racing

Definition

Horse racing is the sport of racing specially bred horses over varying distances, usually on a flat, oval track. The most popular form of the sport is thoroughbred racing, which exists today primarily for legalized gambling. Other forms of horse racing include harness racing and steeplechase. Horse racing is the second most widely attended U.S. sport, trailing only baseball.

History

Horse racing is one of the oldest sports. Nomadic tribesmen of central Asia first domesticated horses around 4500 B.C. We can surmise that, shortly thereafter, horses began to be raced. The ancient Greeks and Romans raced horses; in fact, the image of the Roman chariot race suggests the roots of modern-day harness racing.

The advent of modern racing is typically traced to the 12th century, when English knights returned from the Crusades with Arab horses. Over the next several centuries, these Arab stallions were bred with English mares to produce "racing" horses—animals with a superior combination of speed and endurance. Though horse racing is typically referred to as the "Sport of Kings," this is a misnomer considering the origins of the sport in England. Like cars in our culture, horses were essential for transportation and for work. A fine horse conveyed a sense of status for its owner. Though it was almost a given that members of the nobility and the landowning elite would own a top-flight horse—and challenge one another to match races to settle rivalries or disputes—the common laborer, too, was a proud horse owner and horse racer. As horse racing began to become a professional sport in the early 18th century—with match races giving way to "field" races offering prize money—the sport of racing became a social event. Early on, most of the largest races were held in conjunction with local fairs or annual festivals, and this ensured that both the gentry and the common farmer would be in attendance. Though the two classes typically did not race head-to-head (those of means owned purebred horses; the working class usually owned mixed-breed horses), they did occasionally meet—usually when more numbers were needed to boost the field.

In the early 18th century, the most common kinds of races were handicap events, weight-for-age races, and open sweepstakes. Handicapping involved assessing the track record of all the horses in a race and giving the better horses more weight to carry. This calculation took into account the weight of the jockey as well. Weight-for-age events enabled older, stronger horses to race younger ones—again, additional weight was added to theoretically even out the field. The "open" race, which has come to embody all major thoroughbred racing, was based on the very best horses racing head-to-head.

As racecourses sprang up throughout England and larger purses began to be offered to lure the best horses, the sport became a profitable venture for horse owners and breeders. Given Britain's superior position in world trade, there was a sufficient number of gentlemen in the country who had the wealth and leisure to own and race purebred horses. These men demanded that standards be set in the sport to protect and advance their investment. In 1750 the sport's elite met to form the Jockey Club, an organization that established complete control over English horse racing. Several races were designated as standard sweepstakes races. (As in the United States today, where the Preakness, Belmont, and Kentucky Derby are considered the three elite races, or ultimate tests, for the best three-year-old racers. A horse that wins all three races is said to have won the Triple Crown.) The Jockey Club also took steps to regulate the breeding of racehorses.

Breeding

James Weatherby, who served as an accountant to the Jockey Club, was given the task of researching the pedigree, or family history, of essentially every racehorse in England. In 1791 Weatherby published the results of his search in the *General Stud Book*. Soon, by the early 19th century, only "thoroughbreds," or purebred horses whose lineage could be verified by the *General Stud Book*, were allowed to race. Over 200 years later, the *General Stud Book* continues to be updated and periodically published. All thoroughbreds today can trace their pedigree back to one of three stallions, known as the "foundation sires." These stallions were the Byerly Turk (born in 1679), the Darley Arabian (b. 1700), and the Godolphin Arabian (b. 1724).

Betting

Like many professional sports that originated in England during the 18th or 19th century, horse racing profited from and was largely defined by betting. In England, horse racing has managed to keep fairly clean due to stiff regulations established and administered by the Jockey Club. In the late 19th century, a Frenchman named Pierre Oller developed a betting system known as parimutuel wagering. Under this system, a fixed percentage is initially taken out of the total sum wagered to cover track operating expenses, racing prize money, and state and local taxes. The balance is then divided by the total number of bettors to determine the return on each bet. The "odds," or projected payoff, are then calculated and posted before the start of the race. Odds of 3 to 1 indicate that the bettor will receive $3 for every $1 wagered if his or her horse is the winner. The parimutuel system is used by virtually all major racetracks throughout the world today.

Thoroughbred Racing in America

Horse racing became quite popular in America, particularly in the South, where the plantation culture—defined by large landowners with ample wealth and leisure—largely copied the scene in England. In 18th-century colonial America, many planters (rich southern landowners) went off to study in England. They returned with a penchant for dueling, cricket, and racing horses. But the American scene wasn't organized like Britain's—it wouldn't be until after the Civil War in the 1860s that the first American stud book was published. With the rise of the industrial economy in the late 19th century, horse racing became a big business in the United States. By 1890 there were 314 racetracks operating in the country.

However, there was no governing body for the sport in the United States, and this lack of order enabled organized crime to exercise influence over the sport. A number of tracks were affected by race fixing, and several state legislatures acted to ban the sport. By 1908 there were only 25 racetracks left open in the country. Two developments in the early 20th century essentially saved horse racing in America: legislation that legalized parimutuel betting in a number of states, where track owners agreed to pay the state a percentage of all monies wagered; and the heroics of Man o' War, a dominant three-year-old that, despite narrowly missing the Triple Crown in 1920, brought crowds of spectators back to the tracks.

Today, thoroughbred racing exists in about half the states in America. Elite thoroughbreds compete in a handful of races. The richest, like the Kentucky Derby and the Breeders' Cup, offer over $1 million in prize money.

Two other forms of horse racing, harness racing and steeplechase, have limited followings. Harness racing is an American sport, having developed in the early 19th century. The term "harness racing" actually originated much later among sportswriters, who referred to the sport by the harness placed on the horse. Horses pull drivers who ride in small two-wheeled carts called sulkies. There are two different breeds of horses, trotters and pacers, which are identified by their gaits. A trotter's legs move in diagonal pairs—the front right and rear left together, and the front left and rear right together. A pacer does the opposite—the right front and right rear legs move at the same time, followed by the front left and front rear legs. These gaits are bred into the horses, which are also known as Standardbreds. Like the early thoroughbred races in England, American harness racing got its start at country fairs and festivals, and probably has practical or utilitarian origins—horses were used to pull wagons or carriages, and were an integral part of American culture. When industrialism in the early 20th century ushered in the car as a popular mode of transportation, harness racing began to lose popularity. Still, harness racing welcomed parimutuel betting in the 1940s, and the sport has retained pockets of popularity, particularly in the Northeast, since that time.

Steeplechase originated in England and Ireland during the 18th century. Legend has it that foxhunters began to engage in impromptu races after the hunt. They would pick a far distant object to race to—perhaps the church steeple in the next village—and then set off over hill and dale, jumping brush, fences, and stone walls, and fording streams. The spontaneous sport soon became good training for fox hunting, and eventually a sport unto itself. Organized racing began in England in the early 19th century and has continued to this day. Most courses run from three to five miles long and feature fences, water jumps, and other man-made obstacles that one might encounter on a foxhunt. Aintree, the site of England's famed Grand National, is regarded as the birthplace of steeplechase racing. The sport has a presence in the United States—particularly in the South, where Callaway Gardens in Georgia and Morven Park in Virginia host races on the Sport of Kings Challenge, a multimillion-dollar series of international steeplechase events.

Bibliography

Ainslie, Tom. (1988). *Ainslie's Complete Guide to Thoroughbred Racing*. New York: Fireside Books.

Huggins, Michael. (1999). *Flat Racing and British Society (1790–1914): A Social and Economic History*. Oaklawn Jockey Club (2001). Hot Springs, AR.

"A Quick Guide to Racing," Oaklawn Jockey Club, Inc. Web site, *http://www.oaklawn.com/* (February 17, 2001).

Parker, Michael. (1998). "The History of Horse Racing." Mike Parker Real Estate, Inc. Web site, *http://www.mrmike.com/explore/hrhist.htm*. (February 16, 2001).

Raymond, G. (1983). *Steeplechasing*. New York: Viking Press.

▦ Hurling

Definition

Hurling is a stick-and-ball game played between two teams of 15 players on a large rectangular field. Hurling is known as the national field sport of Ireland, where it is played almost exclusively. Its rich history spans ancient Celtic civilization to the All-Ireland Championship finals today, which annually draw close to 100,000 spectators and a nationally televised audience in the millions.

History

Like Celtic history itself, the roots of hurling are steeped in folklore and myth. The earliest mention of hurling is found in the Irish Annals, which link the game with the Battle of Moytura (1272 B.C.). Legend has it that the island's invaders first defeated the natives in a game of hurling, thus winning lordship over all Ireland. Irish mythology spins tales of the hurling boy wonder, Setanta, nephew of the King of Ulster, who played with a bronze stick and a silver ball. As a result of England's invasion of Ireland in 1169, the game seems to have been taken back to England, where pockets of hurlers still exist, particularly in Cornwall and throughout southwestern England.

The folk version of the sport, known as "Gaelic hurling," or "hurling home," involved residents from neighboring villages. Two sides of as many as a hundred players each might square off over an ill-defined field measuring several square miles. Often the goals were famous markers, such as a large tree or rock. The sport, which is played with a short curved stick, known as a *caman* or *hurley*, and a small leather-covered cork ball, called a *sliothar*, has a historic reputation for roughness that dates back to these "hurling home" matches. Folks who carried a grudge against a neighbor could settle the score by cracking a hurley over his head during "play." Hurling eventually became so popular that many people were neglecting their work, and as a result, legislators in some areas banned hurling from common lands in the 14th and 15th centuries.

Today's game is a direct descendant of "hurling at goals," which was extremely popular in 18th-century Ireland. Wealthy landowners would draft the best hurling players from among their tenant farmers and stage match games. These games were not only for regional bragging rights, but also provided an excellent opportunity for gambling. Betting, ironically, helped promote the development of the game. Huge sums of money were wagered, and because of this, many landlords lobbied for uniform rules to protect their investment. In the late 18th century, basic rules were set forth, and a code of behavior for players was espoused to ensure that order was maintained. Each team fielded 21 players, who, for the first time, played set positions like goalie, defense, halfback, and forward. The playing field was also laid out in a rectangular shape with goals consisting of two posts connected above the ground by a crossbar.

The "golden age" of hurling lasted until the early 19th century, when English and Scottish occupation of Ulster largely eradicated Gaelic culture. With the Act of Union in 1801, England effectively made Ireland its colony, imposing English rule and the Protestant Church over a predominantly Catholic people. When the Irish were devastated in the 1840s by a potato crop failure, which brought widespread famine and disease, many rightly blamed British agricultural and trade policies and wanton indifference to their people's suffering. Soon thereafter, Irish natives began to voice their preference for independence from Britain. By the late 19th century, a strong nationalist movement was under way. The revival of traditional Irish culture became important, as the Irish developed a sense of pride and identity in celebrating their own literature, art, music, and sports.

In 1884 the Gaelic Athletic Association (GAA) was formed, and it began to promote the distinctly Irish sports of hurling and Gaelic football (similar to rugby). The GAA, which is still the national governing body of hurling, made the sport central to each community by organizing play along regional lines. Teams from each parish, or county, played one another in an annual tournament, which soon became a rallying event for the Irish nationalist movement. Today's All-Ireland hurling final, played in Croke Park, Dublin, continues to be an important political and cultural event, attended by Ireland's most prominent political leaders and by crowds that number nearly 100,000.

Beginning in the early 20th century, the sport was introduced to women in the guise of "camogie." Camogie resembles hurling, although the field is smaller (110 meters by 68 meters), the stick, or caman, is smaller than a hurley, and the ball is also lighter than the sliothar. There is also less contact in camogie. Today, the sport is played on a national level, and an All-Ireland camogie championship is contested each year. Like hurling, camogie has come to be identified with Irish nationalism and Gaelic culture.

Equipment

While a hurler's uniform, cleated shoes, and light padding are indistinguishable from a field hockey or soccer player's attire, the hurley and sliothar are two pieces of equipment that make the sport unique. The hurley is a narrow-shafted stick that measures about 3½ feet long. The stick is curved outward at the end, providing a rounded "blade" surface about 3–4 inches wide which is used to catch, carry, or strike the sliothar. The sliothar has a cork center and a leather cover, and measures 9–10 inches in circumference, similar to the size of a field hockey ball. The surface of the sliothar is marked with raised ridges, which make it easier to carry on a stick than a smooth-surfaced ball.

Rules

The hurling pitch is rectangular, measuring about 145 meters long and 90 meters wide (see illustration). The goals at each end of the field consist of two goalposts, which are 16 feet high and set 6.5 meters apart, and a crossbar, set 8 feet off the ground and strung with netting.

In hurling, players can strike the sliothar in the air or on the ground. Picking up and carrying the sliothar is allowed, but for no more than four steps at a time. Though the sliothar can then be bounced on the hurley and back into the hand, players are forbidden to do this more than twice. A preeminent skill in hurling involves balancing and bouncing the sliothar on the hurley while running at top speed. To score, players strike or throw the sliothar off the hurley and either over the crossbar for one point, or

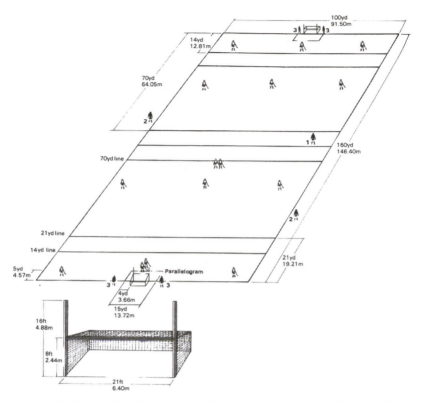

Figure 11. Hurling field. (Reproduced from *Rules of the Game*, by the Diagram Group [New York: St. Martin's Press, 1990], p. 182.)

into the netted goal for three points. A few of the finer rules of hurling include:

A player who is in possession of the sliothar may not score with the sliothar in his or her hand.

However, if the sliothar is in flight, a player may score by striking it with his or her hand.

A player may not pick the sliothar directly off the ground; a roll-lift or jab-lift with the hurley must be used.

A free-puc, similar to a corner kick in soccer, is awarded when a defender knocks the sliothar over his or her endline.

Interference by the defending team in the goal results in a penalty shot, which may be defended by up to three players on the goal line.

The goalkeeper is perhaps the most important player in hurling. The keeper's task is to defend the goal, clear the sliothar, and lead the defense.

There are six players who are chiefly defenders: two cornerbacks and a fullback who represent the last line of defense before the goal, and three halfbacks. Defenders need to mark and block opponents and clear the ball as quickly as possible to the midfielders or up the wings. Two midfielders serve as links between the defensive halfbacks and the offensive forwards. Midfielders must have good passing skills and stamina, as they usually do the most running in the game. There are six forwards who are usually aligned in two rows of three. Strategy typically centers on a lot of movement—forwards switch positions, blocking midfielders and backs, setting picks, and generally creating space into and out of which scoring plays can develop.

Teams are allowed a maximum of three substitutions in a game, so strength and stamina are important player qualities. Most games last 60 minutes and consist of two 30-minute halves, though hurling games at the highest level of play (e.g., the All-Ireland Championships) last 80 minutes.

Bibliography

Gaelic Athletic Association. (2001). "The Game of Hurling," Gaelic Athletic Association Web site, *http://www.gaa.ie/sports/hurling/* (March 7, 2001).

Sugden, John, and Alan Bairner. (1993). *Sport, Sectarianism and Society in Divided Ireland*. Leicester, UK: Leicester University Press.

Worth, Sylvia (ed.). (1990). *The Rules of the Game*. New York: St. Martin's Press.

▦ Pedestrianism

Definition

Webster's defines pedestrianism as "the practice of walking" or a "fondness for walking for exercise or recreation." The term is derived from the Latin verb *pedester*, to go on foot. Pedestrianism grew to be a popular professional sport in the 18th and 19th centuries, predominantly in Britain and America, where competitors engaged in foot races of varying duration and distance, sometimes covering as many as 500–600 miles in events lasting up to six days.

History

The earliest "pedestrians" were probably ancient Greek and Roman foot messengers, who ran distances up to 100 kilometers at a time to deliver important letters and messages. Imperial Rome certainly regarded endurance running as sport, for at the height of the empire, a 237-kilometer race was held in the Circus Maximus in Rome.

Later mention of foot messengers in Europe is found as early as the 11th century in England, and in France and Turkey in the 15th century. General improvements in roadways in the late 18th century made the use of messengers unnecessary.

Good roads, accurately measured courses, a history of organized running events, and the availability of inexpensive and accurate watches all contributed to the rise of pedestrianism as a professional sport in Britain during the first half of the 18th century. Though all of these components were prevalent in other parts of Europe, historians suggest that the fascination with gambling on the part of the upper classes was a pivotal factor in the sport's popularity in Britain.

From the start there was a basic distinction between professional and amateur pedestrians. Professionals came from the ranks of the lower and working classes, and trained and raced solely for money. Working-class youth who showed promise in athletics were encouraged to run professionally—some as early as age 15. While amateur running, particularly cross-country (and its variations referred to as "foxes and hares" and "paper chase"), enjoyed popularity in the English public school system, spreading to Cambridge and Oxford in the early 19th century, the professional sport held the public's attention, hosting the best athletes and the largest events.

With the influx of English, Irish, and German immigrants to America in the 1840s, pedestrianism gained a large following across the Atlantic. Pedestrianism maintained its popularity until the late 19th century, when the lack of organization and ethics among the athletes and their backers turned the public away from the professional sport. In general, this coincided with the rise of amateur organizations and intercollegiate competition, particularly in track and field.

Competition

Most races were arranged by pubs, where the "fancy" or fans gathered. Many taverns constructed running tracks on site so that they could take wagers and supply the crowds with refreshments. A popular form of competition was the match race, where two competitors were pitted against each other. Supporters of a favored pedestrian would give odds on their man and quite often grant a head start to a competitor to heighten the drama of the event. Such a scenario encouraged all forms of dishonesty and deception, as exceptional runners would often travel from city to city, disguising their experience and ability to tempt the locals to bet heavily against them. Such a practice also discouraged record performances, as athletes were usually content to win by the slimmest of margins so as to encourage a steady supply of challengers. While matches ranged from as short as 70 yards to as long as 20 miles, many of the longer events took place between towns or on an out-and-back course. To ensure fair play, backers of both competitors would often trail the race on horseback.

Pedestrians also competed for prize money offered by a promoter or establishment, who would stage invitational races, often at a half-mile horse track. The public would be charged admission, and all the racers would pay an entry fee to discourage noncompetitors. Often promoters would heighten the competition and sweeten the purse by offering a bonus to the winner who could cover the distance within a specified time. The first American pedestrian championships were held at the Union Race Course on Long Island in 1835. There a crowd estimated at between 16,000 and 20,000 watched Henry Stannard run 10 miles in 59:48 to best a field of nine. Stannard won $1,300–$1,000 for winning and $300 for breaking one hour. A 24-year-old farmer, Standard went on to win enough money in purses and match races over the next year to be able to purchase his own resort hotel in Connecticut in 1836. He named his getaway the Pedestrian Hotel.

The most lucrative and demanding pedestrian events were the famed six-day "Go-As-You-Please" races, which gained immediate popularity with the inaugural Astley Belt race, held at the Agricultural Hall in London in March 1878. Funded by Sir John Drysdale Astley, a baron and member of Parliament, the event was billed as the first official world pedestrian championship, with the winner to claim a belt valued at 100 pounds in addition to a portion of the 2,000 pounds in total prize money. Later versions of the Belt race were held at indoor arenas in London and New York, including Madison Square Garden. The prevailing strategy for these races was to run as long as possible each day before walking. Most competitors slept just 2½–4 hours each day—depending on the competition—and usually after a hot bath and massage. Perhaps the most famed six-day competitor was Charles Rowell, a boat boy from Kent, England, who claimed four Astley Belt victories. Rowell proved that a good runner would always beat a good walker, as he perfected an economical running style that enabled him to maintain a 6-mile-per-hour pace for hours on end. With bonus money offered for world records, the mark for the farthest distance continued to improve until George Littlewood, the English champion, covered 611 miles, 570 yards at an 1888 event in New York.

Winning a six-day race that was well attended could earn a pedestrian as much as $5,000–$6,000 in prize money and more than twice that amount in wagers. Star runners could also earn appearance fees at theaters or burlesque shows, where they were billed as an added attraction to the evening's entertainment.

Bibliography

Cumming, J. (1981). *Runners and Walkers—A Nineteenth Century Chronicle*. Chicago: Regnery Gateway.

Milroy, A. (1983). "The Remarkable Record of the Nineteenth Century Pedestrian." *Ultrarunning* (July–August), pp. 24–26.

Nokes, T. (1991). *Lore of Running*. Champaign, IL: Leisure Press.

▦ Roller Skating

Definition

Roller skating is the act of gliding over a smooth, flat surface using specially designed footwear with wheels attached to the bottom—two at the front of the boot and two at the heel. Originating in England, the craze struck America in the 1880s, when roller rinks sprang up in cities throughout the Northeast. Though popular today throughout the world, roller skating has lost some of its following to one of its derivative sports, in-line skating

History

Historians generally trace the invention of roller skates to an 18th-century Dutchman, Joseph Merlin, who fashioned ice skates for dry ground by attaching wooden spools to the skate's supporting plate. Then, in 1863, as cycling began to grow popular in England and France, a British inventor, James L. Plympton, devised another more affordable means of propulsion when he patented the "rocking" roller skate. By shifting one's weight from side to side, a skater could turn and maneuver with ease. Soon roller skates were mass-produced. In England, the sport was especially popular among the upper class and even the nobility, who found "rinking" a stylish and fashionable thing to do.

When the sport hit America in the 1870s, it grew even more popular among broader strata of society. Warehouses installed wooden floors surrounded by seating. Whole families could join in the fun, as the sport demanded modest skill and exertion. Like their counterparts across the Atlantic, skaters didn't need special uniforms—women could wear their long, flowing dresses and men could retain their stylish waistcoats and woolen breeches. Roller skating was considered so wholesome that churchmen in America recommended the sport to their parishioners. For those who wanted competition, there was "roller polo," a form of hockey played on roller skates that originated in Chicago in 1882. Between skate manufacturers and establishment owners, roller skating had become quite an industry. By 1885 an estimated $20 million had been invested in the sport.

However, roller skating on both sides of the Atlantic proved to be a bit of a craze. Mass interest in the sport began to die out by the turn of the century, as more and more families, particularly those in the United States, became enamored with motor cars and the Sunday drive in the country. Still, roller skating continued to be an entertaining and sociable activity, particularly for children and young people. With the introduction of plastic polyurethane wheels in the 1970s, skaters enjoyed greater freedom of movement, and the sport subsequently gained popularity. In the 1980s and 1990s, with the advent of in-line skates—skates with wheels aligned in a single row for greater speed and maneuverability—many roller skaters switched to in-line skating.

Equipment

Roller skating demands a smooth surface—most commonly hardwood or cement. While most roller rinks are located indoors, it is not uncommon to see children roller skating on sidewalks or streets. The roller skate itself is constituted of a leather or vinyl upper boot with a hard plastic bottom onto which two pairs of rollers or wheels are fitted in tandem. Modern-day wheels are made of durable polyurethane with ball-bearing cores, making the skates faster, smoother, and more maneuverable than earlier models.

Most skaters wear protective equipment like knee and elbow pads. In-line skaters wear helmets. Lycra/spandex biking shorts are favored by many in-line skaters. The tight weave of the material protects the skater from "road rash" in the event of a fall.

Rules

As mentioned above, roller skates are fairly easy to operate. The wheels are designed so that whenever pressure is applied over one wheel, the wheel assembly turns in the direction of the pressure. By leaning to the right or left, the skater makes the wheels turn toward the right or the left—the greater the lean, the sharper the turn. In addition to roller polo, or roller hockey, other forms of roller skating competition include:

Artistic skating, which is very similar to figure skating and ice dancing. Singles and pairs compete in graceful, athletic routines;

Speed-skating, which involves racing at various distances, usually around a banked, wooden track; and

Roller derby, a professional contact sport in the 1970s in which teams of skaters would circle a banked track trying to either overtake or block the advance of the opposing team. Roller derby was revived in the 1990s, with athletes using in-line skates.

Bibliography

Phillips, Ann-Vicoria. (1979). *The Complete Book of Roller Skating*. New York: Womman.
Rappelfeld, Joel. (1992). *The Complete Blader*. New York: St. Martin's Press.

▦ Rowing

Definition

Rowing is a sport in which a team of oarsmen race long, narrow boats, known as shells or sculls, on the open water. Popularized in England in the 18th century, the sport has come to encompass two distinctive forms: rowing, or crew, where teams of two, four, or eight oarsmen sit facing the stern of the shell, each rower pulling one oar; and sculling, usually conducted for single, double, or quadruple sculls, where each competitor sits facing the stern of the scull and uses a pair of oars.

History

Rowing dates back to ancient times, when Greek sailors hit upon the idea of attaching the oar to the side of the boat. They found that working a single oar against a fulcrum was a much more efficient way to row a boat than dipping a paddle into the water. Popular movie images of Romans chaining slaves to their warships to power the oars are well founded, although ancient historians also noted soldiers from ancient Egypt and the Roman Empire racing large-oared galleys, perhaps as a form of battle training. Ancient civilizations grew up around waterways, and longboats and galleys were used to transport goods from one settlement or market to another. Though the advent of sail-powered ships and later the invention of the steam engine made rowing for transportation obsolete, the practice of rowing for popular sport and recreation has continued to the present day.

Rowing took hold in England during the 18th and 19th centuries, where a large, relatively calm river like the Thames in London provided an excellent venue for racers and spectators alike. The first competitive rowers were ferrymen, who, when they weren't busy moving passengers and goods across rivers and harbors, were often motivated to race for pride and, at times, prize money. Rowing also caught on with ferrymen in New York, and by the mid-19th century, the proletarian sport was popular in Boston, Philadelphia, and San Francisco. Rowing attracted the entrepreneur, who raised large cash purses for championship races, and it appealed to the promoter, who staged match "duels" between celebrated rowers. Thousands of spectators bet on the rowing, enabling a handful of professionals to earn a living off the sport. Yet, like many other games and events that catered to gambling, rowing became fraught with cheating. A competitor would enjoy a string of victories and the odds would rise in his favor until it was profitable to take a payoff and lose a race.

But professional rowing was largely an individual sport, and when it began to flounder, the amateur and especially the intercollegiate sport began to flourish. In the 19th century, crews of eight, ten, and even twelve were common, particularly in colleges and universities where rowing was regarded as an excellent endeavor to build a young man's character and "nationalistic" (or group) spirit. The first Oxford-Cambridge race was held on the Thames in 1829. The sport's two largest and most famed events—the Doggett's Coat and Badge Race (the oldest rowing contest in the world, held annually on the Thames since 1715) and the Henley Royal Regatta—both attracted the best university and amateur competitors.

The collegiate sport took over in the United States as well. The Harvard-Yale race, first staged in 1852, is the oldest intercollegiate sporting event in America. As an amateur sport, rowing for many years tended to have a rather exclusive following among the upper and upper middle class in America, due largely to its origins in the university system. Historically, elite Ivy League schools like Harvard, Yale, and Cornell have had some of the strongest programs.

Postgraduates who wanted to pursue the sport would do so through select private boating clubs that could afford state-of-the-art equipment and indoor training facilities. Rowing's elitism probably explains the sport's declining popularity in post–World War II America, when more young men began playing and watching team sports than at any time previously. Yet rowing in America experienced a revival in the 1980s and 1990s. The advent of the affordable single-scull rower made the sport accessible to a greater number of people. The passage of Title IX of the Educational Amendments of 1972 also gave rowing a boost. By prohibiting discrimination against women in federally funded education programs, Title IX in effect mandates equal funding for women's collegiate sports.

Rowing has always had a strong following in Europe, where hundreds of rowing clubs provided the sport's point of entry for thousands of participants throughout the 20th century. Rowing has been a sport in the Olympics since 1908. Though the United States dominated international competition for the first half of the 20th century, the playing field was leveled in the 1960s and 1970s, when the Soviet Union and Eastern bloc countries became proficient in the sport. Today there are elite rowers on every continent, though the Europeans and Americans still hold an edge in the Olympic Games and the World Rowing Championships.

Equipment

A modern racing shell for a crew of eight may be up to 60 feet long, but is no more than 2 feet wide. Pair and single sculls are much smaller—the latter about 24 feet long. Shells are designed to be light and maneuverable, built of wooden or fiberglass framing and fitted with small sliding seats for each oarsman. Interestingly, the ancient Greeks also sat on seats that slid so that they were able to use the strength in their legs to drive the boat. And legend has it that Harvard rowers in the mid-1850s greased their pants so that they could slide on immobile seats—a trick that helped them beat Yale one year. For drive and stability, a rower's shoes attach to a foot stretcher, or cross strut, which is affixed to the boat's bottom. Each oar pivots on a rigger, or oarlock, a square metal latch that holds the oar in place. Shells differ from sculls in that shells have a small rudder-like steering mechanism that is operated by either the rower in the bow of the boat or by the coxswain, a nonrowing member of an eight- or four-oar shell. Oars are usually about 12 feet long, with blades of about 2 to 3 feet in length and six inches wide.

Rules

Rowing has its own symmetry and beauty founded in the art of the stroke. The very best crews perfect a synchronized rowing rhythm, where a series of strokes retains a pattern of continuous movement. The stroking motion can be broken down into four distinct actions: the catch, drive, finish, and recovery. The catch is the part of the stroke where the oar enters the water. During the drive, the rower pulls the blade through the water to propel the boat. The blade comes out of the water during the finish, enabling the rower to recover, or come back up the slide to begin another stroke. The power of the stroke is generated by the rower driving down with the legs and pulling back with the shoulders and back. As mentioned above, the sliding seat enables the rower to generate great power through his legs and feet. A stroke rate typically varies between 32 and 36 strokes per minute, depending on water and weather conditions and the length of the race.

Major national and international races are usually contested for single, double, and quadruple sculls, pairs, fours (both with and without coxswain), and eights. A regatta, or sprint, is the most common form of competition, where competitors race side by side on a straight course over a lake or calm stretch of river. Men typically race over 2,000 meters and women over 1,500 meters. A course is usually laid out with six lanes marked by buoys. Though each shell must stay in its lane, a boat will not necessarily be disqualified for wandering out of its lane, provided it doesn't create a wake or obstruction that disturbs or impedes another boat. Regattas are usually conducted in heats, with qualifiers advancing to semifinal and final heats based on either place or time.

Bibliography

Churbuck, D.C. (1988). *The Book of Rowing*. Woodstock, NY: Overlook Press.
Dizikes, John. (2000). "A History of Rowing and Races." Microsoft Encarta Online Encyclopedia 2000, *http://encarta.msn.com* (January 16, 2001).
"Rowing FAQs." (2000). Rice University Crew home page, *http://ruf.rice.edu/~crew/rowingfaq.html* (January 16, 2001).
Seiler, Stephen. (2001). "The Physiology of the Elite Rower." Masters Athlete Physiology & Performance Web page, *http://home.hia.no/~stephens/index.html* (January 17, 2001).

▦ Rugby

Definition

Rugby is a game played by two teams of 15 players on a large rectangular field with an inflated oval ball that may be handled or kicked. The object of the game is to move the ball toward the opponent's goal line. Points are scored by either kicking the ball through H-shaped goalposts at the end of the field, or by carrying the ball over the goal line. Today, rugby continues to be popular in England, where it originated, as well as in the British Isles, France, and in countries that were formerly British colonies or dominions, such as Australia and New Zealand.

History

In its early stages of development, rugby was inseparable from England's other kicking football game, soccer. Throughout the 17th and 18th centuries, the game of English football was little more than a disorganized, violent movement of hacking and kicking (*see* Soccer). Between the mid-18th century and the early-to-mid-19th century the two games began to develop distinct rules, which culminated in the formation of the national soccer governing body, the London Football Association, in 1863 and the national Rugby Football Union in 1871. Both codified rules and established the framework for organized competition.

Rugby's public school origins mirror those of many 18th- and 19th-century sports in England, including soccer, field hockey, and cross-country running. In England, the term "public school" means the opposite of what it does in America. The English public school is an exclusive private institution. At the height of the British Empire's political and economic power in the mid- to late 19th century, England's public schools were invested with the lofty responsibility of creating the nation's leaders of tomorrow—businessmen, bankers, engineers, government officers, teachers, explorers, and so on. The abilities of these men helped advance Britain's expansionist policies, while their character served as a model to the uncivilized or underdeveloped colonials whom they would govern. The English public school curriculum, grounded in the classics, followed the Greek maxim of educating the mind and the body. In this system, team sports were crucial, as they helped to build an individual's strength and character in the pursuit of a collective victory.

Thus, organized rugby began as very much a sport of the upper middle and upper classes. Throughout the mid- to late 19th century, it spread beyond the walls of the public schools to universities and independent amateur clubs. When the sport began to attract paying customers in England—first in the populated south and later in the industrial north—the opportunity arose for players to earn a living playing rugby. Some factories began to hire select employees based on their rugby talents, and tensions soon emerged between the socially exclusive amateur clubs and the industrial-based professional teams. This social conflict first became apparent in 1876 with the formation of the Yorkshire Cup Challenge. The tourney, which was won by a working-class team, spurred more proletarian involvement in the sport. Soon, the amateur traditionalists, beaten at their own sport, were battling those they considered their social inferiors for control of rugby.

The myth of William Webb Ellis figures in this controversy. Ellis, a public school boy at Rugby School, has long been credited with originating the game of rugby as we know it. It was Ellis, according to a stone set in the wall at Rugby School, who, in 1823, "first took the ball in his arms and ran with it thus originating the distinctive feature of the rugby game." Interestingly, this event was first recalled some 60 years after it happened by one of Ellis' schoolmates. This was during the rise of rugby's popularity among the working class in the north of England. The story was circulated by the Old Rugbian Society in an 1895 report, the same year that the society erected a commemorative stone at Rugby. Taken in its historic context, the report seems little more than a response to the threat to rugby posed by the working element in society, a group the Rugbians refer to as "alien" and "inferior." By locating the birth of the sport at their own school, the Rugbians were attempting to reassert their ownership of rugby.

But rugby continued to gain popularity in the north, where clubs routinely ignored an 1886 Rugby Union law which forbade payment to players. In 1895 a number of northern clubs broke from the Rugby Union and founded Rugby League football. Rugby League football developed a separate set of rules which have made it a faster, more wide-open game than Rugby Union. Today Rugby League football continues to be a popular professional game in the north of England. Though Rugby League is also played in Australia, New Zealand, France, and most recently, in the South Pacific Islands, British clubs continue to dominate the world club championships.

When one refers to the sport of rugby today, one typically means Rugby Union football. Rugby Union was spread throughout the British Empire's colonies in the late 19th and early 20th centuries. The game also became extremely popular in France, which staged its first national club championships in 1892. By the turn of the century, England, Scotland, Wales, and Ireland were meeting in an annual championship, which constituted the highest level of Rugby Union play.

Today, the sport is played in over 100 countries, including the United States, where there are more than 1,400 clubs with over 100,000 players. With the establishment of the World Rugby Cup in 1987, Rugby Union became a commercial sport with a tremendous potential for money to be made from sponsorships and television rights. In 1995 the sport's international governing body passed a resolution that allowed national governing bodies the right to pay their players, thus ending Rugby Union's status as an exclusively amateur sport.

Equipment

Though oblong in shape, the rugby ball is a bit larger, fatter, and heavier than a football. A uniform consists of shorts and a large, long-sleeved jersey. In America, children wear "rugby" shirts, which typically have one or more stripes across the front. This style is derived from the traditional rugby jersey, which would have the name of the rugby club emblazoned

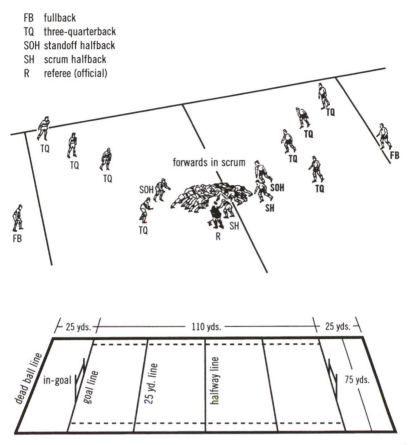

FB   fullback
TQ   three-quarterback
SOH standoff halfback
SH   scrum halfback
R   referee (official)

Figure 12. A diagram of a field for Rugby Union, with two teams in a scrum formation.

on the stripe. Although rugby is a tough sport, most players wear very little padding. Cleated shoes are essential, as rugby is played on a natural grass field.

Rules

A Rugby Union football field is referred to as a "pitch," and is no more than 110 yards long and 75 yards wide (see illustration). The sidelines are called "touchlines." Twenty-five yards beyond each goal line is the dead-ball line, beyond which the ball is out of play. The uprights of the goal are 18 feet, 4 inches apart and are connected by a horizontal crossbar, which is 9 feet, 9 inches above the ground.

Play consists of two 40-minute halves. The positions on a rugby team are based on the distinction between forwards and backs. The forwards are generally larger players. Their task is to get the ball to the backs, who are faster runners. However, all players have defensive and offensive assignments depending on the state of play. The general principles of Rugby Union are as follows:

Forward passes are not allowed. Dropping the ball forward is also prohibited and called a "knock-on."

The ball is advanced by running or kicking it forward.

No blocking is allowed. Generally, all supporting players must stay behind the ball carrier

A tackled ball carrier must immediately release the ball; the tackler must immediately release the tackled player.

Play is continuous; all stoppage of play must be immediately restarted.

A "scrum" restarts play after a ball is dropped or passed forward (see illustration). A scrum is similar to a face-off in ice hockey. All eight forwards from each team take part, with each side banding together and generally pushing the other so that a teammate can heel the ball back out of the scrum to a back to start the team's offense.

A lineout restarts play after the ball travels into "touch," or out of bounds.

A "try" is awarded when the ball is carried or kicked across the goal line and downward pressure is applied to the ball. A try is worth 5 points.

A successful conversion kick taken after a try is worth 2 points.

A successful penalty or drop kick is worth 3 points.

After points are scored, the ball is kicked back to the scoring team.

Rugby Union football games are governed by laws rather than rules. A referee keeps time and ensures that play conforms to the game's laws. Two judges are stationed on each touchline to signal when the ball leaves the field of play and to assist the referee in general.

Bibliography

Dunning, Eric, and Kenneth Sheard. (1979). *Barbarians, Gentlemen and Players: A Sociological Study of the Development of Rugby Football*. Oxford, England: Martin Robertson and Co.
Gardner, Paul. (1996). *The Simplest Game*. New York: Macmillan.
Jones, J. R. (1960). *Encyclopedia of Rugby Football*. London: Sportsmans Book Club.
"A Rugby Primer." (2001). Scrum.Com Web page, *http://www.scrum.com/rugbytoday* (March 12, 2001).

▦ Soccer

Definition

Soccer is a game played between two teams of 11 players, the object being to propel a round inflated ball into the opponent's goal by kicking or hitting the ball with any part of the body other than the hand or arm.

Soccer developed as an organized sport in Great Britain over the latter half of the 19th century and quickly spread to the European continent and around the world. Today, soccer is played by young and old alike, in almost every country in the world.

History

Contrary to popular belief, "football" is not synonymous with soccer. The word "football" came into use in England in the mid-14th century to describe a game not played with the feet but on foot, in order to distinguish it from other games played on horseback.

Soccer's lineage dates back to ancient times. A Chinese military manual dating from the Han dynasty (3rd and 2nd centuries B.C.) includes as one of its physical exercises the game of Tsu Chu. In Tsu Chu, players kicked a leather ball into a small net affixed to the end of long bamboo canes. The ancient Greeks also played a game called Episkiros that involved kicking and throwing a ball on a field. Conquering Romans borrowed much from the game, turning it into a rougher affair that they called Harpastum. It was popular with the Roman legionaries, who brought the game to England during the Roman occupation between A.D. 43 and 409. Later on, a soccer-like game seems to have been associated with seasonal planting and fertility rites. The ball, representing the sun, was ceremoniously kicked across newly planted fields. A rural rite soon was transplanted to the city as a fun pastime. In 1175 a London monk, William Fitzstephen, described how teams of students and trades apprentices played a game of ball on flat ground just outside the city.

But early variants of soccer were often no more than a violent, disorganized mass of opposing forces vying for control of the ball (see illustration, page 108). In "The Anatomie of Abuses," published in 1583 by the Puritan pamphleteer Phillip Stubbs, football is likened to a "bloody and murthering practise," where brutal injury is commonplace:

> sometimes their necks are broken, sometimes their backs, sometimes their legs, sometime their armse, sometime one part thrust out of joynt, sometime their eyes start out; and sometime hurt in one place, sometimes in another … and hereof groweth envie, malice, rancour, cholar, hatred, displeasure, enmitie, and what not els, and sometimes murther, fighting, brawling, contortion, quarrel kicking, homicide, and great effusion of blood, as experience dayly teacheth.

The sport took a significant step toward respectability and organization when, in the early 1800s, public education administrators began to use sports as a form of self-disciple and character building. Dr. Thomas Arnold, the headmaster at Rugby School, was a major proponent of making sports part of the educational process. Arnold's sport of choice was a variant of football called rugby (see Rugby). Popularized between the

1820s and the 1840s, the game of rugby developed along two lines: the "handling game," in which players largely ran with the ball, and the "dribbling game," a precursor of soccer where participants kicked the ball.

Though there were several attempts to produce one master game from the two strains, none was successful. Finally, in 1863, representatives from the leading football clubs in London gathered with the objective of regulating the sport throughout the country. Calling themselves the Football Association (F.A.), they largely favored the skill and athleticism of the dribbling game over the brute strength of the handling game. The F.A.'s first set of rules, published on December 7, 1863, marks the birth of soccer. Prohibitions against running with the ball, tripping, and hacking (or "shinning," where a player checked an opponent's progress with a kick to the shins) were definitive in setting soccer apart from rugby. Other regulations regarding the size and shape of the field and the space between the goalposts, and rules governing kickoffs, in-bounds passes, corner kicks, free kicks, and direct kicks constitute the basis of the modern game.

Throughout the 1870s and 1880s, soccer became enormously popular throughout England and Scotland, and later in Ireland and Wales. Much of the popularity was due to the F.A. creating a Challenge Cup Tournament, open to all clubs in England. Much like today's National Collegiate Athletic Association (NCAA) Basketball Tournament, a good deal of local pageantry sprang up around the F.A.'s winner-take-all tourney. On any given day, a small club from the north could beat a big London club; underdogs dreamed of upsets, and the David-and-Goliath aura around the event produced excitement and boosted attendance. By 1900 the F.A. Cup was drawing 242 teams. In 1901 over 110,000 fans watched the Cup final.

But like many sports in Victorian England, soccer had to wrestle with the question of amateur versus professional. Most of the early club members were former public school and university men of the middle and upper middle classes. However, when the sport spread to the industrial cities of England's midlands and north, the working classes began to play soccer in greater numbers. Companies began to recruit workers with special soccer talents, and many of the most successful clubs outside London were based in factories and carried the name of the company or manufacturer on their uniform. In order to keep the best players on the field, the F.A. ruled in 1885 to allow professionals to play in the Cup tournament. Even when the first professional league, the 12-team Football League, was established in 1888, the F.A. maintained control over the sport. This was important when the F.A. began to export the game through international play. In choosing a national team, the F.A. picked from among the best native-born amateurs and professionals.

But soccer's widespread popularity was ensured before the advent of international play. The sport's rise to prominence in England coincided with the height of the country's maritime and commercial strength. British sailors traveled regularly to foreign ports, and businessmen and engineers often spent long periods of time abroad. Wherever they went, they brought a soccer ball. The game's simplicity helped spread its popularity. Thus, in 1889 employees of the British railway started a soccer club in Argentina, and soon after British students in Sao Paulo, Brazil, began playing the sport with locals. As Britain's business connections increased throughout Europe in the 1880s and 1890s, soccer clubs were formed in Italy, Germany, and Austria.

The Federation Internationale Football Association, or FIFA, was formed in 1904 to govern international play. In 1908 soccer became an Olympic sport, and by 1924, 22 countries were competing. That year, 51,000 fans attended the Olympic final in Paris, where Uruguay beat Switzerland 3–0. World Cup competition was inaugurated in 1930. By that time, FIFA had 41 member nations. Today the association has 204 member nations. These national teams vie every four years for the World Cup, which is considered the world championship of the sport. FIFA also began staging a Women's World Cup in 1991. The United States women won both the 1991 and 1999 championships—the latter before the largest crowd in women's soccer history: 90,185 at the Rose Bowl against China in the final game.

Equipment

Soccer has been referred to as the "simplest game." There are 17 basic rules, and the only equipment is an inflated, leather-covered ball 27 to 28 inches in circumference. When fully inflated, a soccer ball weighs between 14 and 16 ounces. Over the years a soccer player's uniform has changed very little. Players typically wear shorts, a long- or short-sleeved shirt, long athletic socks to cover a pair of shin guards, and a pair of nonmetal studded cleats. Goalkeepers often wear a light pair of gloves to keep their hands warm and to provide a better grip to catch. A goalkeeper must also wear a different colored jersey and shorts to distinguish himself or herself from the other players and from the referee.

Rules

As mentioned above, soccer has a rather small set of rules in comparison to other sports—in all there are 17 "laws" of soccer. The field of play is rectangular—110–120 yards long and 70–80 yards wide for international play (see illustration). The goal is 8 yards wide and 8 feet high.

There are a number of different soccer formations (see illustration). Traditional positions include a striker, or center, and two wings who attack the opponent's goal, four midfielders, or halfbacks, who play both offense and defense, and three defensemen, or fullbacks, who are the last line of defense before the goalkeeper. The goalkeeper is the only player who is allowed to catch and touch the ball—but only while he remains within an 18 by 44 yard penalty area that surrounds the goal.

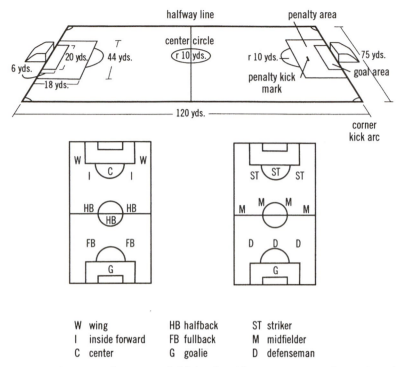

Figure 13. A diagram of a soccer field (top), with two common formations indicated by position (bottom). At left is the "classic" 2-3-5 formation, popularized by England around the turn of the century and the most common formation through the mid-20th century. At right is the "modern" 3-4-3 formation, with an extra midfielder facilitating a more fluid transition from offense to defense.

Players are not permitted to hold, push, or trip an opponent, but they may bump him with the shoulder, and may attempt to intercept passes or kick the ball away from an opponent. For rule violations such as handling the ball, or for fouls like tripping, pushing, or kicking an opponent, the offending team is penalized by awarding a free kick—an unguarded kick from the point of the infraction—to the opposing team. For fouls committed within the penalty area by the defending team, the opposing team is awarded a penalty kick—a free kick directly at the goal.

Soccer, like hockey, has rules prohibiting offside plays. In general, an attacker is offside if there are not at least two defenders between him and the goal at the time the ball is passed to him. He is not offside if he is behind the ball, if the ball last touched an opponent, or if he is in his half of the field. Games consist of two 45-minute halves. Play is continuous and is stopped only when a goal is scored, a violation or infraction is committed, or the ball goes out of bounds. When a ball is driven out of bounds, it is put back in play by a member of the opposing team, who must throw the ball with two hands, over the head, with both feet on the ground. A ball driven over the end line by the defending team is awarded to the opposing team as a corner kick—a kick taken from the corner of the field. A ball driven over the end line by the attacking team is returned to play as a goal kick—a kick taken by the goalkeeper.

Bibliography

Gardner, Paul. (1996). *The Simplest Game*. New York: Macmillan.

Gerhardt, Wilfred. (1979). "The Colorful History of a Fascinating Game." Federation Internationale de Football Web site, *http://www.fifa.com/index.html* (March 3, 2001).

Murray, Bill. (1994). *Football: A History of the World Game*. London: Scholar Press.

▦ Squash

Definition

Squash is a game played on a four-walled court by two (singles) or four (doubles) players. Opponents alternately hit a small rubber ball to the front wall of the court with rackets, the object of the game being to make a shot that an opponent cannot return. Today, squash has gained worldwide popularity. The International Squash Rackets Federation (ISRF) can count over 120 member nations.

History

Squash is a direct descendant of the sport known as rackets, with roots from a variety of racket or hand-and-ball games played throughout Europe in the 16th–18th centuries and even earlier. Town courtyards and church walls served as the playing field for *jeu de paume* in France and *pelota* in Spain. In England, a game known as rackets emerged in the late 18th and early 19th century. Its widespread popularity was such that it was a game common to both backyard taverns and English public school play. Charles Dickens' *Pickwick Papers* depicts inmates of debtors' prison at Fleet playing rackets.

Legend has it that squash—distinguishable from rackets by a smaller court and the use of a soft rubber ball (that can be "squashed" in one's hand)—was created at the Harlow School in England. There, a version of miniature rackets, or "yarder," was popular among boys waiting for a rackets court. The first mention of squash as a formal game appeared in 1890 in the *Badminton Library of Sports and Pastimes*. Throughout the late 19th and early 20th centuries, squash was a sport exclusive to the well-to-do and upper middle classes; squash players either belonged to an athletic club or had private courts built on their estates. Though early courts were not standardized, most used wood planking for both floor and walls. Eustance Miles, a world champion rackets and tennis player, wrote the first how-to book on squash in 1901. Interestingly, while Miles promoted the game's benefit to one's "body, health and mind," he regarded squash as an especially "grand game" for women, thus placing the sport among the relatively few deemed acceptable for Victorian ladies.

The first grand squash championship was the American National in 1907. The British began national and international championship squash play in the 1920s, and in 1928 the England Squash Rackets Association was founded. This body standardized squash's rules and acted as a national governing authority for the sport. Squash really didn't gain international prominence until the late 1960s, when mass production of rackets and balls began to spread the sport to a wider audience. The ISRF was founded in 1967. Universities in America and Europe also began to build squash courts, and this institutionalization of the game made squash much more accessible to the middle class. Today, the sport is played recreationally by an estimated 20 million people worldwide.

Equipment

A squash player's uniform is essentially the same as in tennis. Athletic shoes are also similar, although court shoes used for squash are usually higher cut to afford greater lateral support for what is essentially a faster, more confined game than tennis. Squash balls are hollow, made of soft rubber and measuring about 1¾ inches in diameter. Rackets are typically 25–27 inches long. In the 1980s, rackets with larger heads were gaining in popularity, though there has been a reverse trend recently, as more players opt for greater control. Rackets today are quite light—usually about 140–170 grams—and are typically made of a graphite/titanium composite that affords strength and durability.

Rules

The standard court is 32 feet in length and 21 feet in width (see illustration). A service line is painted across the court 14 feet from the back wall, beyond which a serve must land. Another line stretching from the back wall to the service-court line creates two service areas of equal size. Each side of the court has a square service box in which the player must keep at least one foot while serving. A service line 6 feet above the floor is painted on the front wall. Serves must hit the front wall above this line.

A squash court has boundary lines marked on the front, side, and back walls within which the ball must stay. The line on the front wall is 15 feet high. The back wall line is 7 feet high. Sloping diagonal lines on each sidewall connect the front and back wall lines. Shots hit above these lines, including the ceiling, are out of play. The front wall also has a "telltale," a 19-inch-high wooden or metal band at the bottom bordering the floor. Shots that strike the telltale are also out of bounds.

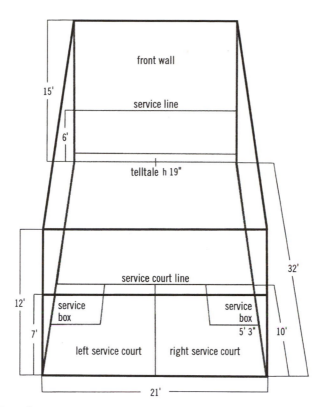

Figure 14. Squash court.

To be successful in squash, one must consistently keep the ball in play. As noted earlier, the ball is put in play by a serve, which must strike the front wall and rebound within a designated service court. In all other play, the ball may strike any combination of walls before or after hitting the front wall as long as the ball does not hit the telltale and as long as it is not allowed to bounce twice before being returned. Points can only be scored by the server on a winning rally. Losing rallies result in a change in service. The first player to score 9 points wins the game, unless the game becomes tied at 8–8. In the event of "eight-all," the player who first reached eight may chose to "set one" or "set two," meaning that the game continues on to either 9 or 10 points.

Bibliography

"All About Squash." (1999). Squash Talk home page, *http://www.squashtalk.com* (February 12, 2001).

Beck, Ron. (2000). "How to Select a Racquet." Squash Talk home page, *http://www.squashtalk.com* (February 12, 2001).

Mitchell, Carolyn B. (1997). *Squash (Know the Sport)*. Harrisburg, PA: Stackpole Books.
Vargas, J.D.C. (2000). "Sports at Harrow." Harrow School Web page, *http://www .harrowschool.org.uk/harrow/sport/htm* (February 12, 2001).
Worth, Sylvia (ed.). (1990). *The Rules of the Game*. New York: St. Martin's Press.

▦ Table Tennis

Definition

Table tennis is a singles and doubles game played across a rectangular table divided by a short net. Players alternately hit a small, lightweight plastic ball with rubber-faced wooden paddles. Volleying continues until one player either misses the ball or hits it into the net or off the table, whereby the opponent scores a point. Table tennis today is truly a multi-ethnic game, played competitively by over 140 nations who are members of the International Table Tennis Federation.

History

Like so many organized sports in this volume, table tennis began in Britain during the 19th century. Legend has it that British army officers stationed in India began playing the game in the 1880s, using makeshift paddles fashioned from cigar box lids and rounded corks from wine bottles as balls. The game was truly after-dinner entertainment, as the officers cleared the dining room table and stacked books across the middle to serve as a net.

Officers brought the game back home to Britain, where the upper classes soon embraced table tennis as a popular parlor game. Several companies began manufacturing versions of the game, known variously as "Gossima," "Flim-Flam," and "Whif-Wham." Parker Brothers hit pay dirt with a variation of the game that used hollow celluloid balls—when they were hit with a wooden paddle, they made a hollow "pong" sound. In 1901 Parker Brothers registered the game as "Ping Pong," and began marketing complete sets that included rackets, balls, and portable netting.

Though the game was popular recreationally, it took a number of years to catch on as a competitive sport. Following World War I, Ivor Montagu, a Cambridge University student who was wild about table tennis, became the first person to write down a uniform set of rules for the game. Montagu was also the driving force behind the formation of the Table Tennis Association in England in 1922. Soon the International Table Tennis Federation was founded in 1926, consisting mostly of a number of European countries plus India. Prior to World War II, the Eastern Europeans—especially the Hungarians—dominated the game, winning the lion's share of the international championships. After World War II, the competitive game changed markedly due to technological improvements in the racket and the revolutionary play of the Chinese.

In 1952 the Japanese introduced the foam rubber–coated paddle—a change that transformed the game into a lightning-quick sport, demanding excellent hand-eye coordination and split-second decision making. Players could now put even more spin on the ball. Asian players also developed the "penholder" grip, in which the handle of the paddle is held between the forefinger and thumb. This configuration allows the player to hit the ball with the same face of the paddle on any stroke.

After China's Cultural Revolution in the 1960s, the country set out to use sports as a showcase for the new communist society. Interestingly, the Chinese have mastered a number of diverse sports, scoring world championship success at table tennis, gymnastics, distance running, rock climbing, and mountaineering. However, the country's mastery of table tennis has been legendary. During the 1970s, they won virtually every major world championship many times over. In 1971 a group of American table tennis players visited China, along with President Richard Nixon and a delegation from the State Department. Dubbed "Ping-Pong Diplomacy," the friendly cultural exchange represented a key warming of relations between a heretofore-isolated communist monolith and a historically mistrusting Western capitalist power. Though the Chinese continued to win their share of gold medals in the 1980s and 1990s, the Swedish men and the South Korean women emerged as rivals.

One can speculate that the game's simplicity—little in the way of equipment is needed, and physically smaller players naturally do quite well, usually better than larger and taller competitors—has perhaps appealed to a more diverse sampling of players than almost any other sport. Today, over half of the International Table Tennis Federation's 140 member nations send players to the world championships.

Equipment

The table measures 9 feet by 5 feet, with the table top 30 inches above the floor. The playing surface is made of three-quarter-inch plywood and divided in two by a 6-inch-high net. This surface is very responsive; a ball dropped from a height of 1 foot will rebound to a height of from 8¾ to nearly 10 inches. The white celluloid ball is hollow, measuring 1½ inches in diameter.

Rackets are made of wood; the head is oval and covered with a sponge rubber that may be "pipped," or covered with extended or inverted pimples. When Japan's Hiroji Satoh won the 1952 world championships with a sponge-rubber racket, he changed the sport forever. For a period of 70 years prior to Hiroji, table tennis had been marked by slow, methodical play. But the rubber-faced racket was much more responsive. Players also began using facings that were dimpled to produce spin. By using a "pips-out" pattern on one side and a "pips-in" configuration on the other, and employing the penholder grip, players could alternatively topspin or deaden the ball on consecutive strokes. This was so confusing to an opponent that rules were created in 1959 that required rackets to be colored red on one side and black on the other. There are also rules regarding the compound and thickness of glue used to affix the rubber facing on a paddle.

Rules

Table tennis involves hitting or volleying the ball back and forth over the net until one player either misses the ball or hits it into the net or off the table, whereby the opponent is credited with a point. A proper serve is executed by holding the ball on the flat, outstretched palm of the hand, throwing it up in the air, and striking it as it falls. The ball must hit the table on the server's side, then clear the net and hit the opponent's side before it can be returned. One player serves until 5 points have been scored, then the opponent serves, and so on. A game is won by the first player who scores 21 points, except when both players are tied at 20–20. In the event of the latter, the service changes after each point until one player has gained a two-point advantage to win the game. Balls that hit the net or the edge of the table are fair; an umpire distinguishes the difference between edge shots and shots that hit the side of the table, which are not allowed.

Championship play consists of five games per match, with the first player to win three games declared the winner of the match.

Doubles play is distinguished by the following rules:

Service must be from the right-hand court to the opponent's left-hand court.

Each partner must hit or return alternate shots.

Each player receives service for 5 points, then, as opponents shift position, serves for 5 points.

The sequence of one partner hitting to a specific opponent must be changed after each game and midway through the deciding game of a match.

As mentioned above, the game today is nothing like it was at the turn of the century. Earlier play was marked by slow, deliberate movement; sometimes a game would take over an hour and matches would last several hours. In fact, rules were instated that placed limits on "stalling." Now, with the sponge-rubber racket, defensive play is largely instinctual and all competitors have become attackers. Most games take only a few minutes, enabling tournaments with over a hundred competitors to be conducted in a fairly short amount of time.

Bibliography

Boggan, Tim. (1976). *Winning Table Tennis*. Chicago: Regnery Gateway.

Boggan, Tim, and Leah Neuberger. (2000). "Table Tennis." Microsoft Encarta Online Encyclopedia 2000, *http://encarta.msn.com* (February 8, 2001).

International Table Tennis Federation. (2000). *Table Tennis Rules: 2000–2001*. International Table Tennis Web site, *www.ittf.com/* (February 8, 2001).

▦ Tennis

Definition

Tennis is a singles or doubles game played on a rectangular court divided by a net. Players use rackets to hit a pressurized ball into an opponent's court in such a way that it cannot be returned. Today tennis is both a popular recreational game and one of the most lucrative professional sports in the world.

History

What we know today as tennis is actually a fairly new game. A British army officer, Major Walter Clopton Wingfield, is generally credited with inventing in 1873 what was then referred to as lawn tennis. However, Wingfield's discovery, which he initially named Sphairistike (Greek for "playing at ball") had its precursors in a number of racket-and-ball games, including squash, badminton, and court tennis. Most historians argue that tennis originated in France in the 12th century in the form of *jeu de paume*, a court game in which the ball was struck with the palm of the hand rather than by a racket. Sometime in the 16th century rackets of varying shapes and sizes came into use, and the game began to be called tennis, probably from the French *tenez*, meaning "to take," or *tendere*, "to hold." Court tennis, also known as "real tennis" or "royal tennis," was popular among the royalty and aristocrats of France and England from the 16th to the 18th centuries. King Henry VIII was said to have been a big fan of the game. A tennis court that he had built at Hampton Court Palace in 1530 is today the oldest real tennis court in the world.

But real tennis was an indoor game—courts were surrounded on four sides by walls and covered by a sloped ceiling. No area was, in effect, out of bounds, and players were partial to odd-shaped rackets used to dig the ball out of corners or smash a return off the base of the wall. In contrast, lawn tennis was to be enjoyed out of doors. While lawn tennis became an instant hit among the British upper class—whose members began building courts at their country estates and playing the game at exclusive London sports clubs—the game also spread quickly around the globe. Britain's prominent position as the world's business leader ensured the game's diffusion among the well-to-do in even the most far-off lands. By 1875 tennis clubs had been founded in Brazil and India, and by 1890 the game was being played in Australia, South Africa, Egypt, Greece, Turkey, the Netherlands, Denmark, and Switzerland.

In the United States, tennis was adopted along with golf as an ideal country club sport (*see* Golf). The first U.S. men's national tennis tourna-

Figure 15. The term "sportswear" had little to do with sport and much to do with fashion when women played lawn tennis in the late 19th century. The illustration shows women playing tennis at the Staten Island Cricket Club in New York. (© Bettmann/CORBIS)

ment was held in the resort town of Newport, Rhode Island. A women's tournament was added in 1887, making tennis one of the first competitive sports in America to accord women equal billing with men. Yet for many, tennis was a symbol of status and wealth; women made fashion statements on the tennis court, and the press at the time delighted in oohing and aahing over the players' clothing at the expense of reporting about the game (see illustration).

The United States, England, Australia, New Zealand, and France were soon the dominant countries in lawn tennis play. Their prowess is illustrated in the history of the Davis Cup, an international tournament initiated in 1900 by Dwight Filly Davis, a student at Harvard, and two schoolmates, Malcolm Whitman and Holcolmbe Ward. After the trio won the first Davis Cup against Britain, teams from either the United States, England, France, or Australia/New Zealand (which competed as one team until 1923) would win the cup through 1973.

Like many organized sports that originated in Britain during the latter half of the 19th century, tennis was largely confined to amateur play. Often the term "amateur" served as little more than an excuse to exclude those whose socioeconomic standing made them undesirable for inclusion in this or that club. If a tennis player accepted payment for any goods or services rendered in relation to tennis (including coaching or giving lessons), he was considered a professional and banned from tourney play. While many professionals could make a good living barnstorming from city to city in the 1920s and 1930s—two stars would usually play one another in a feature match, in addition to entertaining the crowd with trick shots, lightning serves, and so on—these professionals were not allowed to play in any major tournaments. It wasn't until 1968, when Wimbledon opened its doors to all comers, that tennis began its "open" era. Throughout the 1980s and 1990s the game has continued to increase in visibility and impact around the world, as evidenced by greater corporate sponsorship, worldwide televising of the major opens, and lucrative men's and women's tours. Though tennis continues to be popular chiefly among the upper middle and upper classes, world-class play is no longer confined to either America or British Commonwealth countries. Slavs, Russians, Swedes, Argentines, and the Spanish have recently been among the winners at Wimbledon, the French Open, and the U.S. Open.

Equipment

The racket and ball are the two essential pieces of tennis equipment. Tennis balls are hollow and consist of an inflated rubber bladder covered with fabric made of wool and fiber. Rackets are continually undergoing technological changes. Up to the 1970s, all rackets were made of wood. Today, virtually all rackets are made of graphite or a combination of graphite, fiberglass, and perhaps boron or kevlar. The emphasis is on lightness and strength. The maximum length of a racket is 32 inches. There is no uniform size for rackets, which are typically classified by head size: for example, standard, midsize, and oversize. The head of a racket may not exceed 15½ inches in length and 11½ inches in width. In general, larger rackets enable players to generate more power behind their hitting, while smaller rackets afford greater control.

The development of the "widebody" design during the 1980s—whereby racket heads are thicker and stiffer—has also allowed players to get more power behind their serves and returns. These design changes have not only led many players to adopt a "power" game, but they have also, by extension, favored younger players, who possess greater speed and quick reflexes. Whereas many of the best players in the early 20th century played well past 40 years of age, the majority of men now retire before the age of 30. These age and power factors seem even more pronounced for women. During the 1980s, a handful of teenage girls—Steffi Graf, Gabriela Sabatini, and Monica Seles—began dominating the world tennis scene. Today, it's not uncommon to see a 15-year-old reach the finals of a major open tournament.

Rules

The court is 78 feet long, divided in half by a 3-foot-high net. For singles play the court is 27 feet wide; for doubles play the court is 36 feet wide. Most courts are made of asphalt, concrete, clay, or grass.

Play begins with one player serving the ball by tossing it in the air and striking it into the opponent's service box, which is on the diagonally opposite side of the court. A player is permitted two attempts to hit a valid serve—one which doesn't strike the net and must land within the opponent's service box. After each point is played, the service alternates between the left-hand and right-hand side of the court. After a successful serve is made, the ball is volleyed back and forth until one side fails to return the ball by either missing it, letting the ball bounce twice, or knocking it out of bounds or into the net. When a shot is unsuccessful, the opponent scores a point.

Tennis matches are usually the best two out of three sets for women's championship play and the best three out of five for men. Players must win six games to win a set, but they must also win by at least two games. Games are scored to four points, which are designated by the terms 15, 30, 40, and game, with zero points referred to as "love" (probably derived from the French *l'oeuf*, meaning "the egg," which resembles a zero). A tie at 40 is called "deuce." Play continues at deuce until one player leads by two points. Spectators should realize that the score of the server is always given first.

Bibliography

Collins, Bud, and Zander Hollander (eds.). (1994). *Bud Collins' Modern Encyclopedia of Tennis*. Detroit: Visible Ink Press.
"The History of Tennis." (2000). Royal Tennis Court at Hampton Palace Court Web site, *http://www.realtennis.gbrit.com/history.htm* (March 18, 2001).
"King of Games, Game of Kings." (1999). Real Tennis Web site, *http://www.real tennis.com/* (March 18, 2001).
Lawn Tennis Association. (1998). "The History of Tennis." Lawn Tennis Association Web site, *http://www.lta.org/uk/projects/history.htm* (March 18, 2001).
Scott, Eugene. (1973). *Tennis: Game of Motion*. New York: Crown.

■ Track and Field

Definition

Track and field is a sport that consists of various athletic contests involving running races, and jumping and throwing events. Track and field was known simply as "athletics" in the 19th century, as events like the 100-meter dash (requiring speed), marathon run (endurance), long jump (explosive speed), and shot put (explosive strength) were regarded as ultimate tests of athletic skill. The sport has been central to the modern Olympic Games since their inception in 1896.

History

Track and field's program of events is largely derived from ancient athletic festivals held in Greece and the British Isles. Both the original Olympiad in ancient Greece and the Celtic Tailteann Games date from around the 9th century B.C. These pageants played host to the best athletes throughout the land, who contested running, jumping, and throwing events in addition to wrestling, "feats of strength," archery, and, in the case of the Greeks, swimming.

Though cultural and religious trends in Europe tended to downplay athletics throughout medieval times, the sport of pedestrianism began to gain popularity in Britain and Western Europe beginning in the late 17th century (*see* Pedestrianism). While most pedestrians engaged in long walks or runs for distance, some enjoyed short-course competition and sprinting, typically between either two or several competitors and usually linked to gambling. Track and field grew out of pedestrianism in 19th-century England and took two distinct forms, one professional and one amateur.

Professional track and field had no regulation, with many athletes making a living on cunning and skill. There are numerous accounts of sprinters who would travel from town to town in disguise, pretending to have little skill or knowledge of racing until they had convinced several local competitors to run against them and even more spectators to place bets against them. Often these races would be handicap events, with the hapless locals given perhaps 5–10 yards' head start in a 100-yard dash. In this way, a good sprinter could make a decent living. Match races over longer distances were also common, with agents and promoters building up the competition and manipulating the odds to raise the total wager. Though cheating was rampant—often competitors were paid to throw races—the professional sport nevertheless had its heroes who posted impressive performances for the day.

Lewis Bennett, better known as Deerfoot, a Native American runner from the Seneca tribe in upstate New York, toured Britain in the early 1860s. He won a number of races between 5 and 12 miles long, including establishing a world one-hour record of 18,589 meters (about 11.525 miles, or 5:12 per mile) in 1863. George Seward, another American runner who made a living in Britain, is regarded as one of the greatest sprinters of the 19th century, recording an amazing time of 9¼ seconds for the 100-yard dash at a race in Hammersmith, England, in 1844. Though his time was generally accepted as a world record, it was eventually discredited toward the end of the century when no other competitor could come close to it.

Though chronometers were accurate, the conditions under which many races were run varied considerably. Some races were held on an incline, and many began with a "rolling" start, or the competitors would purposely jump the gun. The latter term is actually derived from track and field, where the starter's gun came into vogue in the 1860s as a much more fair and accurate method of starting a race than dropping a handkerchief or a flag.

Though betting and corruption proved the death knell for professional running, which gradually died out by the late 19th century, the amateur sport was by that time in full swing. As with so many organized sports in Victorian England, track and field was a product of the public schools and universities. The first intramural competition was held at Eaton College in 1837. In 1864 the initial Oxford versus Cambridge intercollegiate athletics meet was staged—an event generally regarded as the "foundation meeting" of modern athletics. In the latter quarter of the 19th century, track and field gained popularity throughout colleges and clubs in England and along the northeastern seaboard of the United States.

Though women's track and field would not gain prominence in Europe until after World War II (the 19th-century British frowned upon females running and throwing things, just as they dissuaded women from engaging in most athletic endeavors), the sport caught on among women collegiates in America. In the 1890s, track and field was the most popular sport at Vassar and Smith colleges.

By providing a menu of events that appealed to athletes of varying skill and physique, track and field became an ultimate team sport at many schools. The footballer, wrestler, and baseball player all found common ground on a track and field team.

For the most part, early track and field was fiercely amateur, as officials and coaches vigilantly guarded against the professional element. An amateur athlete could not accept any monetary award for athletic contests, could not accept payment for any occupation related to athletics (this ruled out any coaching, instruction, officiating, scoring, etc., for pay), and, in Britain, could not be employed as a mechanic, artisan, or laborer. These rules effectively excluded from the sport almost any noncollegiate athlete who either wasn't connected to old money or was not a member of the rising professional class. As a result, many of the very best amateurs became professionals out of necessity to earn a living.

Though track and field's first international showcase was the initial Olympic Games staged in Athens in 1896, for a variety of reasons most of the events were less than world-class in terms of competition and times (*see* Olympic Games). Many of the sport's best early marks were achieved at national and collegiate championships.

Evolution of Track and Field Events

Sprinting

The tradition of short-distance running is derived from the ancient Greeks, who held a *stadion* race in the original Olympics. One stadion was the length of a stadium, or about 200 meters. In Britain, the **100-yard dash**, or "century," as it was called, came to be the standard by which men of speed were measured. To run "even time" was to break 10 seconds in the 100. Though several men claimed to have done it earlier, the American John Owen was the first runner to officially break the barrier, running 9⅘ seconds at the Amateur Athletic Union (AAU) Championships in Washington, D.C., in 1890. Interestingly, Owen used a standing start. Several athletes had already developed the crouching ("all fours") start, which is similar to the way sprinters run out of the blocks today. Both Bobby Macdonald, a Maori from New Zealand, and a Yale University sprinter, Charles Sherrill, are generally credited with developing the crouch stance in the mid- to late 1880s.

Though the **400-meter dash** is regarded as a sprint race today, it was more of a middle-distance event in the 19th century. Since track and field originated in Britain, the race was formerly 440 yards, or a quarter mile—a significant distance, as all tracks throughout the world followed England's lead and were constructed either 440 yards to the lap, or the metric equivalent of 400 meters. Pioneering runners who tried to sprint the 440 found that they invariably began to slow around 330 yards; depending on the early pace, the final 110 could be quite agonizing. Two schools of strategy developed for the event—either go all out and try to slow down the least, or pace oneself by running two 220s of equal time. Lon Myers of Richmond, Virginia, was the first runner to consistently break 50 seconds over 440 yards. Competing in the late 1870s and early 1880s, Myers won 15 American titles and 3 English titles, including the British National Amateur 440-yard championship in 1881, where he ran 48⅗ seconds.

Distance Running

Endurance runners of the 19th century ran many fewer trained miles than today's distance specialists. Many ran no more than two to three miles a day in training, believing that a combination of rest, natural ability, and good strategy and guts on race day was the secret to distance running success. Despite their aversion to high mileage running, many of the early running greats were tireless, versatile competitors. It wasn't uncommon for a runner to compete at every distance from 880 yards to 10 miles or longer. Placed within a historical context, England's Walter George is certainly one of the greatest distance runners who ever lived (see illustration). A consistent champion at distances from 1 mile to 10 miles, George also ran match races at 880, 1,000, and 1,320 yards. (In fact, he beat the aforementioned Myers in 1882 at 1,320 and narrowly lost to him over 880.) Though the quest to run a 4-minute mile wasn't realized until England's Roger Bannister broke the barrier in 1954, George actually stirred interest in the feat when he was in his prime in the mid-1880s. George beat the

Figure 16. Walter George (right) and Will Cummings, surrounded by handlers and sponsors, get set to start one of their famous challenge races—this one a 10-miler in 1886 at the Aston Lower Grounds in Birmingham, England.

Scottish champ, William Cummings, with a 4:12¾ before 15,000 spectators at Lille Bridge Grounds in London in 1885. Later that year, he ran an unofficial world record of 4:10⅕ on a track that was found to be six yards too long. That same year George raced 10 miles in 49:29—the first recorded sub–50-minute performance.

Hurdles

There is no mention of hurdling races prior to modern times. The first races were held in British school meets. Originally, three different races were contested over 120, 220, and 440 yards. The 120-yard event was most common—10 hurdles, set at 3 feet, 6 inches off the ground, are spaced 10 yards apart, with a flat 15-yard start and finish. Though the event was standardized in 1866, traditional hurdling equipment did not encourage fast times. Solid sheep hurdles, "rigidly staked into the meadow," were used, and as a result, the hurdling style of the day was conservative and safety conscious. Hurdlers generated little speed or rhythm, as technique over the barriers resembled jumping rather than classic hurdling.

Jumps

Most of today's jumping events would hardly be recognizable in their 19th-century forms. The **high jump** for a time was actually two competitions—standing and running high jump, though competitors in the latter seldom used or converted their vertical speed to horizontal lift. The emphasis was on getting over the bar any way possible. Marshall Jones Brooks, a Londoner, was the first man to jump 6 feet, turning the trick in 1876. But the "artistry" of the high jump was nothing in comparison to the early **pole vault**. Historians speculate that the vault is a descendant of wartime activity, when soldiers used poles to bound across streams or over fortress walls. The Tailteann Games staged a vault-like event, and German gymnastics had developed an exercise similar to the pole vault. The earliest pole vaulting events featured a long hickory pole that was fastened to an iron base. Competitors climbed up the pole, swung from side to side, and threw themselves over a bar. In some cases distance as well as height was measured. By the 1870s, the pole vault began to look something like today's event, though jumpers seldom reached much higher than 9–10 feet. Poles were too heavy and stiff, and vaulting technique was little more than holding the pole 11–12 feet up from the bottom and simply riding it over the bar.

The **long jump** has always been a premier track and field event. The ancient Greeks considered it to be one of the ultimate tests in their all-around pentathlon, which also included the stadion sprint, discus and javelin throws, and wrestling. Many 19th-century track and field meets contested a standing long jump (usually referred to as the broad jump) and a running long jump. Contestants in both events usually used small dumbbells to provide more momentum at takeoff. During the 1880s, the running long jump grew more popular and a bit more challenging, as the takeoff board, which marks the point behind which a competitor must begin a jump, was introduced in 1886. Before that time, a competitor could not commit a foul—all jumps counted and were measured from the point of takeoff.

The **triple jump**, also known as the hop-step-and-jump, underwent a metamorphosis of sorts as well around the turn of the century. Today, the triple jump is regarded as one of the most explosive of track and field events: competitors run all out down the runway, take off and land on one foot (hop), take a long lunging step and land on the other foot (step), and finish with what is essentially a long jump. The Irish and Scots were renowned as the best triple jumpers of the 1880s and 1890s, although accounts of their exploits suggest that they typically followed a hop-hop-step routine. It wasn't until the 1900 Olympics that the hop-step-jump pattern was standardized. Like the long and high jumps, the triple jump also had a "standing" version. Ray Ewry, a farm boy from Lafayette, Indiana, was known as the "Human Frog." The legendary athlete won eight gold medals in the standing jumps at the Olympics (1900–1908)—a track and field gold medal total topped by only Carl Lewis.

Throws

The **discus, shot put**, and **hammer throw** are the three events that have undergone relatively little changes over the past century. The shot put and hammer throw had long been a part of Irish and Scottish folklore, being one of the ultimate tests of strength. Throwing the hammer—a 16-pound iron ball at the end of a thin metal chain—had been one of the few events that was popular with both commoners and nobility. In fact, King Henry VIII is said to have been a fan of the hammer throw, and illustrations exist depicting him throwing the hammer on the grounds of the royal court.

The discus thrower is celebrated throughout classical Greek culture—Myron's *Discobolus* is one of a handful of instantly recognizable sculptures the world over. Interestingly, Greek throwers have never dominated the modern event, and were in fact shown up on their home turf at the inaugural Olympics in Athens (1896). There, Robert Garrett, a collegiate from Princeton, won the discus despite having never thrown the implement in competition. Reportedly, Garrett had trained in the United States with a 20-pound discus. When he hefted the 2-kilogram (about 4.4 lbs.) discus used in international competition, it felt "light as a feather." Garrett bested his nearest competitor 29.15 meters to 28.95 meters. Ironically, Garrett's training methods are used by top discus throwers today, many of whom throw 20–25-pound disci, which at 15 inches in diameter are nearly double the standard 8¾ inches.

The **javelin** throw also has ancient roots, appearing on the program at both the classical Greek Olympics and the Celtic Tailteann Games. Though in medieval times javelins were thrown at targets, the Hungarians, Germans, and Scandinavians began throwing the javelin for distance during the 18th century. A modern javelin has a minimum weight of 800 grams (about 1¾ lbs.), measures between 260 and 270 centimeters (about 8½–8¾ feet), has a diameter ranging from 25 to 30 millimeters thick (about 1–1⅙ inches), and is banded in the center with a nylon grip for throwing. The contemporary style of using a run-up to build momentum behind a throw was pioneered by the late 19th-century great Eric Lemming of Sweden, who held the world record of 49.32 meters (about 160 feet, 4 inches) at the turn of the century.

Bibliography

Cumming, J. (1981). *Runners and Walkers—A Nineteenth Century Chronicle*. Chicago: Regnery Gateway.

Doherty, Ken. (1980). *The Track and Field Omnibook*. Los Altos, CA: Tafnews Press.

Quercetani, Roberto L. (1990). *Athletics: A History of Modern Track and Field Athletics (1860–1990)*. Milan: Vallardi & Associati.

▦ Water Polo

Definition

Water polo is a game played in an indoor pool between two teams of seven players each, the object being to throw an inflated ball into the opponent's goal without touching the bottom of the pool. The game, which originated in England as an aquatic version of soccer, is now played throughout the world and has become one of the most popular spectator sports in the Olympic Games.

History

Water polo is so named because in the earliest version of the game players rode on floating barrels that resembled mock horses and swung at large inflated balls with mallets. The game was just one of a number of swimming-related sports (along with water football, water rugby, and water handball) that became popular in England during the 1870s.

In 1870 the London Swimming Club developed a formal set of rules for water polo, and the first official game reportedly occurred in 1874. Early on, the sport earned a reputation as a rough game. Underwater fights away from the ball were common, as were all sorts of illegal holds applied to impede progress to the ball. The sport was cleaned up in Scotland in the late 1870s with the introduction of rules that prohibited tackling a player and taking the ball under the surface of the water. The hard rubber ball used for water polo up to this point was also replaced with a more forgiving soccer ball.

The Scottish game, which emphasized swimming ability, passing, and teamwork, caught on in England in the 1880s. In the 1890s, water polo spread to Europe, where it became especially popular in Italy, Hungary, and Austria. The sport first appeared in the 1900 Olympics.

In the United States, water polo was embraced by the Amateur Athletic Union (AAU) as a companion sport to swimming. U.S. rules were codified in 1897, and the sport gained acceptance in athletic clubs throughout the East Coast. However, the American game was rougher than the original English version, largely because the game in America was played in smaller indoor pools. A common water polo strategy of the day mirrored football, where teams would mass their players in a floating wedge around the ball carrier and the defense would try to break through or under the escort. The sport reached an absurd level in 1912 when the AAU championship game between the New York Athletic Club and the Chicago Athletic Association ended in a brawl. As a result, the AAU dropped water polo as a competitive sport for several years before American clubs agreed to adopt international rules.

Later in the 20th century, water polo would become a popular women's and men's collegiate sport on the West Coast, as schools in California, Washington, and Oregon came to dominate National Collegiate Athletic Association (NCAA) competition. Today, there are more than 1,000 amateur teams with over 10,000 members of the United States Water Polo Association.

Equipment

Though the ball that is used is very similar in size and weight to a soccer ball, it has a nylon bladder, covered with rubber fabric to keep it from absorbing water.

Because of the rough nature of water polo, most players wear two uniforms, one over the other, in case one is ripped during play. Players wear swim caps that display the player's number. The caps also have ear guards, which prevent injury to the head and eardrums.

Rules

The game is played in a rectangular pool measuring 30 meters long and 20 meters wide (see illustration). Women play in a slightly smaller pool (25 meters by 17 meters). The water in the pool must be at least six feet deep. Water polo goals measure three meters wide and one meter high above the water.

Water polo demands tremendous endurance and aerobic capacity, as all movement in the game consists of swimming, and players (except the goalkeeper) are not permitted to touch the bottom of the pool. Players move the ball by passing it through the air, across the water's surface, or by "dribbling" it in front of them. Dribbling in water polo refers to floating the ball on the water's surface as opposed to bouncing it on a hardwood floor. The ball is passed or thrown at the goal with one hand only, and players are not allowed to punch or hit the ball. Only the goalkeeper may use two hands to stop a shot.

Play consists of four seven-minute quarters (five minutes in international play), and a shot clock is maintained. Each team has 35 seconds to shoot the ball at the goal. If no shot is taken, a free throw is awarded to the opposing team. Goals count 1 point, and scores may run as high as 15 to 20 points for the winner in a fast-paced game.

Players may interfere with an opponent who is holding or moving the ball, and there is generally a good deal of physical contact. But players are not permitted to impede, pull back, or dunk an opponent who does not

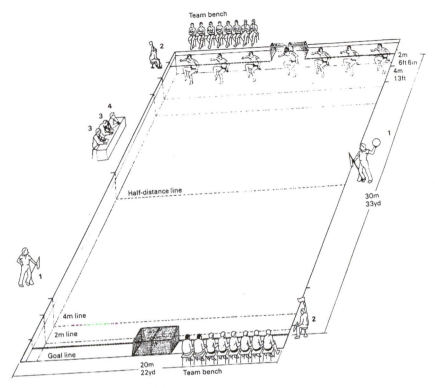

Figure 17. Water polo pool. (Reproduced from *Rules of the Game,* by the Diagram Group [New York: St. Martin's Press, 1990] p. 198)

have possession of the ball. Ordinary fouls are assessed when a player touches the bottom of the pool, grabs the ball with both hands, punches the ball, and so on, and such infractions result in an opponent taking a free throw. Major fouls are assessed for interference, overly aggressive play, or deliberately attacking an opponent, and these infractions result in the opposing team either being given a penalty throw, or the offending player being suspended from the game for 20 seconds. The penalty is served for either the duration, until the offending team regains possession of the ball, or until a goal is scored, whichever comes first. A player who amasses three major fouls in a game is disqualified.

Players stay afloat by using an "eggbeater" kick, which enables them to tread water and also to spring up out of the pool, placing their center of gravity several feet above the water's surface. This movement helps a player to receive or intercept the ball and is essential in getting off a strong pass or shot attempt.

All water polo players have dual roles on offense and defense. Center forwards, or "hole set" players, take position directly in front of the goal.

They specialize in offense, using their size and leg strength much like a basketball center in "posting up," looking for a pass that will enable them to take a close-in shot at the goal. Drivers are usually the fastest swimmers on the team. They are typically relied upon for their quick shooting techniques and strong defensive play. Goalkeepers are much like their soccer counterparts. They guard the three-meter-wide goal area and are permitted to use both hands and to punch the ball to make a save, provided they stay behind their own four-meter line (similar to the penalty area in soccer).

Bibliography

Brown, G. (ed.). (1979). *The New York Times Encyclopedia of Water Sports*. Danbury, CT: Arno Press.

"How to Watch Water Polo." (2000). Water Polo Canada Web page, *http://www.waterpolo.ca/* (January 16, 2001).

USA Water Polo. (2001). "The Origins of Water Polo." USA Water Polo Web site, *http://www.waterpolo.com/* (January 16, 2001).

Worth, Sylvia (ed.). (1990). *The Rules of the Game*. New York: St. Martin's Press.

▦ EUROPE

HISTORICAL OVERVIEW

The 18th and 19th centuries in Europe were marked by changing political and economic systems and the creation of new social orders. The Age of Reason, marked by scientific discovery and greater knowledge about the natural world, led many to begin to celebrate the material over the spiritual. In this context, the divine right of monarchies was questioned, and most ruling families saw their political power either diminished or abolished altogether. Though the French Revolution (1789) prompted a conservative reaction throughout Europe during the late 18th and early 19th centuries, governments generally became more democratic throughout the 1800s, as a growing class of businessmen and professionals gained more political and economic power. This process was intensified after the democratic revolutions in Europe during 1848. Decentralized groupings of states and principalities like Italy and Germany unified in the 1860s and 1870s, largely for economic reasons. Centralized countries standardized currency, banded together to pass trade and commerce laws, and taxed citizens to finance national defense.

As countries in Western Europe began to industrialize, old social orders became obsolete. Peasant farmers moved to the cities to become factory workers. The old aristocracy lost much of its political power, but clung to social status through hereditary wealth and property. Much more important was a rising class of businessmen, who made their wealth and attained their social status through industry and trade.

By the late 19th century, concepts of imperialism and nationalism were coming to define more and more countries. Imperialism describes a country's extension of political and economic power over another country. In the case of Europe in the late 19th century, countries like Germany, Belgium, and France began to compete with Britain for control of parts of Africa and Asia. Strong feelings of nationalism—loyalty and devotion to one's nation above all others—went hand-in-hand with imperialist ideals.

These nation-based values and ideals were reinforced by public education. The concept of education to build a well-schooled, competent citizenry for the good of the nation came to be accepted, leading to a hierarchical system of public education throughout much of Europe. Education at the academy (high school) and university levels was increasingly based on "classical" principles founded in ancient Greek and Roman cultures. The ideals of virtue, order, justice, moderation, reason, and strength of character, mind, and body were imbedded in European styles of art and architecture, in literary tastes, in systems of philosophy and government, and in the concept of sports.

THE LEGACY OF SPORTS AND GAMES IN THE 18TH AND 19TH CENTURIES

Though this period in Europe—particularly during the 19th century—witnessed the rise of competitive sport, in which sports and games began to be played by a uniform set of rules, with winners and losers, the European concept of competitive sport is different from the British. For the British, sport was often a test of national worth and character (see Chapter 3). Many sports and games created and perfected by the British—soccer, rugby, cricket, field hockey, rowing—are collective activities, in which one team challenges another for supremacy. This sporting ethos reflects England's geopolitical and economic position during the 18th and especially the 19th century, when the country envisioned itself as an "empire builder"—a heroic lone island nation pitted against the rest of the world. Though it should be noted that almost every team sport created in England made its way to the continent and was embraced with at least a fair amount of enthusiasm, those sports which were considered central to the European experience (i.e., made a part of the school curriculum and the most popular as club pursuits) were largely individual sports. In Europe, sports like **swimming, diving**, and **gymnastics** were considered vital to the development of character and a sound body and mind. All of these sports have links to classical Greece and Rome, as do **fencing** and **athletics** (*see* Track and Field), two popular school and club sports in Europe.

Europe's taste for things classical is reflected in its promotion of **Greco-Roman wrestling**, a 19th-century European creation that is classical in name only. This classical concept of sport was embodied in the revival of the ancient Greek **Olympic Games**, which were held in 1896 in Athens. Envisioned as a showcase for sport as an ideal means of education and character building, the Olympics would grow to encompass the ideals of peace, cultural expression, and the power of sport as an instrument of social reform and change.

While many of the sports discussed in this chapter have origins that underscore the social and geographic differences across Europe (e.g., **Nordic skiing** as a means of transportation by the masses in the Scandinavian countries, or **ice skating** by commuters on the canals in Holland), all took on recreational and/or competitive aspects that varied by region and social class. **Biathlon**, originally a form of military training in Sweden and Norway, was later adapted as organized competition by middle- and upper-middle-class athletes in northwestern Europe as a cross between ski racing and riflery. Another sport, **orienteering**, which was specifically designed for youth physical education and competition, came to be embraced as exercise and recreation by a broad segment of society. **Mountaineering** was originally a sport of the middle and upper middle classes that appealed to the growing sense of scientific progress and national advancement. But as more and more of the great peaks were conquered, the sport split into several forms: group mountain climbing and hiking, enjoyed by many for recreation and fitness; challenge climbing, attempts to find new and/or more difficult routes up a mountain; ice climbing; and rock climbing.

Though the dichotomy between amateur and professional sportsmen was much stronger in England, there was a similar situation on the continent. Professional wrestling, boxing, rowing, and track and field—engaged in by working-class competitors and spectators—all had amateur school/club counterparts. As in England, professional sports provided an outlet for gambling. Some English sports also attained a much larger following in Europe. After an initial craze among the aristocracy, cycling took off throughout France (*see* Cycling). By 1903, the first year of the annual Tour de France bike race, cycling was well on its way to becoming the French national sport, and it would grow quite popular in Italy as well.

As European society changed from a rural to an urban base, and the economy shifted from agriculture to industry, sports, too, changed. A folk sport like **jai alai**, created in the Basque region of Spain, came to be taken out of its traditional context and transplanted as a professional sport in urban Europe, South America, and the United States. Speed skating was no longer contested only on the Dutch canals, but now took place on man-made ice tracks in Oslo, Vienna, and Munich. The concept of traditional "sports of the people" has become important to men and women all over the world. Because of sport's role in helping to define a people's culture, many ethnic groups who have come under the political control of other countries have made a concerted effort to revive traditional sports in order to help define and celebrate their heritage. Similarly, many rural societies that have been transplanted to urban settings struggle to retain connections to their past. The German **volkssport** movement grew out of the rural/urban social and cultural dichotomy that affected much of society throughout Europe in the 18th and 19th centuries.

▦ Biathlon

Definition

Biathlon is a winter sport that combines cross-country skiing with target shooting. The sport's challenge lies in the unlikely combination of events—an aerobic activity that requires strength, speed, and endurance, and a passive activity that demands intense concentration and self-control. Biathlon has been a Winter Olympic sport for men since 1960 and for women beginning in 1992.

History

Biathlon's ancient origins are revealed in cave paintings found in Norway that date back to about 3000 B.C. These drawings depict hunters on wooden slats stalking animals. We also have later written accounts from the Greeks, Romans, and Chinese that describe hunting on skis. Historical writings from the Roman Empire describe warriors on skis as well. Skiing regiments were active in Russia and Scandinavia as early as the 1500s, and by the late 19th century in Germany, Austria, and Switzerland. A famed David-and-Goliath military story involves the Finnish army, greatly outnumbered but outfitted with skis, repelling the Soviet Red Army from its borders in 1939.

The earliest recorded biathlon event took place in 1776 in Norway between military patrols that guarded the border between Sweden and Norway. This was a team competition that combined shooting skill with skiing. Regular events were held between the two countries throughout the late 18th and early 19th centuries. It wasn't until the early 20th century that biathlon became an individual competition. In 1912 single competitors in Norway skied a race in which 10 rounds were fired in two shooting bouts. The first international biathlon competition was staged as a demonstration sport at the 1924 Winter Olympics in Chamonix, France. Though biathlon appeared as a demonstration event at the 1928, 1936, and 1948 Olympiads as well, participation was limited to members of the military, and it was in fact dropped from the Olympic program after 1948 in response to widespread antimilitary sentiment that followed World War II.

Biathlon experienced a rebirth in the hands of the Union Internationale de Pentathlon Moderne et Biathlon (UIPMB), which worked in the mid-1950s to instate both the pentathlon and the biathlon into Olympic competition as individual civilian sports. As a result, the first Biathlon World Championships were held in Saalfelden, Austria, in 1958 and the sport was sanctioned as an official Olympic event at the 1960 Winter Games in

Squaw Valley, California. These early events were 20-kilometer races (12.4 miles) with four shooting stations. Targets were set at 250, 200, 150, and 100 meters, with the first three executed in a prone position, and the last standing. Large rifles and cardboard targets were used, and competitors were assessed two-minute penalties for misses.

In 1968 the 30-kilometer relay was added to international programs, and the 10-kilometer sprint race became an Olympic event in 1980. The sport entered the modern age in 1977, when organizers changed the standard equipment from large army rifles to more manageable small-bore (.22 caliber) rifles. This change made biathlon accessible to more athletes, particularly women, and added precision to the shooting event. In the 1980s, the skate-ski step revolutionized the sport, making racing much faster and more exciting. Though biathlon continues to be a minor sport in America (there are an estimated 1,000 biathletes nationwide), it is the most popular televised winter sports event in Europe.

Equipment

Rifles are .22 caliber, bolt-action with nonoptical sites. International rules state that "rifles may not be of automatic or semi-automatic design. Loading or unloading may be executed only by the competitor's muscle force." The rifle is carried in a harness strapped to the competitor's back.

The ammunition is standard .22 caliber, with bullets typically made of lead or lead alloy. Targets are metal, and each consists of a white target face plate with five target apertures, behind which are five independently operating "knockdown" falling plate scoring targets, which are black. A hit is indicated by a black scoring target being replaced by a white indicator disc. Target sizes are 115 millimeters (taken from a standing position) and 45 millimeters (prone).

Biathletes use shorter cross-country skate skis, with boots, bindings, and poles identical to those used for cross-country skiing.

Rules

Biathletes ski with a rifle over a set distance to a shooting range, where five shots at five knockdown targets 50 meters downrange are taken from a prone position. Either a time penalty or penalty laps are assessed for each missed shot. The competitor then skis another loop and returns to the range for another round of shooting—this time from a standing position. Once again, penalties are assessed for missed shots. The biathlete then skis a final loop to finish the race.

Because the sport demands such disparate abilities, biathletes must devote a great amount of time to different forms of training. During the summer, speed, strength, and endurance are developed by rollerskiing, in-line skating, biking, and running. Shooting skills are developed by target practice, "holding" (taking a prone or standing position and holding the sights on a target for as long as possible), and "dry firing" (bolting the rifle without ammunition, sighting a target, and pulling the trigger).

Summer biathlon, which entails running and shooting, began as a way for biathletes to keep in shape during the offseason and has grown into an international sport. Events are typically 5–10 kilometers long, with shooting distances of 50 meters on winter regulation targets and penalty loops of 100 meters assessed for each miss. While competitors from 25 to 30 nations compete annually in the Summer Biathlon World Championships, the sport has gained popularity in the United States, where the United States Biathlon Association sanctions a national race series of over 60 events each year.

Bibliography

"About Biathlon." (1996). Allen's Biathlon page, *http://biathlon.net/* (February 8, 2001).
"Basic Training for Biathlon." (1999). Dave's Biathlon page, *http://ul.netgate.net /~tilde/dave/biathlon/* (February 8, 2001).
U.S. Biathlon Association. (2001). "Introduction to Biathlon." U.S. Biathlon Association Web page, *www.usbiathlon.org/* (February 8, 2001).

▦ Bocce

Definition

Bocce is an Italian bowling game played on a long, narrow dirt or grass court. Teams of two players, stationed at opposite ends of the court, attempt to roll as many as possible of their bocce balls closer to the pallino (a small ball rolled down the court to begin play) than the opposing team's closest ball. With origins in ancient Egypt and Rome, bocce is regarded today as a sort of Italian folk game. For many Italian Americans, bocce serves as a vital link to Old World culture.

History

Ancient Egyptian tombs contain what appears to be rudimentary bowling equipment. There are also classical references to the game in 4th-century B.C. Greece. We are also told that, during the First Punic War (264–241 B.C.) between Rome and Carthage, Roman soldiers played a game in which contestants threw larger stones at a "leader" stone. Teams were composed of four, six, or eight men, and the game provided much-needed relaxation between battles. Similar bowling games continued into medieval times in Europe, until 1319, when Holy Roman Emperor Charles IV banned bowling because its popularity was interfering with military training. Later, in the 16th and 17th centuries, the sport was revived and several variations became popular among the upper and growing mercantile classes throughout many Western European cities.

With the industrialization and urbanization of southern Italy in the late 19th century, bocce became a "people's game," as many peasants, relocated to the city for factory jobs, claimed bocce as a folk game. A greater number of players living closer together led to standardization of bocce, and rules were written regarding equipment and play.

Today, the International Bocce Association regulates championship bocce, though most of the best players in the world are from either Italy or France. (The French play a game called pétanque, or boule, which has many similarities to bocce.)

Bocce is regarded as a relaxing, conversational activity rather than a highly competitive game. Friends gather around a game of bocce. This explains the manner in which the game has followed Italian emigrants around the globe. Today, bocce is played in many urban areas in every European country and in North and South America. The U.S. Bocce Federation, which regulates play in America, has created a network of hundreds of clubs throughout the country. In Philadelphia alone there are 17 bocce clubs. For many Italian Americans, bocce is an important part of their cultural heritage. Though bocce has traditionally been a male game, more women and children began to play the game in the late 20th century.

Equipment

Very little in the way of space and equipment is needed to play bocce, referred to as a "sport simpatico e popolare." Though the playing surface should be flat and level, the court can consist of packed dirt, grass, or fine gravel. Because the game was created within an urban context, the dimensions and shape of the court have often been likened to an "alley." A bocce court is approximately 75 feet long and 8 feet wide. A bocce set consists of eight 4½ inch balls weighing about three pounds each, and a pallino, measuring about 1¾ inches in diameter.

Rules

Though the most common form of bocce involves play between two-man teams, the game is also contested between individuals or four-man teams.

In a game between two-man teams, each team positions a player at the end of the court. The first team member rolls the pallino downcourt and then rolls his/her first ball as close to the pallino as possible. The opposing team then must roll a ball closer to the pallino than the starting team. If the opposing team uses all four balls and fails to score a closer throw, then the starting team rolls each of its remaining balls, trying to place them closer than the opponent's closest ball. However, if the opposing team is successful in rolling a ball closer than the starting team, then the starting team must try and roll again to get closer. A player may roll his/her ball to knock an opponent's ball out of the way. A player is also allowed to knock the pallino toward his/her team's balls.

After each team has rolled four balls, the frame is completed. One team is awarded one point for each of its balls that lands closer to the pallino than the closest ball of the opposing team. Only the team with the closest ball can score points. If each team rolls balls that are equidistant from the pallino, neither team is awarded points. The team that scores in a frame begins the next frame by throwing out the pallino. The first team to score 16 points wins.

Bibliography

Freeman, Garth. (1987). *Petanque: The French Game of Bowls*. Leatherhead, England: Carreau Press.

International Bocce Association. (2001). "Basic Rules of Bocce." International Bocce Association Web site, *www.borg.com/~iba/* (April 18, 2001).

Soncini, Louis. (2001). "A Brief History of Bocce." U.S. Bocce Federation Web site, *www.bocce.com/* (April 18, 2001).

▦ Diving

Definition

Diving is the practice of entering the water headfirst, usually at the completion of an intricate airborne routine. Amateur diving competition typically takes place indoors and consists of a series of compulsory and optional dives from an elevated platform. Outdoor high diving, or cliff diving, is the oldest form of the sport. Today, professional divers in Latin America and Asia execute routines from heights of 100 feet or more.

History

One of the earliest historic depictions of diving is found in a tomb in southern Italy known as the Tomba del Tuffatore (the Tomb of the Diver). The burial chamber, which dates back to 480 B.C., has a painting on a roof slab that shows a male athlete diving from an elevated platform. There is also artwork from ancient Egypt that shows diver-like figures jumping off riverbanks. Native Americans in what today is Mexico were also diving off cliffs at the time of the Spanish occupation in the 16th century. During the 18th and early 19th centuries, travelers to Acapulco, Mexico, and the South Pacific Islands returned from their journeys with awe-inspiring stories of native divers who leapt from great heights. Prior to any Western European influence in Hawaii, native boys performed cliff dives as a right of passage. High dives demanded courage and bravery and thus earned the diver an honor not unlike that accorded a successful adult warrior.

Diving as an organized sport began much later. The first book on diving was published in Germany in 1843. Throughout the mid- to late 1800s, diving was popularized by the Germans and Swedes as an extension of or another part of gymnastics. In fact, the Germans took gymnastic apparatus to the beach and performed exercise routines that were punctuated by dives into the surf. Gradually, the concept of diving from a stance evolved. First the British, in the 1880s, engaged in "plunging"—a headfirst, crouching dive that resembled a sprint runner breaking out of the starting blocks. Then Swedish divers began "fancy diving" in the 1890s, where divers would perform acrobatic stunts off a 10-meter-high platform above a pool of water. A series of fancy diving exhibitions by Swedish divers in London was extremely popular, drawing thousands of spectators to Highgate Ponds in London in 1898. These exhibitions inspired the formation of the Amateur Diving Association, the world's first official diving organization.

Soon a series of standards was established for the sport, and springboard diving became an official sport at the 1904 Olympic Games in St. Louis. Platform diving was added to the 1908 Olympics, and in 1912 women began competing in diving at the Olympics in Stockholm. During the 1920s and 1930s, the sport took hold on the club and collegiate level in America, where diving competitions were typically held as part of the swim meet program. As a result, the U.S. men have had great success in Olympic springboard competition (sweeping all the medals in the 3-meter springboard in 1932 and 1964), and have also been among the leaders in platform diving. The best women divers have traditionally come from former and current communist countries such as the Soviet Union, China, and East Germany, where governments have given strong support to women's competitive athletics.

Equipment and Events

In amateur diving, athletes compete in three events—the 1-meter and 3-meter springboard, and the 10-meter platform. Though a springboard supplies a diver with spring to gain height for his or her jump, competitors in the springboard events need to generate power on takeoff to get the height needed to execute a routine, which might include a somersault or a twist. The platform enables a diver to plan and execute a more complicated routine, though the diver must be able to jump with confidence from greater heights. (Ten meters is about 32½ feet.)

Diving Positions

There are four defined positions in diving: the *tuck, pike, layout,* and *free.* Every dive is performed from one of these positions, and, prior to the dive, the *position* is identified, along with a *description* of the dive and the *height* at which it will be attempted. These three factors combine to assign a degree of difficulty to the dive. Standard diving tables rate each dive from a low of 1.2 (e.g., a simple front dive) to a high of 3.5 (e.g., a reverse three-and-one-half somersault off the 3-meter springboard or a front four-and-one-half somersault off the platform).

Types of Dives

Though divers are continually developing different variations of dives, all are derived from six basic groups of dives:

Forward Group: This could be a simple front dive to a forward somersault, or a flying forward dive, which requires the diver to be perfectly straight through the first 90 degrees of the dive, and then collapse into a tuck or a pike.

Backward Group: This dive is executed with the back to the pool, and could range from a simple back dive to a back 3.5 somersault.

Handstand Group: The handstands are the only group of dives performed solely from the platform. All dives begin with the diver in a controlled handstand position at the end of the platform, though the approach (e.g., cartwheel, walk, or kick) and position (backward or forward) may vary greatly.

Twisting Group: Twisting dives can be executed out of forward, backward, or handstand dives, and they range in difficulty from half twists to 4.5 twists.

Reverse Group: Otherwise known as a "gainer," a reverse dive is executed by standing forward, facing the water, and taking off in the same manner as the back dive. This dive is often combined with up to 3.5 reverse somersaults.

Inward Group: The diver begins with back to the water and takes off in the manner of the forward dive. Inward dives range in difficulty from a simple inward dive to an inward 3.5 somersault. A flying inward dive is essentially a reverse of the flying forward dive, with the diver executing a straight dive for the first 90 degrees and then collapsing into either a tuck or pike position.

Scoring

Judges assess a diver on his or her approach, takeoff, technique, and grace during flight and entry into the water. As noted above, a degree of difficulty of between 1.2 and 4.5 is also considered and factored into the scoring, so that an easy dive that is performed to perfection may score as well, if not better than, a difficult dive that is poorly executed. A panel of seven judges awards points based on a subjective scoring formula:

Failed dive = 0 points

Unsatisfactory dive = 0.5–2 points

Deficient dive = 2.5–4.5 points

Satisfactory dive = 5–6 points

Good dive = 6.5–8 points

Very good dive = 8.5–10 points

The highest and lowest marks for each dive are discarded and the remaining five marks are totaled, multiplied by three-fifths, and then multiplied again by the degree of difficulty factor. All men's and women's championship competitions have preliminary and final rounds—divers perform a series of dives in each round, with the highest totals or average scores advancing from the preliminary rounds to the finals.

Bibliography

Canadian Amateur Diving Association. (2000). "The Sport of Diving." Canadian Amateur Diving Association Web page, *www.diving.ca/* (February 16, 2001).

O'Brien, Ron. (2001). "Diving: A Historical Overview." U.S. Diving Web site, *www.usdiving.org/* (February 16, 2001).

Smith, D., with J. H. Bender. (1973). *Inside Diving*. Chicago: Regnery Gateway.

U.S. Diving. (2000). "U.S. Diving Rules and Regulations." U.S. Diving Web site, *www.usdiving.org/* (February 16, 2001).

▦ Fencing

Definition

Fencing is the art or sport in which two opponents engage each other in swordsmanship using blunted weapons. Modern fencing is a recreational and competitive sport, with rules and techniques that are derived from methods originally developed for dueling. Fencing consists of competition with three weapons: foil, épée, and sabre. All are contested for men and women in the Summer Olympic Games.

History

Swordfighting as a sport has existed since ancient Egypt. The ancient Greeks, Romans, Chinese, and Japanese also practiced swordsmanship, primarily as a means of training for combat. Ironically, the application of swordsmanship as an art did not occur until after gunpowder came into general use in combat during the 15th and 16th centuries in Europe. At that time, heavy defensive armor became obsolete, as did the heavy-handed sword-wielding methods of soldiers, who were used to swinging large, sharp rapiers to cleave through the thick armor. As guns became the weapons of choice for military men, civilians began using the rapier for dueling.

During the late 16th and early 17th centuries, the Italians and Spanish became masters at rapier fencing. Throughout the 17th century, the emphasis was on developing increasingly lighter, easier-to-handle swords, and on refining methods of fighting that centered on thrusting rather than slashing. By the early 18th century, the French had developed a shorter, smaller sword. Though the French sword still had an edge, it served little purpose beyond discouraging an opponent from grabbing the blade in the heat of battle. Lightweight styling made intricate offensive and defensive movement possible. When buttoned with a leather safety tip, the sword resembled a flower, hence the name *le fleuret* in French. Le fleuret is essentially the same as a modern-day *foil*, and served as the basis for most modern fencing theory.

The next innovation in fencing occurred in the early to mid-19th century, when dueling began to decline as a means of settling arguments. Because killing an opponent in a duel could lead to a murder conviction and time in prison, duelists began to look for other ways to defeat an opponent without killing or crippling him. The *épée de terrain*, or *épée*, came into vogue as an unedged variation of the foil. It should be noted that dueling, because of its romantic overtones and link to sportsmanship, skill, and honor—fighting with a sword was much more refined and less messy than simply firing a gun at someone—had always been a means of fighting favored by the upper middle and upper classes. The working-class commoner settled disputes in more impulsive fashion, usually by fist fighting or brawling. Fencing as a sport developed along similar class lines—as an amateur sport that flourished in athletic and military officers' clubs through Western Europe and not as a professional sport that appealed to either working-class participants or spectators.

Though swordsmanship had been popular in England from the late 16th to the mid- to late 3th century, this activity could hardly be referred to as an art. Swordfighting often went hand-in-hand with prizefighting. Fighters would often square off in bouts of quarterstaffs or backswords, and, win or lose, both competitors were more likely than not to draw a fair amount of blood. As boxing became a science—one that was easier to learn than fencing—the swordfighting was largely dropped as a popular sport.

The *sabre*, fencing's third variant, developed from military uses, particularly among cavalrymen, who brandished sabres to cut and slash at menacing foot soldiers. Training had always been performed with wooden weapons, and it wasn't really until the late 19th century, at which point the cavalry were becoming obsolete, that smaller, lighter metal sabres were developed for military practice and sport. Around the turn of the century, the Hungarians developed a new form of sabre fencing that emphasized finger control over arm strength, and they would dominate sabre fencing for much of the 20th century.

Fencing's rise in popularity mirrored the growing prominence of intercollegiate sports in America and Britain in the late 19th century and the concurrent advent of amateurism epitomized by the modern Olympic movement. While the early Olympic Games were dominated by the French, Italian, and Hungarian fencers, the Russians mastered all three weapons in the 1960s and, as a result, the Soviet Union won more Olympic medals in fencing than any other nation.

The Amateur Fencers League of America was formed in 1891, and this body governed the sport on the club level in the United States. Though national championships at the collegiate level have been contested in fencing since 1941, the sport's popularity in America has been hindered by a lack

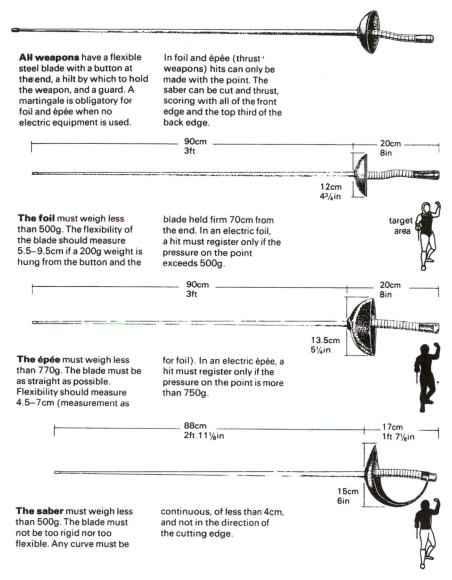

All weapons have a flexible steel blade with a button at the end, a hilt by which to hold the weapon, and a guard. A martingale is obligatory for foil and épée when no electric equipment is used.

In foil and épée (thrust weapons) hits can only be made with the point. The saber can be cut and thrust, scoring with all of the front edge and the top third of the back edge.

90cm
3ft

20cm
8in

12cm
4¾in

The foil must weigh less than 500g. The flexibility of the blade should measure 5.5–9.5cm if a 200g weight is hung from the button and the

blade held firm 70cm from the end. In an electric foil, a hit must register only if the pressure on the point exceeds 500g.

target area

90cm
3ft

20cm
8in

13.5cm
5¼in

The épée must weigh less than 770g. The blade must be as straight as possible. Flexibility should measure 4.5–7cm (measurement as

for foil). In an electric épée, a hit must register only if the pressure on the point is more than 750g.

88cm
2ft .11⅛in

17cm
1ft 7⅛in

15cm
6in

The saber must weigh less than 500g. The blade must not be too rigid nor too flexible. Any curve must be

continuous, of less than 4cm, and not in the direction of the cutting edge.

Figure 18. Fencing swords (left, top to bottom) and respective target areas (right, top to bottom). (Reproduced from *Rules of the Game,* by the Diagram Group [New York: St. Martin's Press, 1990], p. 63)

of unity between the National Collegiate Athletic Association (NCAA) and the United States Fencing Coaches Association (USFCA), which administers the teaching of fencing in the United States. Interscholastic fencing in America has a small following, typically among either progressive schools or private institutions.

Figure 19. Fencing strip.

Equipment

As discussed previously, the three fencing weapons are the foil, epee, and sabre (see illustration, p. 141):

Foil: The foil has a thin, flexible 36-inch-long blade with a square cross-section and a small bell guard. In order to score, a fencer must place the point of his or her foil on the torso of an opponent (known as the target area), including the groin and back.

Épée: The epee has a thicker, stiffer 36-inch-long blade with a triangular cross-section and a larger bell guard. Touches are scored by placing the point of an epee anywhere on an opponent's body.

Sabre: A sabre has a light, flat 35⅛-inch-long blade, slightly curved from end to end, with a knuckle guard. Touches can be scored with either the point or the edge of the blade, anywhere above an opponent's waist.

Fencers typically wear light clothing, usually a canvas or nylon jacket, knickers, and a padded glove on the hand holding the fencing implement. A *plastron* is a quilted pad worn under a fencer's jacket to protect the torso. A wire-mesh face mask is also worn, as is a canvas bib that protects the neck. Both the face mask and the plastron were late 18th-century innovations that contributed significantly to the development of the free-flowing give-and-take style of fencing. Fencers who no longer had to worry about suffering injury could concentrate on strategy and scoring a series of touches rather than on landing one big blow.

Rules and Technique

Fencers compete on a narrow strip, or runway, measuring 14 meters long and 2 meters wide (see illustration above). In general, the object of a fencing bout is to score 15 points on an opponent before being scored upon 15 times. Each time a fencer scores a touch, he or she receives one point. Matches consist of three three-minute periods.

In order to follow a fencing match, one must understand the concept of "right-of-way," which pertains to both foil and sabre fencing. In essence, right-of-way refers to offense and defense and is only relevant when two fencers appear to have scored a point on one another at the same time. In such a case, the referee determines which fencer had the right-of-way—in other words, who was on offense—and awards the point to that contestant.

Fencing is extremely quick—so quick that referees have come to rely upon sensitive electronic equipment to indicate when a touch is scored. In both foil and sabre, fencers wear light metallic vests to cover the target area; small, spring-loaded tips are attached to the point of the foil and the edge and blade of the sabre, and these register a touch when they come in contact with an opponent's target area.

Fencing technique involves fast, balanced footwork and deft swordsmanship. Common methods include attacking, when an opponent lunges forward on the offensive; the *parry*, a defensive motion used to deflect an opponent's blade; and the *riposte*, which is essentially an answering attack, which follows the parry.

Bibliography

De Beaumont, Charles L. (1970). *Fencing: Ancient Art and Modern Sport*. South Brunswick, NJ: A. S. Barnes and Co.

U.S. Fencing Association. (2000). "What Is Fencing?" U.S. Fencing Association Web page, *www.usfencing.org/* (February 20, 2001).

Worth, Sylvia (ed.). (1990). *The Rules of the Game*. New York: St. Martin's Press.

▦ Greco-Roman Wrestling

Definition

Greco-Roman wrestling is a form of grappling in which competitors are not permitted to use their legs in any active manner (e.g., to trip or hold an opponent) and are not allowed to use any holds involving an opponent's hips or legs. Developed in Europe during the 19th century, the sport has maintained its popularity among amateur wrestlers all over Europe and is a major event in the Olympic Games.

History

Though wrestling appeared in the ancient Greek Olympics, no clear lines can be drawn between Greco-Roman wrestling and this early version of the sport. Neither the Greeks, one of the first cultures to wrestle competitively, nor the Romans wrestled in Greco-Roman fashion. The Greeks generally wrestled in two styles: *orthia pale*, or upright wrestling, where the object of the bout was simply to throw one's opponent to the ground, and *kato pale*, or ground wrestling, which is similar to the type of wrestling common among interscholastic grapplers in the United States today.

The name "Greco-Roman" has much more to do with a sense of idealization of classical Greece and Rome by late 18th- and early 19th-century European culture. At that time, new public buildings were dominated by Greek and Roman architectural design; the study of philosophy, education, and the beginnings of political democratic thought were based on Plato, Socrates, and the Greeks; and the judiciary and criminal and civil codes in Western Europe were shifting away from monarchical dominance in favor of the ideals of Roman law. Sports were no different. In a movement that eventually resulted in a reintroduction of the Olympic Games in the late 19th century, many 19th-century sports in Europe took on a classical undertone (*see* Olympic Games).

Greco-Roman wrestling was extremely popular throughout Western and Eastern Europe by the mid- to late 19th century. Vienna, Munich, Prague, Warsaw, and Paris all hosted international tournaments offering rich prizes. It should be noted that Greco-Roman wrestling was a club sport, engaged in by middle- and upper-middle-class professional types, many of whom had either been educated through the European university system or were members of the military. In most cities, the country's military ran athletic clubs to keep officers in top physical condition and to provide a sense of esprit de corps through organized sports competition. In fact, wrestling, gymnastics, and fencing were the most popular club sports.

Greco-Roman wrestling's popularity is also suggested by its standing as a medal sport in the first modern Olympic Games in 1896. Freestyle wrestling—what we regard as amateur wrestling in the United States today—wasn't included in the Olympics until 1904. Greco-Roman wrestling also had a professional side, as did many other sports in the latter half of the 19th century. Skilled grapplers from the working or lower classes could make a good deal of money on the professional wrestling circuit, which performed throughout Europe. With money on the line—and the lack of a uniform code of rules—these bouts were often characterized by violent moves; body slams, chokeholds, and the occasional head butt were the order of the day. Freestyle and pro wrestling in America were also popular in the late 19th and early 20th century. It should be noted that the sport was legitimate, with winners and losers decided by skillful moves and clean competition—a far cry from today's professional wrestling, which is little more than staged theater and laughable, lowbrow antics.

Though freestyle wrestling, where grapplers may apply holds below the waist and use their legs for holds, has outstripped Greco-Roman wrestling in terms of popularity, the latter sport is still quite popular throughout Europe, particularly in Russia, Eastern Europe, Sweden, Finland, and the Baltic nations. Though the Amateur Athletic Union and later the United States Wrestling Federation have conducted Greco-Roman

Championships since the 1950s, the sport really hasn't had a large following in the United States. This may change as a result of the 2000 Olympics in Sydney, where a farm boy from Wyoming, Rulon Gardner, beat three-time Olympic gold medallist Alexandre Kareline of Russia in a narrow 1–0 decision. Prior to the Olympic final, Kareline, wrestling in the premier heavyweight class, had never lost an international match in a career spanning over 250 bouts and dating back to 1985.

Equipment

Wrestlers compete in one-piece suits of cotton/polyester/Lycra blend, which are light and wick moisture away from the skin. Shoes are light with rubber/polyurethane outsoles for good traction and laced high to provide good lateral support. Wrestlers also wear light strap-on helmets that protect their ears.

Rules

Competition takes place on a padded mat within a circle measuring about 18 feet in diameter. The International Wrestling Federation was formed in 1921, and, as a result, the sport gained standardized rules. Significant changes related to the banning of several dangerous holds, prohibitions against stalling, and limitations of the duration of a match. Prior to these changes, it was not uncommon for matches to last two hours or more. In the 1912 Olympics, Anders Ahlgren of Sweden and Ivan Boehling of Finland squared off for nine hours in the championship match before exasperated officials called the bout a draw and awarded both men a silver medal.

Greco-Roman wrestling is distinguished from freestyle wrestling by rules that restrict all holds to above the waist, using only the hands and arms. Tripping, tackling, and the use of the legs to secure a hold are prohibited. A Greco-Roman wrestler grips an opponent in a standing position and attempts to throw him to the mat—or to turn an opponent already on the mat—so that his shoulders strike the mat simultaneously. This position results in a fall, and the match is ended. Failing to score a fall, both wrestlers continue to grapple over two three-minute periods. (In the event of a tie, the wrestlers continue for a three-minute overtime period.) Score is kept throughout the bout, and the winner is determined by points. In general, there are four ways in which to score points:

Takedown: An aggressor scores two points for throwing an opponent to the mat.

Escape: A wrestler earns one point for an escape by breaking out of an opponent's controlling hold, rising off the mat and turning to face his opponent.

A Reversal: One point is awarded when a wrestler overcomes, holds, and controls an opponent.

Near Fall: The award of 1, 2, 3 or 5 points to an attacker for placing an opponent in "a position of danger," the value of which is based on the hold and its duration.

With holds restricted to the upper body, a wrestler not only needs to be skilled in various upper-body locks and holds, but also must be able to use balance and speed to apply a hold and immediately translate it into a throw. In wrestling off the mat, a wrestler must also be able to arch backward onto his neck to lift and turn an opponent, as the legs cannot be applied to a hold on a competitor. Wrestlers compete within their own weight class. Weight classes range from 54 to 130 kilograms (119–287 pounds).

Bibliography

Farrell, Matt. (2000). "Gardner Beats the 'Russian Bear.'" USOC-Olympics Online, *www.usolympicteam.com* (September 27, 2000).

"The History of Wrestling." (2000). The Mat Web site, *www.intermatwrestle.com/* (February 8, 2001).

International Federation of Associated Wrestling Styles. (2000). *International Wrestling Rules*. Amateur Wrestling Network Web site, *www.wrestle.net* (February 8, 2001).

Martell, William. (1973). *Greco-Roman Wrestling*. Champaign, IL: Human Kinetics.

▦ Gymnastics

Definition

Gymnastics is a sport where individuals practice acrobatic routines that demand strength, balance, rhythm, flexibility, and agility. Though organized gymnastics today is marked by work with such apparatus as the balance beam, pommel horse, vault, and parallel bars, a broader, historic definition of the sport includes calisthenics and routines using such equipment as hoops, ropes, balls, and clubs.

History

Gymnastics can trace its heritage back to the Minoan culture around 2000 B.C., where inhabitants of the island of Crete were said to be skilled at grabbing a bull by the horns, getting tossed head over heels onto the bull's back, performing an array of balancing tricks atop the bull, and then dismounting—often via a forward or backward flip. Ancient Greeks used gymnastics as military training, as general conditioning for elite athletes (what we would today term "cross training"), and as general physical exercise for all young men. The Romans also used gymnastics to train their soldiers, and such modern apparatus as the pommel horse and the vault resemble the wooden horses that the ancient Romans built (complete with saddle) to teach basic cavalry skills. The three sections of the pommel horse still retain the names *neck, saddle,* and *croup.*

As an organized discipline, gymnastics has more recent origins. A Prussian teacher named Friedrich Ludwig Jahn is referred to by many as the

"father of modern gymnastics." In the early 19th century, Jahn began es-
pousing a holistic "art of gymnastics," which he believed would restore
balance to the educational process by adding much-needed physical activity to counterbalance the "cerebral" curriculum that had grown to dominate German schooling. Called *Turnen*, meaning "patriotic gymnastics,"
Jahn's concept was also aimed at developing German cultural pride and
political nationalism, particularly in the face of Napoleon's occupation of
Europe. However, Jahn's ideas also have racist and anti-Semitic elements;
his reverence for the *volk* (German people) over all other religious, social,
or political identifications is uncomfortably similar to the values held by
Nazis over a century later. Jahn's patriotic fanaticism and uncompromis-
ing positions on the correct practice of *Turnen* ultimately placed him at
odds with the Prussian Ministry of Education, which came to outlaw *Turnen* in 1818. The ban wasn't lifted until King Friedrich Wilhelm IV issued
a decree in 1842 which officially recognized physical exercise as an essential component of a young man's education, and stipulated that *Turnen* be
introduced into the curriculum. *Turnvereins* (gymnastic clubs) also became
popular around this time, springing up all over Prussia and throughout
other German principalities.

While *Turnen* stressed the development of a set of skills to be performed
with and without apparatus, other forms of gymnastics were also taught
by educators throughout Sweden, Switzerland, and Italy. The Swedish
school emphasized the development of rhythm, coordination, and balance
by working with hoops, clubs, and balls. Juggling, tumbling, rope climbing, and calisthenics like jumping jacks and squat thrusts fell under the
realm of gymnastic exercises. The International Gymnastics Federation
(FIG) was formed in 1881, and gymnastics was held as a medal event at
the first Olympic Games in 1896. Interestingly, the latter competition featured all of the modern gymnastic events—pommel horse, vault, rings,
parallel bars, high bar, and balance beam—except floor exercises, and also
included rope climbing and the flying rings. "International" competition
was largely confined to Western Europe until after World War II, when the
sport became extremely popular in the Soviet Union, China, Japan, and
the South Pacific.

German, Swiss, and Swedish immigrants brought gymnastics to the
United States in the 1880s. Though for many years the sport's official governing body in the United States was the Amateur Athletic Union (AAU)
(the U.S. Gymnastics Federation was not established until 1962), gymnastics in America was more popular through YMCA clubs, colleges, and
high school physical education programs, where it was considered an
ideal discipline for the development of strength, coordination, and overall
conditioning. During the late 19th and early 20th centuries, gymnastic exhibitions in America were much more common than gymnastic competitions. These events often involved athletes from other sports. For example,

James Naismith, the father of basketball, and Amos Alonzo Stagg, All-American footballer and coaching great at the University of Chicago, both took part in a collegiate and amateur gymnastics exhibition in New York City in 1891. The National Collegiate Athletic Association (NCAA) didn't hold its first gymnastics championships for men until 1938 and for women until 1980. (The now defunct Association for Intercollegiate Athletics for Women conducted championship events from 1971 to 1982.)

Gymnastics really didn't gain popularity in America until the Olympics in the 1970s, when the accomplishments of gold Medallists Olga Korbut (1972) and Nadia Comaneci (1976) were broadcast on television to millions worldwide. During the 1980s, thousands of gymnastic clubs for children sprang up throughout the United States as gymnastics came to be regarded as the ideal sport to develop children's balance and agility.

Equipment and Events

International gymnastics competitions today are very different from those at the turn of the century. Some of the early Olympiads included such events as Indian club swinging and tumbling, while the World Gymnastics Championships in the 1920s and 1930s included such track and field events as the pole vault, long jump, and 100-meter dash. Rope climbing, in which competitors would start from a seated position on the floor and climb a 20-foot-high rope using only their hands, was part of AAU competitions in the United States up until the 1950s, as were tumbling and the trampoline.

Modern gymnastics is referred to as artistic gymnastics. Men's artistic gymnastics consists of the horizontal bar (high bar), parallel bars, rings, pommel horse, vault horse, and floor exercises (see illustration).

Horizontal Bar: A flexible steel bar, measuring about 1⅛ inches in diameter and 8 feet long, and mounted 8½ feet above the floor, the horizontal bar supports swinging and vaulting-type movements. Swinging movements are usually performed with the trunk and legs close to the bar, or with the body fully extended from the hands. In competition, the athlete should be in constant motion, with usually only the hands and soles of the feet touching the bar. Routines typically end with an acrobatic dismount, which might include forward or backward somersaults or twists.

Parallel Bars: The parallel bars are two flexible wooden rails measuring 11½ feet long and positioned 5 feet, 8 inches off the floor. Movements consist of swings, vaults, and slow movements and balance positions which demonstrate strength. The bars are grasped, released, and regrasped with one or both hands, as the athlete works either parallel to the bars or perpendicularly (e.g., swinging around or circling one bar). Usually only the hands and upper arms come in contact with the bars.

Rings: The rings are made of wood, spaced 20 inches apart, and suspended from a height of about 18½ feet. Much like the parallel bars, movements include swings,

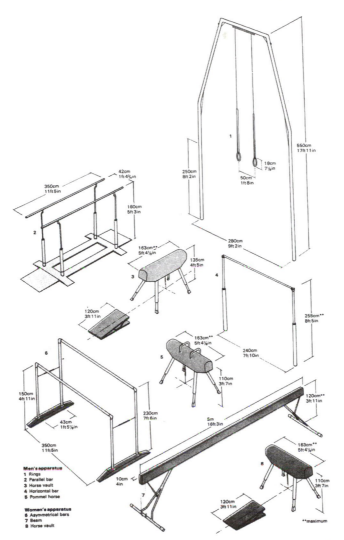

Figure 20. Men's and women's gymnastics apparatus. (Reproduced from *Rules of the Game*, by the Diagram Group [New York: St. Martin's Press, 1990], p. 30)

held positions, and slow movements which demonstrate strength. In advanced competition, athletes are usually required to execute and hold several handstands.

Pommel Horse: The pommel horse is a leather-covered cylinder, measuring 14 inches in diameter and 5 feet, 2 inches long. The pommels, or handles, are set 16–18 inches apart, and the tops of the pommels sit a little over 4 feet off the floor. All movement on the horse constitutes swinging motion—athletes are not permitted to stop, and only the hands should touch the horse.

Vault Horse: The vault horse is the same apparatus as the pommel horse with the pommels removed. The horse is vaulted along its length, with an approach sprint of up to 25 meters long. A "ruether board," a 2-foot by 4-foot spring-hinged board, is positioned on the ground in front of the horse. At the end of the run, the gymnast will leap off the ruether board headfirst toward the horse. Using only the hands, the gymnast pushes off from the horse, achieving enough height to perform somersaults and/or twists before landing feet first on the floor.

Floor Exercise: Often referred to as "free calisthenics," floor exercises constitute a routine of tumbling, ballet-like movement, balance, and held positions that emphasize flexibility and strength. In competition, routines are usually timed between 70 and 90 seconds and performed on a square mat-covered area measuring 40 feet on each side.

Women's gymnastics consists of the balance beam, uneven bars, vault horse, and floor exercise (see illustration).

Balance Beam: The balance beam is made of wood with leather padding. It measures about 16 feet long and 4 inches wide and is positioned 4 feet off the floor. Competitive routines consist of tumbling and stress grace and balance, as all movements must be continuous.

Uneven Bars: The uneven bars are a combination of the men's parallel bars and high bar, with one bar set 5 feet off the floor and the other 7½ feet. The bars are positioned 5 to 6 feet apart and are quite flexible, made of fiberglass with wood covering. Both bars must be used, and the gymnast is allowed no more than five consecutive moves on one bar.

Vault Horse: The women's vault horse is similar to men's, but the equipment and its positioning are on a slightly smaller scale.

Floor Exercise: This too is similar to the men's floor exercise—the same area is used, although the women's routine places more emphasis on grace and dance-like movement. (Routines are accompanied by music.)

Rhythmic gymnastics, which became an Olympic sport for women in 1984, actually grew out of the floor exercise. In rhythmic gymnastics, athletes demonstrate grace, balance, and flexibility while manipulating and maintaining control of an apparatus (ball, hoop, clubs, ribbon, or rope) with both left and right hands. Movement must correspond with the rhythm and mood of the music. Competitors are judged on composition (arrangement and degree of difficulty) and execution.

Scoring

Gymnastics teams consist of seven athletes. Six usually compete in each event, with the five highest scorers counting toward the overall team score. Standards for each event are determined by FIG, and gymnasts must plan their routines to demonstrate these standards. Gymnasts are scored by a panel of 4 to 6 judges, who use a 10-point scale. A routine's level of difficulty figures heavily in a judge's score. A gymnast's overall score is the average of each judge's score, with the highest and lowest score eliminated.

Bibliography

Frederick, A. B. (1996). "Roots of American Gymnastics: A Review." USA Gymnastics Online, *www.usa-gymnastics.org/publications/technique/1996/9/roots.html* (February 10, 2001).

Goodbody, John. (1983). *The Illustrated History of Gymnastics*. New York: Beaufort Press.

Schaap, Dick. (1975). *An Illustrated History of the Olympics*. New York: Alfred A. Knopf.

USA Gymnastics. (2001). "The History of the Sport of Gymnastics." USA Gymnastics Online, *www.usa-gymnastics.org/* (February 10, 2001).

Worth, Sylvia (ed.). (1990). *The Rules of the Game*. New York: St. Martin's Press.

▦ Ice Skating

Definition

An ice skater glides over a smooth surface of ice while balancing on steel blades attached to the bottom of specially designed boots. People have been ice skating recreationally for centuries, though the competitive sports of speed skating and figure skating didn't develop until the 18th and 19th centuries.

History

Prehistoric remains of polished animal bone blades have been found in bogs in the Scandinavian region. These discoveries date the start of skating to at least 3000 B.C. The Scandinavian *Eddas*, a 10th-century collection of folk literature, make reference to the "beauty, arrows and skates" of Uller, the God of Winter, "who runs on animal bones."

Skating as sport grew out of skating as necessity. An intricate system of canals was built in Holland in the 12th century, and canal workers used skates to get to, from, and around the job. Many of these workers engaged in competition for prize money, making them perhaps the world's first speed skaters. Greater speed and grace began to define skating with the introduction of the iron blade in the mid-13th century in the Netherlands. Skating had probably been imported to the British Isles at the time of the Norman Conquest in 1066. Eventually, the sport came to be embraced by nobility there, and the first skating clubs, which came about in the mid-18th century, were elitist in nature. (In Edinburgh, Scotland, in 1742 admission to the club was limited to men of eminent lineage who could skate a circle on each foot and jump over three hats.) The sport became popular throughout Europe in the mid-18th century. Like the cycling craze of the late 19th century, skating for a time was the "in thing" among the well-to-do and socialite set. Robert Jones, an artillery lieutenant in the British army, helped to shape the sport further with his text *Treatise on Skating*. Figure skating, speed skating, and ice hockey (*see* Ice Hockey) all developed as distinct sports during the 19th century.

Figure Skating

England's Henry Boswell developed a skate with an extended heel and shorter turning radius—equipment that facilitated the advent of figure skating. Though the British had for years embraced a brand of skating that emphasized form, the sport of figure skating is very much a child of environment. Confined to small village ponds, skaters in Victorian England had little choice but to circle round and round. Soon they were executing elaborate geometric figures. In Europe, skaters tended to place more emphasis on style and emotion. In Vienna, Prague, and Paris—all bastions of the arts and music—skating was regarded as a form of self-expression similar to dancing and ballet. Jackson Haines, the U.S. figure skating champion in 1863 and 1864, is generally credited with adding verve and emotion to competitive figure skating. Haines' performances were well received in Europe, where he toured extensively throughout the 1860s and 1870s, giving birth to what came to be called the international style of figure skating. As a result of disparate styles in England and Europe, figure skating came to represent a dichotomy of sorts, serving as a test of technique and form while providing a stage for artistic presentation.

Throughout the latter half of the 19th century, skating clubs and associations were created all across Europe. In 1892 Austria, Germany, Great Britain, the Netherlands, Hungary, and Sweden banded together to form the International Skating Union (ISU), which still governs figure and speed skating today. World Championship competition has been held annually since 1896, and figure skating has been a focal point of the Winter Olympics since the Games' inception in 1924.

Figure Skating Equipment

Figure skates consist of a pair of high-laced leather boots with blades that have toe picks on the ends. These picks have serrated teeth which enable skaters to perform spins and jumps. The costuming in figure skating has come to be almost as important as the act of skating itself. Most women skaters wear short skirts and tight, form-fitting spandex tops. Men wear slacks, long-sleeved dress shirts, and sometimes a short waist jacket or vest. There are rules against the excessive use of sequins or beads, which, in pairs skating, can catch on a partner's uniform or injure an eye.

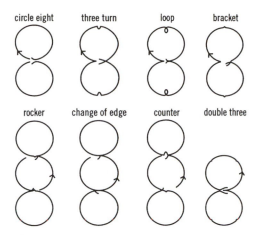

circle eight   three turn   loop   bracket

rocker   change of edge   counter   double three

Figure 21. Compulsory ice skating figures are no longer a part of competitive figure skating competition.

Figure Skating Rules

The major forms of competitive figure skating include men's and women's individual competitions, pair skating, and ice dancing.

Individual competition has changed markedly over the years. Early skaters were judged on compulsory figures, which consisted of tracing a figure eight and its variations (see illustration). A throwback to the British "form" school, skaters would trace identical patterns on the ice three times and were judged on their ability to replicate the exact figures. Compulsory figures were abolished in 1990, when the competition came to consist of a short program (also known as a technical program) and a long program (also known as free skate). The short program constitutes one-third of a skater's total score and lasts 2 minutes and 40 seconds. Skaters must perform eight technical elements, including a series of prescribed spins, jumps, and a footwork sequence. The long program, which counts as two-thirds of the final score, incorporates both technical and artistic elements and lasts 4 minutes for women and 4 minutes and 30 seconds for men.

Though skating began as a male-dominated sport, women were the most celebrated individual skaters of the 20th century, including Norway's Sonja Henie, a three-time Olympic champ beginning at age 16 in 1928, American greats Peggy Fleming and Dorothy Hammill, East Germany's Katarina Witt, and the reigning Olympic gold medallist, American Tara Lipinski.

Pairs skating began in the early 20th century. For several decades, skaters did little more than shadow one another's movements to the accompaniment of ballroom dance music. It wasn't until the advent of the Russians, with their ballet heritage, that pairs skating began to get dynamic and emotive. Romantic expression, speed, and daring characterized the Russian formula, which has proven to be a very good one—first the Soviet Union and then countries from its former republics have won every Olympic gold medal since 1964.

Ice dancing grew out of the ballroom dance craze of the 1930s in England. Dances as varied as the tango, foxtrot, rumba, and waltz are adapted to figure skating performance. Russian skaters have dominated this sport as well, winning all but one of the gold medals that have been contested since pairs ice dancing became an Olympic sport in 1976.

Speed Skating

Speed skating became popular throughout Europe at the same time as figure skating. The first European speed skating competition held outside Scandinavia was contested in England in 1763 over 15 miles. It should be noted that speed skating was a sport of the commoner and working man. Like pedestrianism and running, the roots of speed skating were founded in everyday life—getting from point A to point B—and like those dry-land sports, speed skating also lent itself to match races and competition for prize money.

Several innovations boosted the sport's popularity. In 1850 E. W. Bushnell of Philadelphia crafted the first all-steel skate blade. This did away with constant skate sharpening, making the sport more appealing. The rise of the open-air artificial rink also brought more athletes to ice skating and created venues for more racing. In the late 19th century, major rinks were built in New York, Paris, London, Munich, and Brussels, and smaller facilities sprang up throughout North America and Europe. Speed skating world championships were held beginning in 1893, and the sport has been a part of every Winter Olympic Games since the inaugural edition in 1924.

Though speed skating has always been somewhat esoteric in America, where youth in the winter are drawn more to team sports like hockey and basketball, the sport got a huge boost in 1980 when Eric Heiden, a 22-year-old from Madison, Wisconsin, won a record five gold medals at the Lake Placid Olympics. Since that time, Americans have been competitive internationally with the perennially strong Norwegian skaters.

Speed Skating Equipment

Speed skates are lower cut, usually made of light nylon material. Blades are long and straight—greater contact with the ice generates faster speeds. Though innovations in training have produced better times through the years, improvements in skate technology have also been important. In the late 1990s, virtually all the world records were rewritten with the introduction of the "slapskate," a bolt-and-hinge mechanism that allows a skate blade to briefly disconnect from a skater's boot. This enables a greater part of the skate to be in contact with the ice for a longer amount of time, producing stronger pushoff and greater overall speed. Skaters also wear skin-tight hooded Lycra suits to minimize wind resistance.

For these reasons, the early speed skating greats are difficult to compare to today's stars. For example, the Dutch skater Jaap Eden held the world 5,000-meter record at 8 minutes 37.6 seconds in 1873. In 1998 Olympic 5,000-meter champion Gianni Romme of the Netherlands won the gold medal with a world-record 6:22.2.

Speed Skating Rules

Speed skating is contested on an oval ice track measuring 400 meters. The track is divided into two lanes. Two skaters compete against one another, and both race against the clock, as all competitions consist of a number of heats or rounds. Skaters must switch lanes or "cross over" once every lap to ensure that both competitors cover the same distance. Race distances range from 500 to 10,000 meters, and speeds can reach over 30 miles per hour.

Short-track racing was introduced in the Winter Olympic Games in 1994 and has become an exciting spectator event. Competitors vie in individual, pack, and relay events over a small 111-meter track. Turns are tremendously tight and success is often determined by a combination of strategy and daring. Short-track skaters dress much like in-line skaters, with shin pads, helmets, knee pads, and gloves.

Bibliography

Copley-Graves, Lynn. (1992). *Figure Skating History: The Evolution of Dance on Ice.* Columbus, Ohio: Platoro Press.

Goetz, Karen. (2000). "Ice Skating." Microsoft Encarta Online Encyclopedia 2000, *http://encarta.msn.com* (March 2, 2001).

"Speed Skating." (1998). Washington Post Web site, *www.washingtonpost.com* (March 1, 2001).

United States Olympic Committee. (2000). "Figure Skating History." USOC Olympics Online, *www.usoc.org/usoc/sports* (March 1, 2001).

▦ Jai Alai

Definition

Jai alai is a court game similar to handball in which the competitors throw and catch a hard ball with a long, curved wicker basket strapped to the wrist. Though the game is indigenous to the Basque region of Spain, it has spread to North and South America, Cuba, and the Philippines. In the

United States, jai alai's popularity as a spectator sport during the 20th century has been intrinsically linked to gambling.

History

Though *jai alai* is Basque for "merry festival," suggesting that the game originated as part of a larger festival celebration, the term wasn't used in relation to the sport until 1904, when promoters in the United States wanted to give it an exotic name. Before that time, jai alai was known as *pelota*, the generic Spanish name given to various handball games played in that country. A variant of modern jai alai was probably played as long ago as the 16th century in the Basque region of Spain (located between the Pyrenees Mountains in north-central Spain and southern France). Travel sketches describe a handball-like game that was popular at regional festivals at the time, and children and adults used to play a similar game in rural Basque villages by throwing a ball against a church wall.

The first indoor *frontón*, or auditorium, for jai alai was built in Markina, Spain, in 1798. Jai alai's distinctive equipment reflects its ethnic folk origins. The *cesta*, or basket, which is used to catch and throw the *pelota*, or ball, actually replaced a more costly leather *cesta* that had been used throughout the early 19th century. Legend has it that a boy named Juan Dithurbide, from the French Basque village of Saint-Pee-sur-Nivelle, was the first person to use a basket to play jai alai. One day Dithurbide picked up an oblong, shallow wicker fruit basket and threw a few balls against the wall of a barn. By making modifications to the basket, the boy soon had a product that was lighter and much cheaper than a glove. He began producing them for local children and adults in 1857. Today the wicker *cesta* is made of reeds indigenous to the Pyrenees, and the frame consists of steam-bent chestnut.

Jai alai was introduced to southern France and Italy during the 1880s and to Central and South America by Basque immigrants in the 1890s. By the turn of the century, the game had also gained a following in Cuba, the Philippines, and the United States, the latter country welcoming the professional game as a boon to the entertainment industry. Yet gambling and professionalism hurt the competitive aspect of the game, and jai alai nearly went out of existence in America during Prohibition and the Great Depression. Today jai alai is legal in only three states—Connecticut, Rhode Island, and Florida—and the style of American play, *quiniela*, is tailored to betting schemes.

Though jai alai would become almost a national pastime in Mexico, Brazil, and Argentina, its popularity was adversely affected by the concurrent rise of soccer in the Americas and Europe throughout the early 20th century.

In 1921 the Federation Française de Pelote Basque was formed to codify the various *pelota* games, setting down rules, classifying players, and in-

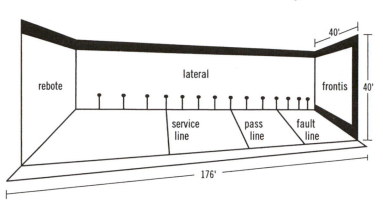

Figure 22. Jai alai court.

stituting a governing structure for the sport. In 1929 the Federación Internacional de Pelota Vasca was created in Madrid to perform the same function on an international level. The world governing body has sponsored a World Jai Alai Championship every four years beginning in 1952.

Equipment

Jai alai equipment consists of a wicker basket, or *cesta*, a *pelota*, and a special *cancha*, or court. The *pelota* is perhaps the hardest ball of any sport. Roughly three-fourths the size of a baseball, the *pelota* is said to be as a hard as a rock. Its core consists of Brazilian virgin de pola rubber, which is layered with nylon string and encased in a stitched goatskin cover. The average court-life of a *pelota* is about 20 minutes, due to the high speeds at which the ball hits the wall during play. (During games, the *pelota* has been clocked at speeds of as high as 180 mph.)

A jai alai uniform is similar to that worn in tennis or handball—court shoes, white shorts and T-shirt, and perhaps knee and wrist pads.

The *cancha* is a three-walled court that is 176 feet long and 40 feet wide and is open to spectators on one of the long sides (see illustration). The walls are 40 feet high and typically made of granite to withstand the impact of the *pelota*. The long side wall is known as the *lateral*, while the front wall is the *frontis* and the back wall the *rebote*.

Rules

Jai alai is played in singles or doubles competition. The object of the game is to serve and return the pelota with the *cesta* to the front wall until the *pelota* is either missed or goes out of bounds. The *pelota* may be played off the front, back, or side wall. To be a legal return, the *pelota* must be caught and thrown in one continuous motion. A player cannot stop the motion of or hold the *pelota*. There are three referees on the *cancha* to enforce these rules. In traditional jai alai, known as *partido*, matches are played to 35 points.

Bibliography

Hollander, Zander, and David Schultz. (1978). *The Jai Alai Handbook*. Los Angeles: Pinnacle Books.

"Jai Alai History." (2000). Jai Alai Players Web page, *www.jai-alai-players.com* (January 5, 2001).

Taylor, Richard. (1987). *Jai Alai*. New York: Doubleday.

Worth, Sylvia (ed.). (1990). *The Rules of the Game*. New York: St. Martin's Press.

▦ Mountaineering

Definition

Mountaineering is a sport in which participants climb up steep, difficult terrain that requires the use of specialized equipment and skill in rock and ice climbing and in ascending and descending high snow-covered mountains. Nontechnical climbs, which require a minimum of safety equipment, are often referred to as mountain climbing, a recreation activity enjoyed by millions throughout the world.

History

People have been climbing mountains since the dawn of history. Throughout time, mountains have been invested with mythical, spiritual, and even romantic symbolism. Often the most inaccessible mountains were both revered and feared. Only in the past two centuries have mountains been regarded as terrain to be scaled for purposes of exploration and sport.

The first ascent of Mont Blanc (Europe's highest peak at 15,771 feet) in the French Alps in 1786 is generally cited as the birth of mountaineering. However, the British, during the height of the British Empire in the late 1880s, referred to Sir Alfred Wills' climb of the Wetterhorn in the Swiss Alps in 1854 as the start of the sport, an assertion that reflects the importance the British placed on mountaineering. At a time when England was laying claim to so many distant lands, the conquest of uncharted mountains seemed a natural extension of their imperial destiny. To the British, mountaineering was not only a courageous, masculine activity that demanded strength, skill, and agility, but it was also a moral and scientifically rational endeavor. Peaks were explored for scientific research and geographic discovery. Just as the strong, technologically advanced nations of the Western world had a moral obligation to spread Christianity and capitalism to "underdeveloped" peoples in Asia and Africa, so too did these nations have a duty to explore and understand the uncharted natural territories of the globe. Lessons learned in exploring the North and

Figure 23. George Mallory (left) and Edward Norton, photographed by Howard Somerville, as part of the first British expedition to Mount Everest in 1922. The three were climbing without oxygen support at an altitude of just under 26,900 feet. Mallory would perish in an attempt to reach the peak of Everest in 1924. (John Noel Photographic Collection)

South Poles or climbing Mount Everest could be key in humans' quest to subjugate nature for their own ends.

Throughout the 1860s and 1870s, British climbers ascended most of the major peaks in the Alps. Mountaineering soon spread throughout Europe, Asia, the Himalayas, North and South America, Japan, New Zealand, and East Africa. By this time, mountaineering had begun to split into two different forms, one based on exploration and the other on sport. Exploration continues today in the first ascents of peaks in the Himalayas, Greenland, and Antarctica. The "sport" climbers began to emphasize the technical aspects of mountaineering. They had no reservations about scaling peaks that had already been conquered, as their objectives were to find routes to the top that were technically more challenging and more dangerous, often involving rock and ice climbing. Unlike the early climbers, these technical specialists recognized that sometimes risks had to be taken to pioneer a new trail.

Mount Everest, the highest peak in the world at 29,029 feet, has presented the greatest challenge to many climbers. Beginning in 1922, numerous exploratory attempts to make the first ascent of Everest— many led by British climbers—failed until Sir Edmund Hillary, a New Zealander, and a Nepali Sherpa, Norgay Tenzing, conquered the peak in 1953. Since 1922 about 1,000 individuals have made it to the summit of Everest—some establishing new routes, several climbing difficult sections solo—while at least 160 have lost their lives on the mountain.

Two recent books about Everest climbs have generated new interest in the sport. Jon Krakaur's best seller, *Into Thin Air*, tells the story of the disastrous May 1996 expedition on Everest in which five climbers lost their lives. Krakaur's book brought to light the dangerous practice of unprepared climbers paying guides to lead them up high, difficult peaks.

Peter Firstbrook's *Lost on Everest: The Search for Mallory and Irvine* tells the story of the 1999 Mallory and Irvine Research Expedition, a collaboration by British and American climbers and scientists whose objective was to determine whether the British climbers George Mallory and Andrew Irvine actually made it to the top of Everest before they became lost and perished on a climb in 1924 (see illustration).

Equipment

Clothing that keeps a climber warm and dry is essential, as alpine conditions often entail climbing and camping in wind chills of well below zero. Cotton clothing is avoided, as it conducts heat away from the body once it becomes moist with perspiration or melting snow. Climbers dress in layers, with synthetic underwear, fleece hats, jackets, gloves, and pants. Typically an outer top and pants shell is made of Gore-Tex or a similar material which is windproof and waterproof, yet breathable.

Today, almost all climbers wear a hard-shell helmet for protection against falling rocks and ice. Footwear is also extremely important. Most wear lightweight plastic boots that are waterproof. For icy conditions, climbers strap crampons to the bottoms of their boots. A crampon is a rigid metal-framed plate with a 12-point cleat for traction.

A climbing harness, which straps around the waist and thighs of a climber, clips into a high-strength nylon rope called *perlon*, which serves as a safety line in the event of a fall. An ice axe is commonly used for balance or to arrest a fall. A climber also carries a wide array of *nuts, chocks, ice screws*, and *snow pickets*, which are wedged into cracks and fissures in the rock or ice to provide an anchor for a climber's rope.

Types of Climbing

Alpinism, or alpine climbing, is the oldest form of mountaineering. The basic skills, techniques, and essential equipment of alpine climbing encompass the basis of all the other forms of mountaineering. Alpine climbing involves the continuous ascent of a mountain peak over the course of one or several days by a team of at least two climbers. In the event of a demanding climb, most teams consist of dozens of assistants, who may act as guides, cooks, doctors, and so on. Usually a base camp is established down the mountain which enables a team to gradually work its way up toward the summit. Leaving base camp, climbers must carry their gear, including water, food, and a lightweight bivouac sack. All those who climb Everest must bivouac, or spend the night precariously perched on a mountain ledge, before continuing to the top.

Ice climbing grew out of alpine climbing. Many of the techniques and safety precautions are the same, though ice climbers must rely on more advanced equipment. Laurent Grivel, a French ice climber, is credited with upgrading the traditional crampon when he added two extra front teeth to the device in 1932. This development enabled climbers to ascend steeper climbs—particularly ice faces—without cutting elaborate configurations of vertical steps. Later, in the 1970s, the curved ice axe pick was created, which made it easier for climbers to drive ice axes into ice. More radically curved picks and ergonomically designed axe shafts have recently been developed which enable climbers to traverse continuously vertical and even overhanging stretches of ice.

Rock climbing also developed out of alpine climbing. During the early 20th century, French and German mountaineers began to train on cliffs and boulders. Soon they were doing it for sport. More than the other forms of climbing, rock climbing demands excellent balance, finesse, and flexibility to complement the mountaineer's requisite endurance, strength, and coordination. When climbing lesser cliffs (50 meters or less), climbers use a technique called top-roping, in which the safety rope is anchored above. Higher climbs demand multiple ropes, and climbers typically anchor these to the rock face as they climb. The most common types of rock climbing include the following:

Friction climbing: moving up smooth, gradually sloping rock slabs.

Face climbing: holding onto flakes or edges of rock to scale a sheer wall.

Crack climbing: jamming fingers, hands, feet, arms, and so on into rock fissures.

Overhang climbing: marshalling quick bursts of energy to swing past rock overhangs.

Americans of all ages who are interested in mountaineering or rock climbing typically join a regional club where they can meet climbing partners, share information about gear and specific climbs, and take part in group expeditions and climbs. Most organizations are members of the American Alpine Club and go by names like "mountaineering club," "rock club," "outing club," "alpine club," or "mountain club."

Bibliography

Firstbrook, Peter. (1999). *Lost on Everest: The Search for Mallory and Irvine*. Chicago: Contemporary Books.

Unsworth, Walter. (1992). *Encyclopaedia of Mountaineering*. London: Hodder and Stoughton.

Webster, Ed. (2000). "Mountain Climbing." Microsoft Encarta Online Encyclopedia 2000, *http://encarta.msn.com* (January 5, 2001).

▦ Nordic Skiing

Definition

Nordic skiing is an all-encompassing term which refers to any type of skiing that uses free-heel equipment, including cross-country and telemark skiing, biathlon, and ski jumping, also known as ski flying. Nordic skiing generally originated from day-to-day activities in ancient Norwegian and Northern European regions. Today, cross-country skiing has a strong following among millions of exercise enthusiasts in Europe and America, while the competitive side of the sport has split into two different events—classic cross-country, and freestyle or skate skiing.

History

In Sweden, Finland, and northern Russia, skis found preserved in bogs date back 4,500 to 5,000 years. Rock carvings of people on skis, dating from around 2000 B.C., have been found near the Arctic Circle in Norway. Norse sagas also tell of early informal ski competitions, which not only tested athleticism but also measured one's strength and bravery, as skiers had to climb and descend mountainous terrain and cross vast frozen lakes. Skis were used in Scandinavia for transportation and hunting, and their maneuverability proved ideal for military purposes. The Norwegian military is generally credited with staging the first modern organized Nordic ski races in the early 18th century (*see* Biathlon). By the mid-19th century, civilian clubs in Scandinavian countries soon took up cross-country skiing and started to organize races.

Until the mid-19th century, ski jumping was always done in combination with cross-country skiing, where a jump was taken at the end of the competition, or within a distance race, where one or more jumps would be encountered. According to the Scandinavian *idraet* (sport) tradition, the purpose of winter athletics is to produce a competitor who is not only strong and fit, but morally upright as well. By this credo, the winner of an individual race is not as esteemed as the best all-around athlete, who has both speed and endurance, and can jump for distance and with grace. The Nordic Combined event, where skiers compete in a series of jumps for distance and style, then race cross-country, is still a part of today's Winter Olympic Games.

Sondre Norheim, a Norwegian outdoorsman, is credited with inventing the distinctive sport of ski jumping in the 1840s. Competitions began in the 1860s and were typically held in conjunction with cross-country races at winter carnivals. Norheim is also responsible for developing the first binding that stabilized the boot on the ski.

Two factors are generally cited for the spread of Nordic skiing outside Scandinavia. Norwegian emigrants who left their homeland in the mid-1850s to settle in Western Europe, Australia, New Zealand, and North America took their sport with them. The Scandinavian influence in America can be traced from the farmlands of Minnesota all the way out to the Northwest—particularly around the gold mining camps in California, where skiing was a major form of transportation and recreation. Miners were known to engage in crude downhill races. To get to the top of the ski hill, they would ride ore buckets on a conveyor belt.

Fridtjof Nansen, who skied across the southern tip of Greenland in 1888, also spread the sport abroad. When Nansen's travel account, *Paa Ski over Gronland*, was published in German in 1890, it set off an immediate interest in skiing among the wealthy outdoorsmen of Western Europe. While Nordic ski clubs sprang up all over Europe, the craze also led to the development of a new form of skiing that was more suitable for Central Europe's more mountainous terrain, particularly the Alps. Swiss and German mountaineers, who wanted to conduct ski tours of the Swiss Alps, adapted Nordic ski techniques to steep terrain, and alpine skiing was born.

In 1910 Norway convened an international ski congress to establish guidelines for the sport and to organize competition. Later, in 1924, the

Federation Internationale de Ski (FIS) was founded, and the sport continued to grow in Europe. Before the advent of downhill ski resorts during the 1930s and especially after World War II, Nordic skiing was far and away the most popular form of skiing, and, in fact, the only type of competitive skiing. When the Winter Olympic Games were first held in Chamonix, France, men's Nordic events were the only skiing races that were staged.

The age of specialization in skiing really didn't arrive until the late 1940s and the 1950s, when the tourism and resort industry began to take off in Europe and the United States and the new consumer industry in the West began mass producing sports equipment. While skiers from cold-weather countries in Europe have dominated literally all World Cup and Olympic Championship Nordic events, the sport in America got a huge boost when Vermont's Bill Koch won the silver medal in the 30-kilometer race at Innsbruck, Austria, in 1976. Koch's accomplishment coincided with the fitness boom in United States, and soon millions of Americans were on cross-country skis. Today, a second generation of children is learning how to ski through the Bill Koch Ski League, a federation of local ski clubs around America that teach the basics of competitive classic and freestyle Nordic skiing each year to thousands of children between the ages of 3 and 14.

Nordic Ski Equipment

Today's Nordic skis are a far cry from the standard-issue wood slats of yesteryear. Though there are a wide variety of skis, all are made of essentially the same materials: a hard plastic top, polyethylene on the bottom, with a core of wood or foam encased in several layers of fiberglass. As a rule of thumb, the heavier and taller the skier, the longer the ski; shorter skis provide greater maneuverability. There are three basic styles of Nordic skis:

- Classic touring skis range in length from about 160 to 210 centimeters (5¼ to 7 feet) and are designed for diagonal-stride skiing.
- Skate skis are narrower, a bit thicker and shorter than touring skis, ranging in length from about 170 to 190 centimeters (5½ to 6¼ feet).
- Telemark skis resemble touring skis, but are more rugged, with metal edges for making sharp turns on downhill runs. Telemark skis are designed to cover backcountry terrain; therefore they are usually slightly wider than touring skis to support the weight of a backpack and other gear. Telemark skis also have specially stripped bottoms that enable skiers to climb steep terrain without slipping backward.

All competitive Nordic skiers use wax, which is applied to the middle of the bottom of the ski to aid a skier's glide. Entire books have been written on the subject, and most racers have as many as 15 to 20 different types of wax to address the different weather and snow conditions. Since the early 1980s, waxless skis have become extremely popular among recreation skiers. Waxless skis have scales on the base of the ski that perform much the same function as wax.

Ski boots are usually made of a combination leather/nylon upper with a hard plastic sole and a metal clasp or plate which clips into a binding that is attached to the top of the ski. Touring ski boots are generally wider in the toe and higher cut, while a light touring or tour racing ski boot is narrower and lower cut, resembling a running shoe. Skate ski boots are similar to the light touring models, though they clamp into an integrated binding system, which provides the lateral stability needed for skating. Telemark boots are much heavier and sturdier, similar to hiking boots.

A good pair of poles is extremely important, as over one-quarter of the thrust developed by a competitive skier comes from poling action. Up until the 1970s, most poles were made of bamboo cane, which was light but not as strong as fiberglass. Today, top skiers use poles made of aluminum, carbon fiber, and even graphite/kevlar, which is extremely light, strong, and durable. All poles are equipped with a small plastic "basket" several inches above the metal point at the end of the pole. The new light "half basket," which resembles a small, hard plastic semicircle, functions to keep the tip of the pole in the snow during the end of the poling thrust. These half baskets work much better on groomed trails than the old round basket, which tends to bounce the tip of the pole out of the snow.

What we regard as traditional Nordic ski wear probably has as much to do with the adoption of the sport by mountaineers in Western Europe as it does with 19th-century Norwegian clothing. The traditional knickers, woolen knee socks, and a greatcoat or parka have given way to Gore-Tex jackets, polypropylene tops, and Lycra-style bottoms and one-piece suits that are light and warm, and keep the skier dry.

Ski Technique

The most significant development in Nordic skiing over the past half century has been the introduction of skate skiing, which came to the attention of the ski world in 1975, when the winner of the famed Engadine Marathon in Switzerland used the skating technique. In skate skiing, the competitor keeps one ski in a track, while using the other to push off like a skater or rollerblader. Skating is much faster than the classic diagonal stride, where skiers use two tracks, alternating skis to glide and push off. By the late 1970s, the skating stride was being used so effectively by the Finns that it was referred to as the *Finnstep*. Today at the Winter Olympics, there are separate classic and skate, or freestyle, events. Men compete over distances of 15, 30, and 50 kilometers (9.3, 18.6, and 31 miles), while women ski 5, 10, and 30 kilometers (3.1, 6.2, and 18.6 miles).

Ski Jumping

As noted earlier, ski jumping became a distinctive sport in Norway in the mid-19th century. Its spread throughout Europe and America mirrors that of cross-country skiing, though, because of the daredevil aspect of ski jumping and the need for special equipment and man-made jumps, the sport does not have a mass following among recreation athletes. Rather, the sport's history is bound in competition, and therefore much of its development has focused on the quest for longer, more aerodynamic jumps.

A ski jump really consists of four separate actions: the *inrun*, where competitors ski down a steep ramp that curves upward at the end before takeoff; the *jump* itself; the *landing*, which is executed down slope on the steepest part of the hill; and the *outrun*, or the halt, where a jumper slows down and comes to a stop.

Jumps are classified by the distance that an average competitor would be expected to jump under normal conditions. The most common competitive jumps are 70 meters (230 feet), 90 meters (295 feet)—which is called a "normal" hill—and 120 meters (394 feet), called a "large" hill. A jumper's goal is to cover as much distance as possible in the air while displaying the best form and technique throughout. A panel of five judges evaluates the style of a jumper while in the air and upon landing and awards points accordingly, with the highest and lowest scores discounted. Distance and style are generally weighted equally. Competitors usually take two rounds of jumps.

Ski flying is an offshoot of ski jumping, where competitors are judged solely on distance. Interest in ski flying has developed around the latest innovation in jumping, referred to as the "V-style" approach. Prior to the mid- to late 1980s, the Finns had developed the most dominant style of jumping. The jumper would take off with parallel skis, hips bent and arms along the side, creating an aerodynamic and stylistically admired form. But in 1986, Jan Boklov, a Swede, revolutionized the sport when he began jumping with his skis spread in a V-shape. Though this new style produces significantly longer jumps, and, therefore had been adopted by all the top competitors by the 1990s, it yields fewer style points than the ideal of even parallel skis.

Bibliography

Allen, E. John B. (1993). *From Skisport to Skiing*. Amherst, MA: University of Massachusetts Press.

Caldwell, John. (1985). *The Cross-Country Ski Book*. Brattleboro, VT: Stephen Green Press.

Mansfield, Dick. (1986). *Runner's Guide to Cross Country Skiing*. Syracuse, NY: Acorn Press.

McKhann, Mary. (2000). "Skiing," Microsoft Encarta Online Encyclopedia 2000, *http://encarta.msn.com* (February 4, 2001).

⊞ Olympic Games

Definition

The modern Olympic Games are an international sports competition held every four years in which elite athletes from over 200 nations compete in a variety of events. Though derived from an ancient Greek tradition, the modern Olympics celebrate the achievement of the individual by promoting the ideals of moral integrity, fair and open competition, and physical and intellectual excellence. Though political and commercial aspects of the Games have at times overshadowed the athletic competition, today's Olympics continue to be the premier showcase for world-class sports.

History

We know about the ancient Greek Olympics from the writings of a handful of Greek historians and poets. Legend has it that the Games were part of a great religious festival held every four years in honor of Zeus, the Greeks' most powerful god. The Games were held at Olympia, the site of Zeus' temple, and were part of a common Greek cultural heritage (e.g., common religion, language, and sports tradition) that served to unify a host of independent city-states. Beginning in the 8th century B.C. and continuing well into the 4th century A.D., the ancient Games staged a slate of events that included running, wrestling, boxing, swimming, and equestrian events.

Interest in the ancient Olympics was rekindled in the mid- to late 19th century, when archaeologists in Greece began to discover classical Greek ruins and anthropologists began to piece together more evidence about ancient Greek culture. This coincided with a movement in 19th-century Western Europe that celebrated classical (e.g., Greek and Roman) ideals in art, music, architecture, and education. Baron Pierre de Coubertin, a French educational theorist, is generally credited with reviving the Olympic tradition. Coubertin disagreed with the French education system, which he felt put too great an emphasis on intellectualism at the cost of neglecting the body's development.

Coubertin's ideas corresponded with Victorian England's "muscular Christianity" movement, which linked moral and intellectual development with physical fitness. In the late 1880s, Coubertin toured the English public school system and met William Penny Brookes, a physical education enthusiast who had founded an Olympic festival for youth in Shropshire, England, in 1850. Brookes' creation, called the Much Wenlock Games, included running, jumping, soccer, and cricket. During the 1860s, the Much Wenlock Games grew to encompass adult competition, and became international in scope when the German Gymnastics Society began to send athletes to compete. Brookes even founded the National Olympian

Figure 24. The start of the 100-meter dash at the first Olympics in Athens, 1896. American Thomas Burke, second from left, would win the race. Note the interesting stadium architecture in the background.

Association, with the goal of creating an international Olympics, primarily to promote physical education in participating countries.

Though Brookes was unsuccessful, he undoubtedly influenced Coubertin, who in 1894 organized an International Athletics Congress (IAC) in Paris, which was attended by 78 delegates from nine countries. The IAC, a forebear of today's International Olympic Committee (IOC), voted to hold an international athletic competition in 1900. But Coubertin, who was anxious to see his ideas put to action, convinced the delegates to push the date up to 1896 and to stage the first modern Olympics in Athens, Greece—a symbolic gesture made to give the modern games legitimacy by establishing a link with classic tradition. Despite political unrest and financial hardship in Greece—the Greek government had to rely upon a large donation from a millionaire to cover the cost of constructing a modern state-of-the-art athletic stadium—the 1896 Games became a reality (see illustration). Competition was held in cycling, fencing, gymnastics, target shooting, swimming, tennis, weightlifting, wrestling, and track and field.

But the 1896 Games were a far cry from today's elite event. There was little mention of the Games in the press, and fewer than 300 athletes attended. The New York Athletic Club, which had more national-class track and field athletes than any other club or college in America, failed to send any athletes. A handful of 10 athletes, mostly from either the Boston Athletic Association or Princeton University, wound up winning 9 of the 11 track and field events. So weak was the overall field that Princeton's Robert Garrett won the discus gold medal despite never having thrown the implement in competition prior to the Olympics.

Early on, the Olympic Games suffered from being staged in conjunction with larger international events. In 1900, the Games were part of the World Expo in Paris, and in 1904 they were held in concert with the World's Fair in St. Louis. It wasn't until 1912 in Stockholm, Sweden, that the Olympics began to take shape as a truly international event of sporting excellence. That year, over 2,500 athletes from 28 countries competed in 102 events. By this time, the Olympics had also taken on many of the ideals that define what has come to be known as the "Olympic spirit." In 1908 Coubertin listed the following as motivation for holding the Olympics:

as a cornerstone for health and cultural progress;

for education and character building;

for international understanding and peace;

for equal opportunity;

for fair and equal competition;

for cultural expression;

for beauty and excellence; and

for independence of sport as an instrument of social reform, rather than government legislation.

Soon thereafter, the Olympics adopted its signature five-ring logo and created a motto: *citius, altius, fortius*, which is Latin for "swifter, higher, stronger."

For much of the early history of the Olympics, this motto applied only to men. Until very recently, the IOC has been largely a conservative, male-run body. Victorian views of women as either weak or frail, or morally unsuitable for rough, physical sport lasted well into the 20th century. Though women began competing in Olympic tennis in 1900, swimming in 1912, and track and field in 1928, most of these programs were limited in comparison to the men's roster of events. Until 1968 women weren't allowed to swim any distance in competition over 400 meters, and they weren't allowed to run farther than 800 meters in track and field until 1972.

In fact, a rival sports body founded by women in France, the International Federation for Women's Sport (FSFI), operated in the 1920s and 1930s to showcase women's sporting ability. FSFI held several "Women's

Olympic Games," which were totally separate from the IOC-sanctioned event. Not until the 1970s and 1980s would women begin to be accorded equal treatment with men in regard to contesting Olympic championship events.

Olympic history is rich with the achievements of American athletes. Some famous figures include sprinters Babe Didrikson, who won the women's hurdles and javelin in 1932, and Jesse Owens (see below); swimmer Mark Spitz, who won a record seven gold medals in the 1972 Olympics in Munich; speedskater Eric Heiden, who won five golds at the 1980 Winter Games (*see* Ice Skating); and Carl Lewis, a jump/sprint specialist who won a total of nine gold medals, including four consecutive Olympic long-jump titles.

Though the Olympics have proven to be a unifier in times of loss and political unrest—particularly after World Wars I and II—the Games have also been used as a political tool by countries and factions who wished to make a worldwide statement about an important issue or event.

Politics of the Olympics

Germany played host to the Olympics in 1936, and Adolf Hitler capitalized on the spectacle to show the world the order, efficiency, and might of Nazism and Teutonic culture. Many blacks and Jews from America were reluctant to compete in Berlin, reasoning that their attendance would lend support to the racist Nazi doctrine of Aryan supremacy. In the end, an African American, Jesse Owens, upstaged the German regime, winning the 100- and 200-meter dash and defeating German champion Luz Long to win the gold medal in the long jump.

Events from the late 1960s through the 1980s overshadowed the athletic competition and threatened the very fabric of the Games. In 1968 African Americans contemplated boycotting the U.S. Olympic team to protest the poor socioeconomic conditions of blacks in America. Though the boycott never came about, Tommy Smith and Jon Carlos, who placed first and third in the Olympic 200-meter dash, registered their dissatisfaction with the U.S. government by giving the "Black Power" salute while on the victors' podium during the playing of the national anthem.

In 1972 Palestinian terrorists infiltrated the Olympic Village in Munich and kidnapped members of the Israeli wrestling team. All nine athletes were killed in the terrorists' escape attempt, a result that blackened the Games and the host German government. The politicization of the Olympic Games continued in 1976, when 32 African nations boycotted the competition in Montreal to protest the participation of New Zealand. The latter's rugby team (though not present at the Games) had played against apartheid South Africa in violation of an IOC ban on athletic competition with the latter country. The political situation at the Games approached the ludicrous in 1980 and 1984. First, the United States led a

62-country boycott of the Moscow Olympics, ostensibly in protest of the Soviet Union's invasion of Afghanistan. Then the Soviets led a 17-nation Eastern bloc boycott of the 1984 Games in Los Angeles in retaliation for America's embargo four years before. Following the 1984 Games, the IOC took a harsher stance on boycotts and, for the most part, such protests have stopped, as countries realized that boycott activities seldom had any effect.

Rise of Commercialism

Today's Games have grown to be marked by commercialism. During the late 1980s and early 1990s, IOC rulings facilitated the participation of most professional athletes, making competition truly world-class in several events. Ironically, many well-paid professional athletes, such as American baseball players, European and Latin American soccer stars, and many professional cyclists, still find it impractical to compete, either on account of other professional obligations or because the value of an Olympic gold medal fails to approach their multimillion-dollar salaries.

Still, perhaps the biggest story of the Olympics over the past decade has been the seemingly unbounded advertising potential of the Games and the IOC's increased wealth as a result. World television rights for the Games now generate close to a billion dollars in revenue, and the Olympic logo is "leased" every four years to a host of corporate sponsors, who pay many millions of dollars to reproduce the five rings on their products.

The Winter Games

Though figure skating was held at the 1908 and 1920 Summer Games, and ice hockey was played at the 1920 Olympics as well, there were no separate Winter Olympic Games until 1924, when an inaugural competition was held in Chamonix, France. The most popular Winter Olympic events include downhill and Nordic skiing, figure skating, speed skating, and bobsled and luge. Due to the growth of the winter recreation industry, several new events have recently been added to the Winter Olympics, including snowboarding and trick skiing.

Because of the nature of the sports, which demand cold-weather climates and mountainous terrain, the Winter Olympics are almost always hosted by a small city. This has tended to give the Winter Games a rural charm and personal touch that the Summer Olympics do not have.

The Olympic ideals of peace, brotherhood, and harmony were perhaps never better illustrated than at the Lillehammer Games in Norway in 1994. That year, the host Norwegians dedicated their Games to the war-torn Bosnian city of Sarajevo, which had held the Games just 10 years earlier in 1984. In a truly Olympian gesture, Norwegian speedskater Johann Koss, who won three gold medals, donated his skates and all of his Olympic earnings from the Norwegian government to the Olympic Relief Fund.

Bibliography

Guttmann, Allen. (1992). *The Olympics: A History of the Modern Games*. Urbana: University of Illinois Press.

Hickok, Ralph. (2000). "The 19th-Century Olympic Movement." Hickok Sports.com, *www.hickoksports.com/history/ol19thc.shtml* (January 24, 2001).

Quercetani, Roberto L. (1990). *Athletics: A History of Modern Track and Field Athletics (1860–1990)*. Milan: Vallardi and Associati.

Schaap, Dick. (1975). *An Illustrated History of the Olympics*. New York: Alfred A. Knopf.

▦ Orienteering

Definition

Orienteering is a sport where competitors navigate through the woods to a series of predetermined checkpoints using only a topographical map and a specially designed compass. Though the sport began in the Scandinavian countries during the late 19th century, it is now enjoyed as a form of recreation and competition by men and women from over 50 countries throughout Europe, North America, and Asia.

History

Orienteering began in Scandinavia as a form of military training. The terms "orienteering" and "orientation" were used by the army to mean finding one's way through unknown territory with the aid of a map and compass. The first orienteering competitions date from 1895 and involve contests between military garrisons stationed in the United Kingdom of Sweden and Norway. Though orienteering was soon adopted by civilian society, its ties to the military remained strong throughout the mid-20th century. Skiing regiments in Finland repulsed a Soviet invasion in 1939 by using map and compass to turn dense, little known woodlands to their advantage. Leaders of the Norwegian resistance movement who escaped to Sweden during Germany's invasion of Norway in 1940 used orienteering to lead bands of guerilla fighters against the occupying Nazi army. Their tactics were so effective that Hitler banned the sport of orienteering in occupied Norway.

The first public orienteering competition was held by the Tjalve Sports Club in Oslo, Norway, in 1897. The winner covered a course of 19.5 kilometers (12.1 miles) with three control points in rugged wilderness terrain in 1 hour, 47 minutes, and 7 seconds. The sport came to Sweden in 1901, and soon after the seeds of orienteering's international popularity began to develop in that country. Major Ernst Killander, the president of the Stockholm Amateur Athletic Association (1917–1934), is considered the father of modern orienteering. Killander was dismayed to witness what he considered a lack of interest in running and track and field on the part of

Sweden's youth. In 1918 Killander began staging cross-country running races in which competitors had to choose their own routes using map and compass. Though one needed diverse skills to excel in the sport—strength, endurance, mental agility, and good navigational skills—for the same reason orienteering appealed to a broad audience. Given Killander's position of authority, the early orienteering competitions garnered a lot of press, which in turn spurred interest in the sport. Killander went on to establish all the basic rules and techniques of orienteering, including types of courses, regulations regarding map and compass, age group and handicap competition, and so on.

Orienteering became an international sport in the 1930s, as first Sweden, Norway, and Finland began competing among themselves, and then the sport caught on in Switzerland, the Soviet Union, and Eastern Europe. Though the growth of orienteering was slowed by World War II, in May 1949 the Swedish Orienteering Association held the first international conference on the sport. A little over a decade later, in 1961, representatives from 10 European nations came together to form the International Orienteering Federation (IOF). By 1966 the sport was conducting world championship competition. Today, the IOF has 41 member nations and 8 associate members, including the United States. Orienteering is popular throughout America, especially in the Northeast, where one is within driving distance of an event every weekend of the year. Orienteering, in some form or another, has also been adopted as part of the curriculum at many middle and high schools, as the sport invariably draws on skills needed to master geography, math, and, of course, physical education.

Internationally, the highest levels of competition have been dominated by men and women from the Nordic countries—out of 220 total medals contested in the 30 world championships between 1966 and 1995, competitors from Sweden, Norway, and Finland won 162, or nearly 75 percent. And yet there are many more people who regard orienteering as recreation, to be enjoyed as a chance to get out in the woods and explore, to work up a sweat while sharpening one's navigational skills. In a world where so much has been discovered—where there are fewer unknowns than at any time in human history—orienteering enables everyone to be an explorer.

Equipment

Clothing and footwear used for orienteering depend upon the terrain, level of competition, and type of orienteering (see below). Generally, most people dress as they would to go on a hike—in warm, light clothing that is water and wind repellent, with hiking shoes that provide good lateral support and traction. Serious orienteering competitors are more likely to dress as a runner would, wearing lighter trail-running shoes.

Maps and compasses have improved significantly since the turn of the century. Early orienteering events used maps with little detail—usually at a scale of 1:100,000 with hash lines rather than true contours to indicate height. Full-color contour maps for orienteering, scaled at 1:15,000 or 1:10,000, weren't developed until the 1950s. Early compasses were either the conventional "watch" type or simple box compasses. Today's protractor compass, which is encased in a transparent base, has a straight edge and various markings to take measurements on a map and to help determine location and direction. The protractor compass was developed in the 1930s.

Rules

"Foot" orienteering is the most common form of the sport. Most events range from 1 to 15 kilometers (0.6–9.3 miles), with variations in terrain determining the classification, or degree of difficulty. Officials set the course in advance, marking control points or checkpoints with specially colored flags. Most foot orienteering events are point-to-point challenges, where participants must find their own routes to each control point in a predetermined sequence. "Score" orienteering involves finding as many control points in random order in the least amount of time possible. Relay events are also contested. Teams of two, three, or four participate, with each member making his or her way through a different course.

Other types of orientation include:

Ski orienteering, where competitors ski over cross-country ski trails;

Mountain bike orienteering, where participants ride mountain bikes, either over demanding off-road trails or on bridle paths; and

Trail orienteering, where disabled participants can compete on equal terms with the able-bodied. In trail orienteering, also known as "control choice" orienteering, up to five controls are hung at each site. Emphasis is placed on map interpretation, the objective being to identify control sites by referring to the map and control description alone. Scoring is based on the number of control sites correctly identified.

Bibliography

British Orienteering Federation. (1997). "The Early Days of Orienteering." British Orienteering Federation Web page, *www.cix.co.uk* (February 20, 2001).
———. (1997). "The Four Orienteering Disciplines." British Orienteering Federation Web page, *www.cix.co.uk* (February 20, 2001).
Palmer, Peter. (1998). *The Complete Orienteering Manual*. Doune, England: Crowood Press.

▦ Swimming

Definition

Swimming is the act of propelling oneself through the water using the arms, legs, and torso in concerted repetitive motions called strokes. There are four principal swimming strokes: the crawl (often referred to as the overarm crawl or freestyle technique), breaststroke, backstroke, and butterfly. While millions the world over swim for recreation, there are essentially two forms of competitive swimming: long-distance or endurance swimming, which is performed in the open water; and speed swimming, which is usually contested at an indoor pool.

History

Humans have been swimming since ancient times. Mesopotamian art from the third millennium B.C. depicts men swimming much as an animal might, keeping their heads above the water with the dog stroke. The Greeks and Romans were a bit more sophisticated when it came to swimming. The recurrence of the Latin words *iactare* and *alterna*, which indicate the action of raising one's arms alternately above the surface of the water, provide evidence that the Romans used at least some form of the crawl. Plato, the Greek philosopher (3rd century B.C.) considered a man who did not know how to swim as uneducated—this was in keeping with the ancient Greek concept of a man's education and character development as equal parts intellectual and physical—"alphabets and swimming."

Being such a natural activity, swimming developed similarly in different parts of the world. Artwork and early historic writings suggest that inhabitants of Egypt, West Africa, Japan, and Central America have all been swimming for recreation and competition and by necessity (e.g., to hunt or to prepare for or conduct war) for over a thousand years.

The history of swimming as an organized competitive sport is a great deal shorter. The popularity of swimming waned in Europe during the Middle Ages, as many believed that immersion in water could bring on or transmit an epidemic disease like the bubonic plague. During this time swimming was probably more prevalent in the Pacific Islands. In 1603 the emperor of Japan decreed that swimming would be an integral part of the nation's school curriculum. This edict prompted interscholastic competition and the start of nationally organized swim races in Japan.

But it wasn't until the mid-19th century in Europe that amateur swimming clubs began to be formed. Members of these clubs were professionals and businessmen—people we would refer to today as the middle class, though in 19th-century Europe their status was much higher in relation to the masses of industrial workers and rural poor, who hadn't the leisure time to devote to a competitive sport.

By 1837 the National Swimming Society of England was holding regular competitions in London, which at the time sported at least six man-made pools. An account of a Swimming Society event in 1844 illustrates the European swimming style of the time. The society had invited two famed Native American swimmers from the Ojibwa Nation—colorfully named Flying Gull and Tobacco—who "thrashed the water violently with their arms, like sails of a windmill, and beat downward with their feet, blowing with force and forming grotesque antics." Though the Native Americans used the crawl to devastate the breaststroking British, neither the English swimmers nor the spectators who were present that day seem to have been impressed by what to them should have been a revolutionary stroking technique. And yet throughout the 19th century, European swimmers continued to use primarily the breaststroke, probably because endurance swimming at that time was held in higher regard than racing against the clock.

Then as now the English Channel crossing was considered the ultimate test of the long-distance swimmer. Captain Matthew Webb, a showman and inveterate self-promoter, was the first to make the Channel crossing in 1875, covering the 20-mile distance in 21 hours and 45 minutes. Webb reportedly sang, ate steak, and downed an occasional beer along the way. When he encountered a heavy storm en route, Webb was unflustered, though strong currents forced him in the end to swim a total of 38 miles—a hardship that only served to add to his storied accomplishment.

It wasn't until later in the 19th century that speed swimming became more popular. Though the amateur swimming scene in England continued to grow throughout the mid- to late 19th century—by 1880 the Amateur Swimming Association of Great Britain numbered over 300 clubs—most competitions in England were won by "professional swimmers," so named because they gave swimming lessons on the side for money. When these professionals were banned from racing by the Amateur Swimming Association in 1886, competitive swimming began to develop through the endeavors of amateur swimming clubs.

In 1889 the first European Championships were conducted by the Erste Wiener Amateur Swim Club in Vienna, with only two events contested—races over 60 and 500 meters. Swimming races were also held at the inaugural Olympic Games in Athens in 1896, where contestants vied over 100, 500, and 1,200 meters in the open waters of the Bay of Zeus.

Throughout the 20th century, the number of swimming events that have become a part of most scholastic, club, and national and international competitions has grown in relation to the development of the various swimming strokes (see page 178).

Equipment

Competitive swimmers wear a swimsuit, cap, and goggles. The cap is worn over the ears and hair for protection and to reduce drag through the water. The goggles protect a swimmer's eyes from chlorine and other chemicals that are typically added to pool water.

Improvements in swimwear have been dramatic since the 19th century, when bulky cotton or woolen one-piece suits and trunks were standard.

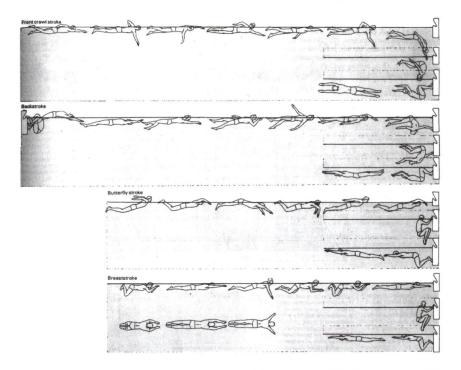

Figure 25. Major swim strokes. (Reproduced from *Rules of the Game*, by the Diagram Group [New York: St. Martin's Press, 1990], p. 195)

Today swimsuits are made of light material like Lycra or spandex that clings to the body while permitting a free range of motion.

Today almost all competition is conducted in indoor pools. Standard pool sizes are short-course, which are 25 yards or meters (the size of most high school and YMCA pools), and long-course, which are 50 meters (used in international competition).

Rules

Swim meets are organized competitions, typically between two or more teams. Swimmers compete in a slate of events. Most events are broken down into a series of increasingly competitive races, or heats. The top finishers in each heat advance to the next round, while the slower competitors are eliminated.

Events take place in the freestyle, backstroke, breaststroke, butterfly, and individual medley (a race involving all of the major strokes in the following order: butterfly, backstroke, breaststroke, and freestyle). At most competitive levels, including national and international competition, the following events are contested: freestyle races over 50 meters, 100 meters, 200 meters, 400 meters, 800 meters, and 1,500 meters; the backstroke, breaststroke and butterfly—all over 100 and 200 meters; and individual medley events at 200 and 400 meters.

Relay races are also contested, where four-member teams take turns swimming equidistant legs. Relay events include the 4 × 100-meter freestyle, 4 × 100-meter medley, and 4 × 200-meter medley events.

Competitive swimmers train every day, typically covering between 10,000 and 20,000 meters per day and adding flexibility exercises, weight training, and cross-training techniques depending upon the season. Most swimmers train by performing sets of repetitions where the distance, time, and rest interval of each repetition are planned and monitored. Performances throughout the 20th century have improved to such a degree that the times of a 1920s Olympic champion are routinely beaten by the best teenage girl swimmers today.

In addition to sprint and endurance swim races, other games and competitions involving swimming developed, including water polo (*see* Water Polo) and synchronized swimming. The latter was actually referred to as "scientific and ornamental swimming" in England in the late 19th century when men first engaged in what was characterized as a routine of stunts and acrobatics in the water. Synchronized swimming later became popularized as a women's sport in America and Europe through water show performances in the 20th century. Synchronized swimming made its Olympic debut in 1984. Today there are over 60 nations conducting national synchronized swimming programs.

Swim Strokes

While competitive swimmers know how to swim all the strokes, most work hard at perfecting the overarm crawl and then specializing in one or two other strokes (see illustration).

As discussed earlier, the **crawl** is the fastest of all the strokes and is most often chosen in freestyle competitions. A swimmer executes the crawl in a prone position by combining the six-beat flutter kick with alternate arm pulls in which each recovers out of the water and reenters the water ahead of the body. In competition, the swimmer's head remains in the water. Breaths are taken with the head rolled to one side so that the mouth is just out of the water. The stroke didn't become popular in international competition until the early 20th century, particularly after Duke Kahanamoku, the famed Hawaiian surfer, won the Olympic 100-meter race using the crawl in 1912.

The **backstroke**, as the name implies, is executed in a supine position. The swimmer combines the flutter kick and alternate arm pulls in which each arm is extended beyond the shoulders and pulled to the hips alternately. The backstroke is the only competition that begins in the water with a push off the wall of the pool. The backstroke first appeared in the

1900 Olympics and has changed very little since then. In fact, one of the most significant developments in backstroke technique occurred in the late 1990s, when the Australians found that they could get more horizontal thrust by slightly bending the arm as it came around under water.

The **breaststroke** is executed in a prone position and combines the frog kick—a glide with the arms outstretched overhead—and a double-arm pull downward and to the side. The stroke is faster underwater—a discovery that led to some competitors trying to navigate an entire race underwater and passing out as a result. In 1957 international rules banned the underwater breaststroke.

The **butterfly** is a fairly new stroke that grew out of the breaststroke. In the 1930s swimmers began to use a double overhead arm stroke to give them a boost as they went into their turns. Though the butterfly was initially considered too tiring to employ over an entire race, it proved faster than the breaststroke, and throughout the 1940s, a butterflier using the frog kick could usually beat a good breaststroker. This led to the butterfly and breaststroke becoming two distinct events in 1953. Today the butterfly is executed by combining a double overarm pull, with the arms and face coming out of the water on the recovery, and the dolphin kick—a kind of undulating motion from the hips and toes.

Bibliography

Colwin, Cecil. (1992). *Swimming into the Twenty-first Century*. West Point, NY: Leisure Press.
Gundling, Belah, and Jill White. (1988). *Creative Synchronized Swimming*. Champaign, IL: Human Kinetics.
Whitten, Phillip. (2000). "Swimming." Microsoft Encarta Online Encyclopedia 2000, *http://encarta.msn.com* (February 2, 2001).
Worth, Sylvia (ed.). (1990). *The Rules of the Game*. New York: St. Martin's Press.

▦ Tobogganing

Definition

Tobogganing refers to a variety of activities involving sliding down steep ice-covered tracks of banked turns and straightaways on a small sled. The three main types of toboggans used in competition are the skeleton, luge, and bobsled. Luge and bobsled are two of the most exciting Winter Olympic sports.

History

The term "toboggan" is derived from the French-Canadian word *tabaganne*, which in turn comes from the Algonquian word for sled, *odabaggan*. Native Americans in the St. Lawrence River Valley crafted sleds with runners made of long birchwood poles with upturned ends. These toboggans were functional, used to transport goods over snow and ice. A snowshoer would pull the sled on the flats, then sit or stand on the back as it glided downhill. Like the Native Americans, peoples indigenous to the cold-weather regions of Europe—particularly Scandinavia and Russia—used sleds at least 1,000 years ago to transport goods and for recreation. Norse legends recount sled races down frozen mountains.

Use of the toboggan for recreation dates to more recent times, beginning in the 1870s and 1880s in the alpine resorts of St. Moritz and Davos, Switzerland. There, the sport became popular with tourists, and also among people with disabilities, many of whom visited the Alps to recover from various ailments and found tobogganing to be one of the few sports that could be enjoyed in a seated position.

In 1881 national competition in Switzerland began on a 3,000-meter run between the resort towns of Davos and Klosters. As resorts began to design curving, downhill runs that demanded greater skill and courage from participants, specialty tobogganing clubs sprang up throughout the Alpine regions of Switzerland, Austria, Germany, and France. Competitors began experimenting with different sleds, and the sport soon spawned three unique events: luge, bobsledding, and skeleton.

Skeleton is a solitary sport. Though a skeleton (also referred to as a *cresta*) is most similar to a Flexible Flyer, the light, maneuverable sled embraced by generations of boys and girls in America, it supports perhaps the most dangerous of the sledding sports. Competitors lie headfirst, face-down, and hands-back on the skeleton, approaching speeds of nearly 80 miles per hour in their descents.

Skeletons measure just 3 feet in length and 16 inches wide and weigh between 70 and 100 pounds, depending upon the slider's body weight. They are made of fiberglass and steel, with two small, deep-grooved runners at the back of the sled. Competitors wear skin-tight Lycra-polyester suits for aerodynamics and special spiked boots, which are used to gain momentum out of a running start, and also to help steer the sled. To negotiate corners and keep the sled from hurtling over banked curves, a rider resorts to "head steering" techniques; weight is shifted to the rear of the sled over the runners (the legs of most riders hang over the back of the sled by about 2 feet), while the front is steered by swinging from side to side. Changes in direction are accomplished by tilting the head and shoulders to one side or the other. A rider's boots also are spiked in the toes. By digging a toe into the ice, a rider gains control, though this technique is used sparingly because it also sacrifices speed.

Ironically, skeleton racing began to wane in the early 20th century, as bobsledding became more popular. (Early bobsleds were little more than two skeletons placed end to end.) The sport has really made a resurgence since the 1980s, when Europeans began to reintroduce the skeleton as a complement to the luge (see below). Today, men and women from over 20 nations, including the United States, compete in annual Skeleton World Championship and World Cup series competition. In 2002 the sport will return to the Winter Olympics, where it was contested in 1928 and 1948.

The **luge** is a sport in which competitors slide on a small dual-runner sled while lying on their backs with their feet at the front. The word "luge" is actually derived from a southern French dialect word that means sled.

Though appearing to be a reverse version of skeleton, luge equipment and techniques are actually quite different. A luge is nothing more than two runners with two steel blades, a "sling" seat, and two bridges of fiberglass that support the runners. As with all the sledding sports, a premium is placed on aerodynamics. Competitors can spend hours polishing their blades with different wax compounds in order to create the least amount of friction between the sled and the track. Luges cannot exceed about 50 pounds in weight. Rules enacted by the International Luge Federation in 1985 instituted a handicapping procedure of sorts.

Lighter competitors are allowed to weight their sleds for speed. Lugers wear clothing similar to that of skeleton competitors, though there are no spiked boots. The luger begins in a seated position. Competitors lean back as soon as the luge gains speed, steering the sled by applying pressure with their legs on the curved part of the end of the runners and by pressing their shoulders on one side of the sled or the other.

The luge was introduced as an Olympic sport in 1964. Both men and women now compete in singles and two-person events. Athletes from Germany have dominated luge, largely because of advances made by German engineers in sled design.

The same can be said of the **bobsled**, which has come a long way from the wood sleds of the 1880s. Those early bobs consisted of wood planking, braced together and laid over two skeleton sleds, with a crude pivoting mechanism in the front which was steered by two strings. A metal piece in the back could be plunged into the track to act as a brake. By the turn of the century, wood was giving way to steel sleds, which acquired the name "bobsleds" because of the way teams would bob back and forth to increase their speed on the straightaway.

Though we are used to considering Olympic competitors as world class athletes, such was not the case with the early bobsledders, many of whom were little more than well-to-do adventure seekers who could afford to vacation in the Alps and purchase a sled. (Bobsledding has never been the kind of sport that a casual enthusiast can simply go out and try. Today, state-of-the-art sleds cost as much as $35,000.) Though the four-man bobsled became a medal sport at the 1924 Winter Olympics, and the two-man was added to the program in 1932, early competitors did very little training for these events. It wasn't until the 1950s and 1960s that sporting federations began to take bobsledding seriously. Once again, engineering had something to do with an advance to the sport. Sports physiologists who studied the bobsled found that the start of the race—the art of pushing the sled and "loading in"—was extremely important. In general, a one-tenth of a second lead following the 50-meter sprint/push at the start translates to a three-tenths of a second advantage at the finish. Teams began recruiting track and field athletes and gymnasts who were strong and fast. A 1952 rule that limited the weight of a bobsled team to 390 kilograms for two-man (about 850 pounds, including the sled) and 630 kilograms for four-man (about 1,350 pounds) ended the era of the super-heavyweight crew. The combination of more athletic crews, who trained year-round, with advances in sled technology led to faster and faster times.

A four-man bobsled team consists of two pushers, a brakeman, and a pilot, who steers the sled; on two-man teams, both members must push in addition to either braking or steering. Though top speeds typically reach 80 miles per hour on runs of about one mile, most world-class competitions are determined by hundredths of a second, with the top 10 teams often separated by little more than a half-second. Since the 1970s, the Germanys (first East and West Germany—now the Federated Republic) have dominated the sport, winning the most Olympic and World Championship medals.

Today, the bobsled has come to be viewed as the ultimate winter team sport, to which strength and speed from other sports are transferable. Hence the emergence in the sport of countries like Jamaica, Japan, Australia, and New Zealand.

While the United States has made gains in bobsledding, winning several medals at recent World Championships, the sport has been hindered in the United States by several factors. There are only two bobsled runs in the country—one in Lake Placid, New York, and the other in Provo, Utah. This limits participation and makes training costly, as athletes either have to travel and rent accommodations on site, or live in these rural areas. The lure of rich professional sports in the United States has also captured many of the best strength and speed athletes. The United States Bobsled and Skeleton Federation (USBSF), the sport's governing body in the United States, conducts a youth program which consists of recruitment events around the country and the sponsorship of national developmental training camps in Lake Placid. Young men and women who want to succeed in bobsledding take much the same route as junior alpine skiers, attending bobsledding school, where they continue their normal schooling in conjunction with an intense program of conditioning and skill training related to bobsledding.

Bibliography

Federation Internationale de Bobsleigh et de Tobogganing. (1997). "Bobsleigh: The Race and the Sled." Federation Internationale de Bobsleigh et de Tobogganing Web site, *www.bobsleigh.com/* (February 18, 2001).

———. (1997). "History of the Sport of Bobsleigh." Federation Internationale de Bobsleigh et de Tobogganing Web site, *www.bobsleigh.com/* (February 18, 2001).

USA Bobsled and Skeleton Federation. (2000). "The Sliding Sport of Skeleton." USA Bobsled and Skeleton Federation Web site, *www.usabobsledandskeleton .org/* (February 18, 2001).

USA Luge. (2000). "History of Luge." USA Luge Web site, *www.usaluge.org/* (February 20, 2001).

▦ Volkssport

Definition

Volkssport is a German-derived term that means "people's sport." Volkssport is neither one single sport nor a well-defined group of sports, but rather a reference to popular noncompetitive forms of exercise like walking, biking, swimming, running, cross-country skiing, skating, and so on—all sports that can be enjoyed by individuals on their own, or by groups. Today the volkssport movement is popular throughout Europe, where public health and exercise are encouraged through a systematic program of recreational sports.

History

The concept of "people's sport" has gained prominence throughout many parts of the world over the past few decades, as cultures have explored their traditional folk roots. Prior to the industrial revolution in Europe, which began in the late 18th and early 19th centuries, society was agrarian in nature, based on the relationship between the gentry, or landowner, and the peasant farmer. While the upper-class gentry engaged in such sports as hunting, fishing, horseback riding, falconry, and the like—so-called "noble pursuits"—the peasantry had their folk festivals, which were often tied to the harvest and the passing of the seasons. Though these festivals featured "folk" games like sack racing, tug-of-war, log tossing, relay racing, and so on, they also featured a good deal of partying and quite often violent or crude behavior. For this, the folk culture and its games got a bad rap from the upper classes, which regarded them as lowbrow, and indicative of pagan ceremony.

As people moved to urban areas and socioeconomic relationships became structured around manufacturing and consumerism—owners, factory workers, and small shopkeepers—links with folk culture were lost. Sports became organized and based in schools and clubs. As has been discussed throughout this book, many organized sports were initially accessible only to amateurs, meaning the middle and upper middle classes that had the means and leisure time to compete for pleasure. The urban working classes—severed from traditional hierarchical rural society and its folk pastimes—began to play organized sports for money; ultimately, as with sports like soccer, rugby, prize fighting, and pedestrianism, the working classes could claim as their own many sports that had been created by their social betters.

It wasn't until the late 19th and early 20th century that cultural separatists and independence fighters began to consider traditional culture (e.g., music, literature, dress, language, etc.) and its folk sports as sources of ethnic and cultural pride—aspects of one's heritage that are unique and worthy of revival and celebration. Hence in 1884 the Gaelic Athletic Association began promoting hurling among Irish Republicans as a sport of liberation from British rule. Basque separatists have embraced traditional forms of pelota, and in Brittany, a movement to revive *gouren* wrestling was instigated by Breton nationalists fighting for political autonomy from France. Many of these traditional sports came to be linked once more to cultural festivals, which were revived to celebrate a people's differences in opposition to the sameness or standardization of modern culture.

It should be noted that such folk movements, which break distinctions between classes of people by celebrating a common heritage, are not distinct to Europe, but rather have been repeated around the globe, particularly when an indigenous culture attempts to reassert itself politically, socially, and economically. The majority of the independence movements in Latin America, Africa, and Asia in the 20th century have had strong elements of cultural rediscovery and reassertion as the formerly colonized peoples have worked to forge a national identity. The revival of the martial arts in Asia, or of traditional wrestling in Africa, or the increasing popularity of sepak takraw in Malaysia and Indonesia are all movements in response and direct opposition to the imposition of organized Western sports on a colonized people—systematic cultural diffusion that occurred throughout colonized Africa, Asia, and Latin American in the 19th and early 20th centuries.

Organized Volkssport

In 1972 the International Federation of Popular Sports was created in Munich, Germany, "to encourage public health through non-competitive, outdoor sports programming." A second goal of the group is "to contribute toward peace and understanding among nations by fostering international friendship through volkssport."

This movement has helped popularize a number of common aerobic sports like running, walking, swimming, biking, skating, skiing, and so on. Local, regional, and national volkssport festivals in Western Europe are held on weekends, with each festival often holding several or a series of events. Participants vie for achievement awards that are designed to provide incentive to exercise regularly. Hence the competition is with one's self, as each participant records accomplishments like total distance covered in practice, or total number of events completed. Germany, Austria, Switzerland, and the Scandinavian countries have national organizations, and there are thousands of local volkssport clubs. While some clubs compete against each other in "athletics" (e.g., a series of "common" sports events like swimming, distance running, long and high jumping, bicycling, volleyball, etc.), others simply provide an opportunity for folks of all ages to keep company while getting steady exercise.

Walking remains the most popular organized volkssport worldwide. Starting in the 1980s, volkssport began to gain followers in the United States, with many informal clubs staging long-distance walks that appeal to a wide range of people.

Bibliography

Baker, W. J. (1982). *Sports in the Western World*. Totowa, NJ: Rowman and Littlefield.

Burke, Peter. (1978). *Popular Culture in Early Modern Europe*. London: Temple Smith.

International Federation of Popular Sport. (2000). "What Is the Internationaler Volkssportverband?"

International Federation of Popular Sport Web site, *www.ivv.org/* (February 16, 2001).

LATIN AMERICA

INTRODUCTION

Indigenous culture in Latin America underwent a major transformation in the 16th century when Spain and Portugal colonized literally all of South and Central America. Though most traditional sports and games lost their cultural significance under Iberian rule, variations of many games continued to be played by children and adults for many generations.

HISTORICAL AND CULTURAL PERSPECTIVE

Prior to the arrival of European explorers, a South American continent rich in soil and natural resources sustained the development of several advanced civilizations. The Mayas, known for their monumental works of art and architecture, controlled much of Central America beginning in 500 B.C. and continuing until the 13th century. Mayan civilization encompassed a string of independent city-states located in the area of Yucatán, modern-day Honduras, Panama, and Guatemala. Further north in Mexico, the warring Aztec culture flourished from the 14th to the 16th centuries. In South America, hill states and coastal kingdoms based on farming and fishing were flourishing in the Andean highlands as early as 900 B.C. During Europe's Dark Ages, Tiahuanaco, located in modern-day Peru, ruled much of what is today Bolivia, Peru, northern Chile, and Argentina. Their rich textiles and pottery were precursors to the creations of the great Inca civilization (12th–16th centuries), whose achievements in metallurgy, agriculture, engineering, and government are admired by cultural anthropologists and historians to this day.

Spanish and Portuguese explorers changed the face of the continent during the 16th century. Starting in 1500, when Portugal's Pedro Alvares Cabral reached the coast of Brazil, both Spain and Portugal began setting up trading posts all along the continent's shoreline. The search for gold and silver led the explorers and their armies inland, where Hernando Cortes clashed with the Aztecs (1519) and Francisco Pizarro fought the Incas (1531). Both battles resulted in destruction for the indigenous peoples. Throughout the continent, guns, disease, and forced labor served to decimate the native population, which decreased an estimated 95 percent, from 25 million in 1500 to just 1 million in 1605.

Spanish government, religion, and economy would have a profound impact on South America through the 19th century. A feudal-like system of local government was established throughout much of the South American continent, with the wealth, political power, and land concentrated in the hands of a foreign-born elite. Livestock and large-scale farming were introduced. Sugar, coffee, and cotton plantations dominated the landscape in Central and South America and in the Caribbean, though their products and profits went to Europe. Throughout Latin America, the Roman Catholic Church helped to legitimize Iberian rule and to advance its culture by transforming traditional religious beliefs. Catholic missions throughout the continent taught Spanish, Latin, and Catholicism. And, as in Africa, European missionaries discouraged the continued practice of many traditional games that were linked to native celebrations and rituals.

By the 18th and 19th centuries, the culture that had emerged in Latin America was deeply influenced by Europe. Although much of the continent underwent a wave of political revolutions in the early 19th century that overthrew Spanish and Portuguese rule, the resultant political change had little impact on the majority of the population. The system of government, the economy, and the social order remained largely unchanged, as a native-born elite simply assumed power that had formerly been held by Europeans. It is within this context that traditional Latin American sports and games are discussed below.

TRADITIONAL SPORTS AND GAMES

▥ Speed, Strength, and Endurance Sports

Running. The Tarahumara Indians of Mexico are famous for their endurance running skill. Running was considered to be a way one celebrated nature, and for most native Latin American tribes, the ability to run for long periods of time without tiring was also an age-old hunting or tracking skill. Runs of 100–150 miles—always over difficult, hilly terrain and often at high altitude—were commonplace for the Tarahumara. Sometimes, either to relieve monotony or to introduce another skill to the activity, the runner would kick a ball, with the object being not to let it stop rolling. Though participants would race over long distances, the process of running itself was more significant for the participants than reaching the finish line first or recording a fast time. Descendants of the Tarahumara practice both types of running today, and, true to their ancestors, they resist invitations to compete in races in America and Europe.

Relay Racing. Indigenous Latin Americans had a cooperative concept of work that was in opposition to the European ideal of individual accomplishment and industry leading to personal wealth. This cooperative ethos was reflected in their games. Running relay races was common in Latin America long before European track and field was staging such events. The Ge Indians of South America engaged in log relays, where participants would carry short logs weighing as much as 200 pounds over courses as long as several hundred yards. Others raced in teams around natural boundaries like lakes and mountains. Again, there is no evidence that these "races" were against time, or to see who would win or lose, but rather to accomplish a feat of endurance.

Tug-of-War. Similar tests of collective strength involved tug-of-war and "push-of-war"-type contests, where groups would attempt to either pull the opposing group over a line of rocks or a furrow in the ground, or try to push them back, usually to a natural boundary like a large rock or tree.

Swimming. Native Latin Americans, especially those indigenous to the Caribbean region, were also adept at swimming. Many natives had perfected strokes like the crawl long before the Europeans, and their ability to swim with speed was unrivaled, as indicated by the success enjoyed by several Latin American swimmers who toured England in the mid-19th century (*see* Swimming). Caribbean natives were also good endurance swimmers. Many engaged in the tradition of "island racing," where participants would circle an island or a group of islands, often swimming as much as 10–20 miles at a time.

Wrestling. Natives of Guyana, Venezuela, and northern Brazil all have traditions of wrestling, either individually or in groups. These peoples didn't seem to wrestle as a means of conflict or to settle differences. Rather, as in Africa, much of the wrestling process appears to have been symbolic, either linked to celebrating the earth's fertility, giving thanks for a rich harvest, or purifying a place or site. Wrestling technique was based more on balance than brute strength. Participants, starting from a standing position, attempted to throw opponents onto their backs.

▦ Ball Games

Meso-American Ball Game. The Mayas, Aztecs, Olmecs (a civilization preceding the Mayas that dated back to the second millennium B.C.), and many smaller tribes throughout Central America and northern South

America seem to have played a game referred to today as either "Meso-American ball game" or "hip ball." (The Mayas called it "Pok-ta-Pok," the Aztecs "Tlachi.") Played on a walled rectangular court by both men and women, hip ball required participants to hit a heavy rubber ball using only their hips, knees, or buttocks. The object of the game was to propel the ball across the opponent's end line, though most courts were also equipped with a stone ring mounted on both sides of the wall of the court. Should one of the teams hit the ball through the ring, that team automatically won the game.

Though versions of the game are still played in regions of Mexico today, traditional hip ball seems to have had a number of symbolic purposes. We know that warring cultures used the game to settle disputes, or to pit captured peoples against one another. In some cases, the members of the losing team were sacrificed. The game also seems to have been linked with agriculture, particularly in celebration of the harvest, or as a means to guarantee fertility. Most courts were oriented east to west, with the height and angle of walls also signifying astronomical or seasonal importance.

Basketball. Natives of the Andes played a game similar to basketball, in which participants tried to throw a rubber ball into a basket mounted on the top of a pole. Again, the game seems to have been linked to the harvest, with the ball signifying the sun, and its arc to the basket, the trajectory of the sun across the sky.

Hand-and-Ball. The Tucuna tribe, from the Amazonian region of Brazil, played a game like badminton, where participants stood in a circle and struck a shuttlecock-like implement made of corn husks with the palms of their hands. The object of the game was to keep the shuttlecock from hitting the ground. Several other tribes, including the Ge, played a game similar to paddle ball, where players volleyed a small rubber ball back and forth with wooden paddles. Again, the object of the game was to keep the ball from touching the ground. Similar games are still played today in parts of South America.

Hockey. Both men and women seem to have engaged in a game similar to field hockey, where each side tried to hit a round stone or ball made of dried reeds with a curved stick through the opponent's goal. As with other cultures around the world, the game appears to have been related to fertility rituals and harvest, with the fields often set to be plowed or planted, and the ball representing fruit or the sun.

Stickball. Though more popular in North America, a primitive version of lacrosse, or stickball, was also played by indigenous tribes in South America. Often entire tribes or villages would meet, sometimes to settle a dispute. Using small 2–2½ foot rackets, or short clubs with wide, rounded heads, each side would attempt to hit a round rock or a small wooden ball into the opponent's goal, which might be a tree trunk or a large rock.

▦ Skill Games

Archery. Up through the Spanish conquest of Latin America, most native men were skilled in archery as a major means of fighting and hunting. Though colonial rule and the switch to an agrarian economy made the bow and arrow largely obsolete, many rural inhabitants continued to practice archery for sport and to hunt for subsistence. Also, isolated cultures, particularly in Amazonia and in the equatorial rain forests, continued to survive off the land as hunter-gatherers. The most common archery games included attempting to hit a moving target (usually a log or similar round object rolled down a hill), shooting as many arrows in the air as possible at a time, throwing fruit or balls of woven reeds in the air and attempting to pierce them, and shooting at distant targets—either horizontally or from the ground at an object in the top of a tree.

Hoop-and-Pole. Another hunting skill game indigenous to the American Southwest and the Mexican plains involves a hoop and a pole or spear. One participant rolls the hoop across an open field, while the other throws a pole or spear ahead of its path. The object of the game is to place the pole so that it rests either on top of or under the hoop when it stops.

SPORTS AND GAMES FOLLOWING COLONIAL RULE

Though Spain no longer ruled Latin America by the mid-19th century, the continent was still closely tied with Europe and Britain, with whom it traded much of its agricultural produce and rich metals. The ruling elite also emulated European culture. By the late 19th century, the upper classes were playing polo, tennis, and golf. The richest landowners were also investing in thoroughbred horses. Racetracks sprang up in urban areas in Brazil, Argentina, Mexico, Venezuela, and Peru. As in America and Europe, horse racing became a popular spectator sport as well as a focus for gambling activity.

Sports that were popular with the working class in Latin America mirrored the sporting scene in Europe as well. Soccer became a national pastime in many countries. Argentina, Brazil, and Uruguay developed national teams that were the equals of the best soccer clubs in England. Mexico City, Rio, and Buenos Aires all hosted major prizefighting venues. During the biking craze of the late 19th century, many cities in Latin America also built velodromes, thus establishing a biking tradition on the continent that would continue into the 20th century. Field hockey and racket sports like pelota and later jai alai also became popular in Latin America.

Bibliography

Arbena, Joseph L. (ed.). (1988). *Sport and Society in Latin America*. Westport, CT: Greenwood Press.

Armstrong, John M., and Alfred Metraux. (1963). "The Goajiro." *Bureau of American Ethnology Bulletin* Vol. 143, No. 4, pp. 369–383.

Blanchard, Kendall. (1999). "Traditional Sports, North and South America." In David Levinson and Karen Christensen (eds.), *Encyclopedia of World Sport*. New York: Oxford University Press.

Katz, Friedrich. (1972). *The Ancient American Civilizations*. New York: Praeger.

Leyenaar, Ted J., and Lee A. Parsons. (1988). *Ulama: The Ballgame of the Mayans and Aztecs*. Leiden, Netherlands: Spruyt, Van Mantgem & De Does.

Oxendine, Joseph. (1988). *American Indian Sports Heritage*. Champaign, IL: Human Kinetics.

Skidmore, Thomas E., and Peter H. Smith. (1984). *Modern Latin America*. New York: Oxford University Press.

▦ NORTH AMERICA

HISTORICAL OVERVIEW

During the 17th century, Europeans had created settlements in eastern Canada and in the northeast, mid-Atlantic, and a portion of the southeast of what is today the United States. Throughout the 18th century, these territories grew in economic importance as suppliers of resources and goods for Europe. While England ultimately gained control of the Canadian territories from France in the late 18th century, it lost sovereignty over the American colonies.

Following the Revolutionary War in America, the newly independent United States continued on a path of commercial growth that reflected its regional social and economic differences. Manufacturing and small-time farming in the North were based on a Puritan work ethic, while an agrarian culture that developed in the South was organized around raising cash crops, specifically cotton and tobacco. Slavery was a key component of the southern economy. The movement to abolish slavery in the United States would of course serve as a major impetus for fighting the Civil War (1861–1865).

The latter half of the 19th century in America was marked by greater industrial development in the Northeast and expansion westward. A railroad to the Pacific was constructed, along with hundreds of towns and cities throughout the Plains that served as links in the chain of transcontinental commerce. Mining settlements sprang up throughout the Northwest to exploit the region's natural deposits of silver, copper, and gold. In the midst of this activity, the United States waged a shameless war on Native Americans, killing thousands of men, women, and children, seizing their land, and all but wiping out their indigenous culture.

By the close of the 19th century, the United States was well on its way to being a world power, and Canada, though still under British dominion, was already one of the world's chief agricultural producers.

NORTH AMERICAN SPORTS AND GAMES OF THE 18TH AND 19TH CENTURIES

Several cultural factors were influential in the development of sports and games in North America. For the most part, the American colonies took their cue from England regarding games and pastimes. Though the strict religiosity and the Puritan work ethic that defined New England society were a reaction of sorts to English Protestantism, its values of strength of character, sobriety, self-reliance, and self-perfection led northerners to take the moral high ground in sports participation. For example, sport was not to be frivolous, or simply fun, but rather had to serve a purpose—great or small. Thus the colonists made games out of many of their daily chores and larger seasonal tasks. Later in the 19th century, when American football became extremely popular in northeastern schools and universities, the game was touted as a great character builder and as a "shaper of men." Similarly, boxing, which was to become a popular club sport in the early 20th century among youth in northeastern cities, was supported by boys' clubs—many with links to the Catholic Church—as a sport that taught discipline and respect for hard work. The whole YMCA movement, which began in the American Northeast in the late 19th century, had as its moral objective the development of sound body and mind. The sports of basketball and volleyball were created by and disseminated through YMCA channels to promote physical fitness on a mass level.

America's southern culture also contributed to the country's concept of sports and games. Many of the gentry who owned plantations in the South were schooled in England, and they brought back such pursuits as horse racing, fencing, wrestling, and boxing. Even cricket was played in some areas of Virginia and the Carolinas. Lower-class whites in the South had their own low-brow versions of these sports (e.g., brawling instead of wrestling, racing nonthoroughbred horses, cockfighting, and forms of boxing that also entailed sword fighting). Sport was a mark of masculinity in the Old South, and gambling (e.g., on cockfights and horse racing) provided a common ground for the two segments of society to meet.

One can draw parallels between the old Gaelic/European tradition of the seasonal festival, which featured sports, games, and a good deal of partying, and the southern county fair, which provided similar entertainment. It should be noted, too, that even black slaves were allowed to engage among themselves in cultural events (many of which had African origins) and in sports like wrestling, foot racing, and cockfighting.

Native Americans weren't as fortunate. Beginning with the European discovery of the continent in the 16th century, there was an uneasy coexistence between white settlers and Native Americans that was interrupted periodically by episodes of violence. U.S. political and economic objectives ultimately led to the near annihilation of Native American culture, as native tribes were either slaughtered in the country's westward advance, or crowded onto reservations and marginalized as American citizens. Only in the past few decades have Native Americans acted to reclaim their culture. This volume discusses a traditional Native American cultural event known as powwow, where folks gather together to engage in sport, game, and celebration.

As the United States industrialized and urbanized, sports increasingly became linked with the ways in which people worked and lived. Baseball had mass appeal and was derived from anglicized town ball, a folk game that was typically played on the town common. By the late 19th century, many factories, businesses, and municipalities had their own amateur and semiprofessional teams. Northeastern and midwestern cities hosted professional ball clubs whose games were regularly attended by thousands of men and women. The Canadian sport of ice hockey built a similar following throughout the provinces and the northern midwestern United States.

During the 19th century, there were other mass sports in North America. These were pastimes that engaged all classes of society. Both basketball and football were played on the school, club, and professional level. Softball was created in the late 19th century and rapidly became one of the country's most popular forms of organized group recreation. Curling, a sport that originated in Scotland, became extremely popular in Canada, where by the 1880s many towns had a curling club, and almost every club maintained a rink with several curling sheets.

As in England and Europe, there were a number of sports in America that distinguished the elite or upper classes from the working class. During the mid- to late 19th century, only the well-to-do attended college. There they practiced rowing, tennis, track and field, and lacrosse—sports that were largely unknown to the lower classes. (Lacrosse, ironically, was derived from several variations of a similar Native American game.)

Both the new and old moneyed classes in America, who made fortunes in industry and finance, found ways to display their wealth and status through sport as well. Exclusive country and boating clubs provided a venue where men and women could show off the latest fashions while engaging in such elitist sports as tennis, golf, croquet, squash, and sailing.

▦ American Football

Definition

American football is a game played between two teams of 11 players using an inflated oval ball on a rectangular playing field 120 yards long and 53⅓ yards wide. Each end of the field is marked by a goal line and an H-shaped goal crossbar. The object of the game is to move the ball across the opponent's goal line by running or passing, or to kick the ball over the goal crossbar for a score, and to prevent the opposing team from scoring. With origins in European soccer and British rugby, American football, which evolved in the latter half of the 19th century, quickly caught on with collegiate and amateur athletic clubs throughout the United States.

History

History records the first official football game as having taken place between Rutgers and Princeton in New Brunswick, New Jersey, in 1859. However, the complexion of that game was very different from American football today. The teams squared off with 25 players to a side in a game that constituted an amalgam of soccer and rugby. Players were not permitted to run with the ball or to pass it forward; the ball had to be drop-kicked or kicked "as it lies" in order to advance it and score. There was no concept of possession, or of downs or a line of scrimmage. When a stalemate was reached—which was often—players from both sides locked arms and huddled around the ball, forming a "scrum." The clash of the two masses succeeded in either popping the ball free or heeling it back to a teammate. Each team had a goalkeeper, legions of fielders, who guarded sections of the field, and bulldogs, who followed the ball up and down the field. The first team to score (kick) six goals won.

While early football's kick-the-ball roots had connections to European soccer, rugby was also influential (*see* Soccer; Rugby). By the 1850s amateur and collegiate rugby clubs had already sprung up in the northeastern United States. But the game could be tremendously rough—in 1860 officials at Harvard banned rugby at the school after one contest got out of hand.

Still, Harvard would figure prominently in the birth of American football. In 1873, when a small group of eastern colleges gathered to discuss rules for the sport, Harvard declined. Instead, the school developed its own set of rules, which were indebted more to rugby than to the soccer-type game that was being played at the time. Then, when Harvard played McGill University of Montreal, Canada, in Cambridge in 1874, it was exposed to a more wide-open version of rugby that had been popularized in Canada. A player could pick up the ball and run with it whenever he wished, and touchdowns were counted as well as goals. (In "pure" Rugby Union, a touchdown only provided the chance to kick a free goal. If the kick missed, the touchdown didn't count.) The Harvard team liked what it saw and adapted these exciting features of the Canadian game. Soon, these measures began to gain acceptance, particularly after Yale played Harvard in 1875.

Then, in 1876, Walter Camp entered Yale as a freshman. On the football field, Camp had speed and strength, and could kick and punt the ball for distance and placement. At Yale he played halfback for six years (at the time there were no rules limiting a player's eligibility), serving as captain for three years. During that time Yale built a 25–1–6 record. Later, between 1888 and 1892, he served as head coach at Yale, during which time his teams were 67–2. Regarded as the "Father of American Football," Camp is best known for his lasting influence on the game. Eleven of his teammates or players he coached went on to become first coaches at other schools, thereby spreading the game throughout the collegiate ranks. His most famous student, Amos Alanzo Stagg, is considered one of the game's greatest coaches. Stagg coached an incredible 71 years, including 41 at the University of Chicago.

Camp also attended every national rule committee meeting from 1878 to his death in 1925, and he either proposed or helped formulate virtually all of the basic rules of American football, including rules limiting players to 11 on a side, the introduction of the line of scrimmage, and the concept of alternating possession of the ball based on a series of downs and yardage gained. (See discussion of rules on page 200.)

It is interesting to note that two dominant perceptions of American football that came to shape the sport's culture had their origins in the early game: football as character builder of young men, and football as violent, aggressive sport.

Clearly football's pioneers perceived the same qualities in the sport that coaching legends like Vince Lombardi and Knute Rockne would be preaching to future generations: that football demanded strength, courage, dedication, unrivaled teamwork, and the commitment to sublimate the quest for individual accomplishment and glory to the overall team goal of winning.

The following passage by Walter Camp, written in 1892, could have been written years later by Lombardi:

> When it comes to football, mind will always win over muscle and brute force. What a gentleman wants is fair play and for the best man to win. If he accepts these principles, he will find his own character greatly enriched.... There is no substitute for hard work and effort beyond the call of duty. That is what strengthens the soul and ennobles one's character.

With such moral and ethical lessons to teach, it's no wonder that football enjoyed great popularity throughout collegiate and scholastic institutions. After gaining acceptance in the Ivy League schools and neighboring northeastern colleges in the 1870s and 1880s, football caught on like wild-fire in the South and Midwest during the 1890s. Larger schools like Michigan and Dartmouth gained prominence by traveling cross-country and playing series of games that served to spread the popularity of the sport. By 1899 there were an estimated 5,000 college, high school, and amateur teams playing football, constituting about 120,000 players.

But football was a rough and quite often dangerous game. The most successful plays were based on mass movement like the "flying wedge." Introduced by Princeton in 1884, the flying wedge was nothing more than a mass V-formation, with the ball carrier tucked into the center of the V. The steamroller aspect of the play itself could cause serious injury to a defender caught in the onslaught. The play became especially violent when teams began to counter the formation by sending players leaping, cleats first, over the wall of blockers.

As crowds began to flock to the college game—it wasn't uncommon for contests to draw 10,000–15,000 spectators at the large universities—more and more institutions began to see the sport as a moneymaker. This led to flagrant professionalism; numerous players either gained employment through university connections or were paid outright to play. These football mercenaries rarely set foot on campus at any time but game day, and often played under aliases in order to switch allegiance at any time to whichever school offered the most money. One infamous player, known as Martin Thayer, was exposed as having played 13 years at nine different schools.

By the turn of the century, violence and corruption were threatening to ruin the game. Dr. Nicholas Murray Butler, president of Columbia University, labeled the college game as "madness and slaughter," while a colleague at New York University, Chancellor Henry MacCracken, argued that football "has no social significance, except to give ruffians on our campuses an opportunity to express themselves." A survey of college presidents and medical doctors published by Charles Thwing in the *Journal of the American Medical Association* reported that the majority of those surveyed wanted the game to be abolished.

There were 12 reported deaths in the college game in 1902, and after a player was killed in an NYU–Union College game in front of a newspaper reporter, the media began to rail against the sport. The situation reached a head after the *Chicago Tribune* published a series on football in 1906 that documented the preceding year's death of 18 collegiate players, 46 high schoolers, and 9 semipros. Colleges began dropping the sport.

It took actions that were presidential in stature to reverse football's slide into oblivion. President Theodore Roosevelt, an alumnus of Harvard and an ardent fan of the sport, summoned a conference of coaches to the White House following the 1905 season. Discussing the need for sweeping change to the sport, this gathering acted as the impetus for the soon-to-be-established National Collegiate Athletic Association (NCAA) Rules Committee. Prior to the 1906 season, representatives from 28 member schools met to enact a far-reaching set of rule changes to counter violent play and dangerous conditions. Revisions included:

1. Legalizing the forward pass. This move lessened the incidence of mass pile-ups as teams had to position defenders off the line of scrimmage.
2. Creating a "neutral zone" which separated both lines by the length of the ball. This change made the incidence of offsides and fouls less prevalent and easier to call.
3. Requiring a minimum of six men on the line of scrimmage. This change made it impossible for teams on offense to mass all their players in a dangerous wedge around the ball carrier.
4. Raising the yardage for a first down from 5 to 10.

A second major revision to the rulebook followed in response to the unabated incidence of death and injury and the negative public opinion surrounding it. (In 1909 33 deaths and 246 serious injuries were attributed to playing football.) Again, many of these revisions are fundamental to the game as it is played today:

1. Outlawing the flying tackle.
2. Requiring seven men on the line of scrimmage.
3. Prohibiting the pushing and pulling of the ball carrier and the interlocking of hands.
4. Permitting the forward pass to be thrown to any point, provided the passer was at least five yards behind the line of scrimmage.
5. Dividing halves into quarters of fifteen minutes each.
6. Allowing players who are removed from the game to return.

Equipment

The equipment needed for the game itself includes an oblong spheroid ball and an assortment of protective gear. The term "pigskin" derives from an early version of the ball, which was in fact an inflated pig's bladder. Today's ball is made of cowhide, drawn tightly over inflated rubber tubing. A row of stitches or lacing on the ball—originally used to access the tubing for frequent repair—is today most instrumental in gripping the ball to throw a forward pass.

Protective equipment has evolved to make playing the game much safer. The helmet wasn't adopted by most players until the 1910s and 1920s, and then the headpiece was little more than a thick, form-fitting leather cap that extended over the ears. Earlier players wore protection that resembled modern-day wrestling headgear. Pioneering players also wore light padding on their hips, legs, knees, shins, and shoulders. Technology has made synthetic material, particularly plastics, which are much more durable and in many ways lighter than the canvas-leather padding of yesteryear. Such advances are particularly evident in the modern helmet with face mask and in specialized shoes, which are either cleated for traction on grass fields, or rubber-soled for speed on artificial surfaces.

Rules

As discussed earlier, the rules of American football gradually evolved throughout the late 19th and early 20th centuries. Faced with a game that was, at times, boring and increasingly rough, a handful of coaches and leading proponents of the game met intermittently in a series of rules conventions and conferences beginning in 1878. Though these meetings were crucial in standardizing the game of football, it is interesting to note the objectives that football's forefathers pursued at these gatherings—to make the game safer and more exciting—and how similar these concerns are to those of today's professional football owners, who, over the past 20 to 30 years, have implemented rules on blocking, sacking, and pass coverage to protect the quarterback and to open up, or liven up, the passing game.

In 1878 Walter Camp and his contemporaries moved to limit to 11 the number of players on each side. They also created a "line of scrimmage," with a player in the center of the line (the "snapperback") designated to pass the ball back with his foot to the quarterback, who was allowed only to pass it off to a halfback or fullback. The term "quarterback" derives from the position of the player—a quarter of the way behind the line of scrimmage between the fullback and the snapperback. The concept of one side having possession of the ball and the other setting up to defend its goal triggered the rapid development of strategic plays designed to advance the ball.

In 1882 a rule was enacted that required teams to advance the ball five yards in three downs, or surrender the ball. In order to track a team's progress toward a first down, the field was subsequently laid out in five-yard chalk lines, thus giving it the appearance of a gridiron.

Meanwhile, football's system of scoring slowly set itself apart from rugby. In 1883 a field goal was valued at 5 points; a "field goal after touchdown" counted for 4 points, a touchdown was worth 2 points, and a safety counted for 1 point against the team forced to make it. As the game developed, it became obvious that a touchdown was more difficult than a field goal, and scoring rules were adjusted accordingly. In 1897 a touchdown was raised to 5 points, while a kick following a touchdown was reduced to 1 point (the modern-day "extra point"). The field goal fell to 4 points in 1904 and to 3 in 1909. In 1912 the touchdown rose to its current scoring value of 6 points.

Bibliography

Leckie, Robert. (1965). *The Story of Football*. New York: Random House.

Smith, Ronald A. (1988). *Sports and Freedom: The Rise of Big-Time College Athletics*. New York: Oxford University Press.

Twombly, Wells. (1976). *Two Hundred Years of Sports in America*. New York: McGraw-Hill.

▦ Baseball

Definition

Baseball is a game played between two teams of nine players each using a bat and ball on a field having an infield, or diamond—a 90-foot square with a base positioned at each corner—at one end. The bases mark the route that an offensive player must take in order to score. For over a century now the game has enjoyed great popularity among people of all ages in the United States, where it has been regarded as the national pastime. Today baseball is played throughout the world, particularly in North and South America, the Caribbean, and Southeast Asia.

History

There is evidence of stick-and-ball games like baseball being played in ancient Persia, Egypt, and Greece. These games often carried religious or ceremonial significance. Games of this type were probably spread throughout Europe by the Romans and later in the Middle Ages by crusaders. There are accounts of a game played in church courtyards in 12th-century France that used four milking stools for bases. University students in 16th-century England played a similar batted-ball game that featured a base path of four stakes arranged in a square. Europeans brought stick-and-ball games to the American colonies in the 1600s.

By the early 19th century, a number of stick-and-ball games had caught on in America. Contrary to popular legend, Abner Doubleday did not invent baseball in Cooperstown, New York, in 1839. Nearly a century before, in 1751, the British game of cricket was played in Philadelphia. And throughout the northeastern colonies, an English game called rounders had gained popularity. The earliest mention of rounders as linked to baseball comes in William Clerke's *Boy's Own Book*, an account of popular sports and games published in London in 1829. In reciting the rules for rounders, Clerke points out that Americans called it "towne ball" or "baseball." The rules for rounders certainly have many similarities to modern baseball: two teams of nine players take turns hitting and fielding; a run is scored when a batter circles a square marked by four bases, or posts; and an out is recorded when a batted ball is caught either on the fly or after one bounce. In early America, rounders was played in several variations. In urban areas it was often known as One Old Cat or Two Old Cat, and played with just one or two bases. In rural communities throughout New England rounders took the form of town ball—so named because it was often played on the town common.

In town ball, the diamond was a 60-foot by 60-foot square. Bases were marked by large flat stones, with the fourth base positioned slightly off to the left of the batter. (Later, to counter the incidence of sprained or broken feet, stones were replaced with canvas bags filled with sand.) Teams would usually number 8 to 20 players, with every player getting a chance to bat before the game would move to the next inning. Town ball was a rough and tumble game. Players might use a crudely carved stick of wood or an axe handle for a bat, and a ball was often little more than a slug or bullet covered with yards of string or yarn. And the practice of "plugging" or "soaking" a baserunner—recording a putout by throwing directly at the runner—led to early variants of the bench-clearing brawl.

By the 1840s, baseball was established as a common form of recreation throughout the country. In 1842 the first organized baseball club, the Knickerbocker Baseball Club, was formed in New York City. Alexander Cartwright, a surveyor and a member of the Knickerbockers, is credited with giving structure to the game by laying out the standard baseball diamond and developing 20 basic rules for baseball which were first published in 1845.

Cartwright's rules, known in practice as the "New York Game," form the basis for the modern game of baseball. The "diamond," with the bases spaced an equidistant 42 paces, or 90 feet, was a revolutionary concept. By drawing two foul lines from home plate, Cartwright designated an area of fair play (prior to this, the ball could be hit in any direction) and established space where spectators could gather to watch the game without interfering with play. The New York Rules also created the concept of innings, with each player going to bat in turn. Teams were limited to nine players. Regulations stipulated "pitching" the ball to the batter, and a fielder could now force out a runner by throwing the ball to a teammate on base. All disputes and differences related to the game were to be decided by an independent arbiter, an "umpire," from whose decision there was no appeal.

On June 19, 1846, the Knickerbockers played the New York Club at the Elysian Field in Hoboken, New Jersey (see illustration). Despite playing by their own rules, the Knickerbockers lost 23–1. Nevertheless, baseball's popularity continued to grow, particularly among the working classes. Schoolteachers, clerks, farmers, and factory workers met in formal and informal groups alike to play the game. Baseball spread rapidly in the 1860s, particularly during the Civil War, when Union soldiers played the game wherever they went in the South and Mid-Atlantic.

Figure 26. An illustration of one of the early baseball games at the Elysian Field in Hoboken, New Jersey. (Reprinted from the Collections of the Library of Congress)

In 1859 the Fashion Race Course in Brooklyn had hosted the first game before paying customers. Over 2,000 fans paid 50 cents each to watch two amateur teams, the Brooklyn Excelsiors and the Brooklyn Athletics. Newspapers and periodicals began to assign reporters to cover games, and entrepreneurs began to rent or purchase land on which to stage contests. The practice of playing baseball in an enclosed park began at Union Grounds in Brooklyn in 1862. Park owners could charge admission, and sell food and drink within the park without competition from vendors. While the games were exciting, betting on the outcome of the contests generated even more interest surrounding the sport. In fact, gambling terms were part of the New York Game, which referred to a time at bat as a "hand," a run scored as an "ace," and two runs driven in as a "deuce." Gamblers were "fancy men," or fans. Many players bet on games in which they played—even the umpires got into the act.

After the war, baseball was quickly established as a profitable business. The National Association of Base Ball Players (NABBP), the sport's early governing body, ruled in 1868 that players could play for pay. In 1869 the Cincinnati Red Stockings, the first true professional team, traveled the country, beating every local team it met en route to a 65–0 record. Their success suggested that fans in a number of cities were hungry for top-flight professional baseball, and that specialists could play the game as a full-time job. Thus the National Association of Professional Baseball Players was born in 1871.

Though the National Association disbanded in 1876 due to mismanagement and allegations of heavy betting, the National League (NL) was formed the same year. Beginning with clubs in eight midwestern and northeastern cities, the National League regulated the activities of all owners. Players were required to sign contracts, and all forms of gambling were banned to give the league and its games legitimacy. While the NL has persisted, in one form or another, to this day, several rival professional leagues came and went during the 1880s and 1890s. In 1901 the minor Western League was renamed the American League (AL). The NL formally recognized the AL in 1903, when the leagues' champions agreed to meet at season's end in what is today called the World Series.

While the professional game has enjoyed a great following in America, the crowning of baseball as the national pastime is rooted in the game's local popularity—a sport deemed "as American as apple pie." For several generations in the late 1800s and early 1900s, a town's pride and identity were founded in its ba. ball team. While playing for the town team was the ultimate honor—a badge of maturity—for a young man, almost every boy and girl played some form of pick up or sand lot baseball at one time or another. Baseball was also central in the workplace. By the turn of the century, it was common for businesses to organize amateur teams made up of their employees. Occasionally, businesses would hire professional players, known as "ringers," to improve their teams. Factory baseball teams, which played in industrial leagues, were the precursors of today's softball teams.

Equipment

Modern baseball equipment includes a wooden or aluminum bat, a hard, leather-covered ball, padded leather gloves for fielding the ball, and cleated shoes for traction. Catchers wear protective gear including a helmet, face mask, chest protector, and shin guards. Rules govern the size and construction of equipment and uniforms. In general, the ball, which is made of a cork center that is wrapped in layers of rubber and string, measures about 9 inches in circumference, while the bat may be no more than $2\frac{3}{4}$ inches in diameter and no greater than 42 inches long.

Baseball equipment has changed dramatically since the 19th century. Early versions of the ball used heavy material in the core, and were neither wound nor stitched as tight as modern balls. As a game wore on, the ball tended to soften and lose its form—hence the term "dead ball" era. Gloves weren't used until the 1880s, when catchers began to wear unpadded models. There are accounts of early catchers slipping raw meat inside to cushion the shock of the ball.

Rules

It is difficult to generalize the rules of 19th-century baseball because the game changed so fast. Though Cartwright's New York Rules established a foundation for the way the game is played today, there were many adaptations throughout the latter half-century. The New York Game stipulated that the first team to score 21 aces won, but each team had to play an equal number of hands, or innings. For many this game took too long, particularly for the working-class player, who had limited time for recreation. Hence the 1860 rules adopted the practice of playing nine innings with three outs to a side each inning. Yet several rules derived from rounders persisted years after Cartwright's regulations were published. In 1866 most teams still played the "bound game," where a ball caught on one bounce was ruled an out. It wasn't until around 1870 that the majority of teams began to play by the "fly game," which required a fielder to throw a runner out on one-hop grounders. Early rules also allowed substitution "at any time," leading several players to sub themselves in off the bench to catch foul pop-ups hit their way. This rule was changed to permit substitutions only when the ball is dead.

Most of the major rule changes in the 1870s and 1880s related to pitching. In baseball's earliest days, umpires didn't call balls or strikes at all. With runners on base, a batter might watch 50 pitches go by, waiting for a wild pitch or a passed ball to advance the runners. In 1876 balls and strikes were called, but pitchers had the luxury of a nine-ball count, and batters were entitled to call their own pitches—high or low. Legend has it that when a batter stepped up to the plate, an umpire would ask, "What's your pleasure, sir?" Prior to the 1880s, pitchers were required to deliver the ball underhand or sidearm. By the mid-1880s, pitchers were allowed to throw overhand, and the number of balls for a walk was gradually reduced from nine to four.

Bibliography

Rosenburg, John M. (1966). *The Story of Baseball*. New York: Random House.

Stewart, Douglas. (1998). "The Old Ball Game." *Smithsonian Magazine* (October 1998), pp. 99–106.

Twombly, Wells. (1976). *Two Hundred Years of Sports in America*. New York: McGraw-Hill.

Ward, Geoffrey C. (1994). *Baseball: An Illustrated History*. New York: Alfred A. Knopf.

⧗ Basketball

Definition

Basketball is a fast-paced game played on a rectangular court (usually indoors) between two teams of five players. A team tries to score more points than the opposition by tossing an inflated ball through a goal, which consists of a metal-rimmed basket placed 10 feet above the floor and mounted on a rectangular backboard. Basketball is perhaps the most popular team sport in the world, played by men and women of all ages and abilities in more than 200 countries.

History

Basketball is truly an American game, having been devised by a physical education instructor, Dr. James Naismith, in Springfield, Massachusetts, in 1891. Luther Gulick, chairman of the physical education department at the School for Christian Workers (now Springfield College), asked Naismith to create an indoor game that would hold students' attention and keep them in shape during the long northeastern winter. The game also had to be safe. Sports like indoor soccer and an early variant of box lacrosse had left many of Naismith's students battered and bloodied. These concerns led to basketball developing as a noncontact sport, emphasizing grace and speed.

From the very beginning, players were prohibited from hitting, holding, shoving, or tackling opponents, though they were allowed to intercept passes and block shots. The basket was situated 10 feet off the ground to dissuade players from massing around it and defending it with their bodies. The first game was played among 18 members of Naismith's class. After outlining 13 basic rules (which Naismith would publish in 1892 as basketball's first rulebook), the group split into two nine-man teams. Legend has it that the name "basketball" was coined that day by Naismith, who, after asking the school's janitor for a pair of boxes or crates to use as goals for the game, had to settle instead for two half-bushel peach baskets. Though the first game was a resounding success—the players worked up a sweat and enjoyed the competition, and no one got hurt—we would probably think otherwise if we were to watch a re-creation of this historic game. Players used a soccer ball and were prohibited from running in any way with the ball—they could pass but weren't allowed to dribble. After 30 minutes of play, the two teams had scored just one basket between them.

But the framework for basketball was established that day, and over the next 20 to 25 years (1890s–1910s), changes in rules and advances in equipment acted to shape the game into one with which we are familiar today. By 1897 each basket counted 2 points and each free throw was worth 1 point. In 1900 the free throw line was marked 15 feet from the hoop, where it remains today.

A short time later, in 1905, a metal-rimmed hoop with open netting replaced the peach basket. This sped the game up, as contestants no longer had to wait each time a basket was made for the referee or an attendant to climb a stepladder to retrieve the ball. Several years earlier, the wooden backboard attached to the basket had been introduced, enabling players to bank shots and, in general, opening up the game's offense. Advances in the shape and material of the ball also greatly influenced the style and flow of the game.

Though today's players are much more skilled at dribbling and passing than were players in the early 20th century, this was due largely to the imperfections of the early basketball rather than to a lack of dedication or innate athleticism. Slightly larger than soccer balls, the first basketballs were rubber inflatable bladders covered by a thick leather casing. The casing was laced together to provide easy access to the bladder in the event of repair. Unfortunately, dribbling the ball on the lacing made for adventuresome bouncing, and the leather tended to lump up or deaden in spots after prolonged use. Players weren't even allowed to dribble the ball until 1910. Legend has it that some clever players at Yale University began to "pass" the ball at the floor and grab it on the rebound. Upon witnessing what he termed one of the game's "prettiest" plays, Naismith added this activity, which he called a "dribble," to his official rulebook. It wasn't until 1942, when basketball manufacturers added cloth lining to the leather for support and uniformity, that the ball assumed a constant, uniform size and shape. Thereafter play was more consistent, scoring increased, and skill levels improved.

Basketball's popularity grew like that of no other sport. Each member of Naismith's class was a trainer or instructor at a Young Men's Christian Association (YMCA) gym. By the turn of the century, the YMCA had already established an extensive network of facilities throughout the United States and Western Europe. With an official endorsement by the YMCA, the game of basketball became a wintertime fitness curriculum of sorts. Taken together, the impact of Naismith's students, in essence a cadre of trainers for the game of basketball, and the immediate creation of a rulebook (first published in 1892 and regularly revised) were both immediate and far-reaching. Just three years after its inception, the game was being played in 15 countries. In 1897 the first five-a-side college game was played between Yale and Pennsylvania University, with the Elis winning 32–10.

Basketball also became one of the few team sports that was accessible to women (see illustration). In 1895–1896 Vassar and Smith fielded women's teams, and many more physical education instructors at colleges throughout the Northeast and Midwest began promoting the game as an ideal exerciser.

By the early 1900s, basketball was contested as an intercollegiate sport in nearly 100 schools, most located in the East and Midwest. Basketball was also gaining popularity at the high school and club level. In 1904 basketball was conducted as an exhibition at the Olympic Games in St. Louis, thereby further legitimizing the game and providing another boost to its popularity. By 1913 Naismith's rules were printed in 30 languages and followed by an estimated 20 million players worldwide.

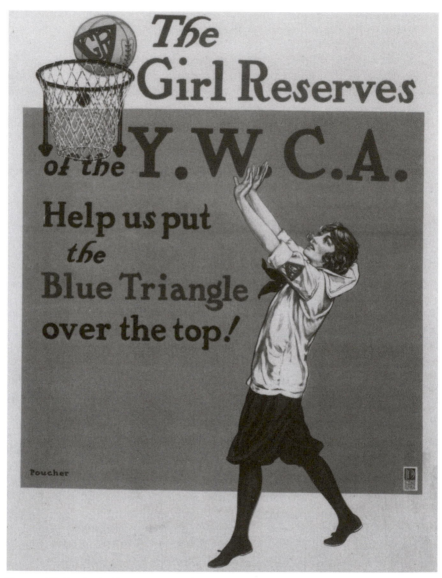

Figure 27. Basketball became the most popular team sport for young American women at the turn of the century. This wartime poster illustrates the YWCA's role in this process. (Reproduced from the Collections of the Library of Congress)

Equipment

Basketball equipment has changed considerably since the earliest days of the sport. Though most players still wear some form of shorts and tank-top shirt as a uniform, today's court shoes, which aid side-to-side movement, jumping, and traction on hardwood floors, are a far cry from the leather "flats" worn by players at the turn of the century. One tradition that hasn't changed and that seems to have been pioneered by the sport is the practice of numbering uniforms. Because referees and record keepers had to identify players who committed fouls, most teams wore numbered uniforms. The game also seems to have initiated the now standard sports practice of wearing white uniforms for home games and dark for away contests—once again so that referees could quickly identify a player in the heat of a game.

Better equipment also made the game easier to follow and more entertaining. As discussed earlier, improvements made to the ball broadened the scope of play and heightened the game's skill level. Dribbling became an art, and a broad array of plays were designed to spring off the dribble. (In fact, rules were amended in 1916 that allowed players to shoot after dribbling.) Early on, backboards were made of wire screen and placed behind each basket so that spectators kneeling in the balcony above a gymnasium couldn't help steer balls into the baskets. But soon wooden backboards were mounted above baskets to help players bank the ball into the hoop. A short time later, as attendance at basketball games began to take off, backboards began to be made of thick glass so that fans seated behind the basket could still follow all the action.

While dimensions of individual courts vary even today (a playing area 84 feet long and 50 feet wide is now most common for high school and collegiate play, and professional basketball uses a slightly longer court of 94 feet), courts were rarely alike in the early days of the game. This led to many teams adopting styles of play and tactics that were suited to the dimensions of their home court.

Rules

As discussed previously, the rules of basketball were codified right from the start when Dr. Naismith published the first rulebook in 1892. From the beginning the game was recommended for women, too. In 1892 Senda Berenson Abbott, a Lithuanian-born physical education instructor at Smith College in Northampton, Massachusetts, introduced Naismith's game to women at the school. It's interesting to read the initial women's rulebook today and to draw inferences from its pages regarding society's gender roles and biases at the time. Because men's basketball was regarded as too physically demanding for women, Berenson Abbott made significant changes to the game. The court was divided into three equal sections, with players required to stay in an assigned area. Players were prohibited from grabbing and batting the ball from the hands of another player. Women were also prohibited from holding the ball for longer than three seconds and from dribbling the ball more than three times.

Though proponents of the early women's game were concerned with potentially rough, unladylike aspects of basketball, the sport has always considered the issue of contact between players and wrestled with rules to regulate it. Today, illegal contact between opposing players is ruled a foul, resulting in either a change of possession or a chance to take one or more free throws. But early on, a foul had much direr consequences for the offender and his or her team. A player's second foul once meant removal from the game until the next field goal was scored. If a team committed three consecutive fouls, the opposition would be awarded a field goal. Beginning in 1908, a player who committed five fouls was disqualified from the game. Based on the severity of the foul, rules were soon set so that players who were fouled were either awarded two shots or one shot plus a bonus shot, which was attempted only if the first shot was made. Rules also stipulated that offensive play could be too aggressive, as fouls were soon called for charging.

In 1915 the Amateur Athletic Union of the United States (AAU), the National Collegiate Athletic Association (NCAA), and the YMCA formed a committee to standardize the rules of basketball. This spurred further growth of the sport in clubs and colleges across the country, and it boosted interregional and eventually national play.

Bibliography

Devany, John. (1976). *The Story of Basketball*. New York: Random House.

Peterson, Robert W. (1990). *Cages to Jump Shots: Pro Basketball's Early Years*. New York: Oxford University Press.

Twombly, Wells. (1976). *Two Hundred Years of Sports in America*. New York: McGraw-Hill.

▦ Canoeing

Definition

Canoes are durable craft designed to sail in a variety of water conditions. Today, there are basically two kinds of canoes: the traditional Canadian canoe, a long, narrow wood or fiberglass boat with an open deck; and a kayak, a smaller, flatter boat with an enclosed deck. Both were developed by native North Americans and were essential for day-to-day life. Today, canoeing and kayaking are two of the fastest growing sports in America.

History

Dugouts and birch bark canoes were used by northern Native Americans for many centuries prior to contact with French explorers and fur traders in the 16th and 17th centuries. The dugout was so named because it was created by shaping and hollowing out a log. The birch bark was more similar to a modern canoe—essentially thick tree bark covering wood framing. Each boat had a shallow draft that was ideal for navigating through rough water. The canoe's design and relatively light weight also enabled rowers to carry it on shore and around dangerous rapids or dry, impassable stretches. It should be noted that although modern-day canoes are descendants of craft used by Native Americans to hunt and fish, many other cultures around the world have used versatile, canoe-like boats.

The kayak was developed in the northern Arctic region by the Aleut and Inuit. Traditional kayaks consisted of animal skins strung tightly over wood framing. A kayak's design reflects its origins in the icy Arctic Sea. Kayaks are several feet shorter than canoes and have a much shallower draft. A kayak's deck is enclosed, and the kayaker typically sits in a cockpit-like seat. Built close to the water, fast, maneuverable, and watertight, a kayak wasn't easy to flip in the water; when it was, it could be easily righted, as the kayaker used a long steadying paddle with blades on both ends.

Canoes were not used for recreation until the mid-19th century—ironically, about the time they became no longer practical for transportation. A Scottish lawyer, John MacGregor, is generally credited with establishing canoeing as a recreation sport. In 1845 he designed the "Rob Roy," a type of canoe/ship that had a partially enclosed deck, mast, and sails but also used paddles. In 1866 MacGregor founded the Canoe Club, which in 1873 became the Royal Canoe Club in England. MacGregor and his friends turned canoeing in the late 19th century into an elite club sport in England and Europe.

Canoeing developed along a similar path in North America, where the upper class and growing upper middle class took canoes on outdoor getaways and wilderness adventures. Beginning in the late 19th century in the Northeast (Adirondacks) and continuing into the early 20th century in the West (Yellowstone) and Pacific Northwest, Americans embarked on a back-to-nature movement, accompanied by the creation of "wilderness" camps and resorts and the newfound popularity of the great outdoors vacation. This activity would contribute to the creation of an American national park system in the early 20th century and the start of an ongoing interest in protecting the country's wildlife and natural resources.

Due to the sport's popularity in the early 20th century, representatives from 19 nations met in Denmark in 1924 to form the Internationale

Representationschaft des Kanusport (IRK), canoeing's initial international governing body. The IRK got canoeing accepted as a demonstration sport in the 1924 Olympics in Paris and as an official medal sport in Berlin in 1936. Today, men and women compete in a variety of singles and pairs events over "flat-water" and "white-water" courses. The white-water races are similar to slalom events in skiing—competitors must pass through a series of gates, including "reverse" gates, which must be passed backwards. Penalty times are assessed for hitting or missing gates.

The U.S. Canoe Association was founded in 1968 to govern and sanction long-distance racing. Marathon canoe races take place throughout the United States, primarily during the springtime when rivers are highest. One of the best-known canoe races in the world is the annual International White-Water Race, begun in 1948 and held on a 23-mile course down river from Salida, Colorado.

Equipment

Basic canoes and kayaks are discussed previously. Paddles are made of wood or fiberglass. A canoeist uses a short paddle with a blade on one end. A canoeist must shift the paddle from side to side to row the boat forward. A kayaker uses a long paddle with blades on both ends. Held in the center, the kayak paddle enables the rower to more easily shift his or her stroke from one side to the other.

Both canoeists and kayakers usually wear a lifejacket. Kayakers, because they are closer to the water and usually paddle in rougher conditions (white water or open sea), usually wear some type of wet suit designed to keep the body warm even when wet. In white-water rapids, a competitive kayaker will wear a helmet as well.

Consulting a nautical map or guidebook for information on water currents and depth is also important. For canoeists, many rivers are rated by degree of difficulty (e.g., Class I, for the calmest, to Class VI, for the roughest).

How to Paddle a Canoe

In a Canadian canoe, paddling from a kneeling position (knees on the bottom of the boat) is usually the most efficient way to move the boat, though one may also paddle from a seated, upright position in calm water. There are three basic strokes: power strokes, turning strokes, and stabilizing strokes.

Power strokes propel the boat forward, stop it, or push it backward.

Stabilizing strokes are used to balance the boat and keep it from tipping over.

Turning strokes place force on either side of the boat to either change direction or counter a stroke.

Bibliography

Adney, Tappan, and Howard I. Chappelle. (1993) *The Bark Canoes and Skin Boats of North America*. Washington, DC: Smithsonian Institution Press.

Newell, Bruce (1994). *Pocket Guide to Basic Canoeing*. Helena, MT: Greycliff Publishing Co.

Slim, Ray. (1992). *The Canoe Handbook*. Harrisburg, PA: Stackpole Books.

Solway, Kenneth (1998). *The Story of the Chestnut Canoe: 150 Years of Canadian Canoe Building*. Halifax, NS: Nimbus Publishing Co.

▦ Curling

Definition

Curling is a sport in which two teams of four players slide stones along a sheet of ice toward a "house," or circular target area within which all scoring takes place. Curling originated in Scotland, where it was the national pastime before immigrants brought the sport to North America, Europe, and New Zealand. By the early 20th century, the sport was being played by an estimated 1.5 million people in over 33 countries.

History

Though Scotland's climate is more temperate today, the region's winters were harsh five to six centuries ago when the sport was believed to have originated. Small flat stones known as *loofies* (Scottish for "palm of the hand") have been discover in drained lake and pond beds in Scotland that date from the early 1500s. The term "curling" is probably derived from the Scottish *curr*, which means "to make a low or hoarse murmuring sound." As the stone slides down the ice, it makes a similar rumbling sound. To "curl" may also refer to the path of the stone, which trails slightly to the left or right depending on the spin motion employed by the thrower.

By the mid- to late 16th century, the sport had either already made its way to Europe, or a similar game had been developed there, as Holland's Peter Breughel's painting, *Hunters in the Snow* (1565), depicts scenes that resemble curling. Throughout the 17th and 18th centuries, the sport was played throughout Scotland with varying rules that reflected local and regional differences. Formalized, uniform rules were not enacted until the mid-1850s and were brought about by two important technological changes. Improved modes of transportation, namely, the steam train and the stagecoach, shortened the distance between localities, making interregional play more common. The mass production of sporting goods led to the standardized sizing of equipment, meaning that all curling players soon used the same size stone. With the formation of the Grand Caledonia Curling Club in 1838, the sport created a national governing body. Five years later, in 1843, the club received royal patronage, further legitimizing its charge.

From the late 18th century through the 19th century, Scottish soldiers and emigrants spread curling throughout the world so that by the 1900s the sport had a presence in England, Sweden, New Zealand, Switzerland, Norway, Italy, France, Russia, the United States, and Canada. In the prairie regions of Canada the sport became especially popular, as starting in the 1870s thousands of Scottish settlers carved out homestead farms in the provinces of Manitoba, Saskatchewan, and Alberta. In Canada, the climate was ideal for curling, as was the seasonal nature of the economy. Farmers worked extremely hard in the spring, summer, and early fall. In the winter, they had plenty of time to devote to curling. Across the border, in the Dakotas, Wisconsin, Minnesota, and throughout the Great Lakes region, curling took hold. Today, there are over 135 clubs with over 15,000 curlers in the United States. The largest club in America is based in St. Paul, Minnesota, and has over 700 members. The World Curling Federation was founded in 1966 and contests a world championship each year. Curling became a Winter Olympic sport for both men and women in 1998.

Equipment

As discussed earlier, curling stones today are standard, made of granite rock, disk-shaped with a handle attached to the top. Weighing 42 pounds, the rock has a concave bottom (curving inward) which places only the rim of the stone in contact with the ice.

Today curlers wear special shoes, which allow them to slide on the ice without losing their footing. One shoe has a rubber sole to grip the ice; the other shoe has a slippery, low-friction substance like Teflon on the outsole. Curlers also use brooms to sweep the ice in front of the stone. Sweeping the ice reduces friction, thereby allowing the stone to slide farther. In earlier times, it was probably necessary to sweep the ice to remove foreign objects like sticks, branches, pebbles, and bits of snow and ice. Today, most curlers use long-handled brushes made of hog or horse hair or nylon rather than brooms, as the former are much more efficient than fiber-bristled brooms.

The curler throws the stone by crouching down, placing the right hand on the stone and the left hand on the broom for balance. Swinging the stone forward, the curler pushes off with the right leg and then shifts his or her weight to the left leg, which is under the center of the body directly behind the stone. With the right leg extended behind the body the curler slides down the ice, extending the right arm and releasing the stone. The stone is released with a slight turn to the left or right which makes it curve, or curl, as it approaches its target.

Rules

Most curling today is done indoors on ice rinks. Clubs that own their own rink typically maintain six to ten playing areas. A sheet of curling ice

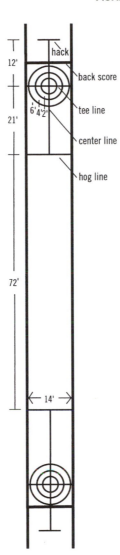

Figure 28. Curling sheet of ice.

is 146 feet long and 14 feet wide (see illustration). Embedded in the ice 4 feet from the end of the sheet is a foothold known as a *hack*. Each end of the sheet also has a circle 12 feet in diameter known as the *house*. The house has three concentric rings, each marked with different colors which denote levels of scoring. A *tee* marks the center of the rings. A line called the *hog line*, located 33 feet down the ice from the hack, indicates how far a player can glide before he or she must release the stone. Once released, the stone must pass beyond the hog line (72 feet) on the other end of the ice to remain in play.

A curling game consists of ten periods, called ends. During an end, each player on each side slides two stones from one end to the other. In general, players either aim their stones close to the tee, or attempt to knock the opposing team's stones away from the tee. The object of the game is to complete each end with as many stones as possible closer to the tee than any of the opponent's stones. Stones must rest inside the house to count. Only one team can score in each end, and one point is awarded for each stone that is closer to the tee than the other team's nearest stone.

Success in curling depends upon strategy and the mastery of a variety of shots which are warranted by various circumstances. Though curling originated in Scotland, almost all the techniques and strategy used today were developed by Canadians in the late 19th and early 20th centuries. The Canadian game has come to be defined by *hits*, or throws which are aimed at moving an opponent's stone, rather than *draws*, which are simply throws that come to rest on their own. Some of the most common curling shots include:

Draw shot: a shot that comes to rest on its own.

Takeout: a shot which knocks an opponent's stone out of play.

Come-around draw: a shot that curls around behind another stone. This protects the stone from being displaced by a subsequent shot.

Freeze: a shot that comes to rest in front of and touching an opponent's stone. If the opponent's stone is behind the tee, this shot makes it difficult for the opposing team to displace it without knocking its own stone out of contention.

Bibliography

Lukowich, Ed, Eigil Ramsfjell, and Bud Sumerville. (1990). *The Joy of Curling: A Celebration*. Toronto: McGraw-Hill.

USA Curling Association. (2001). "The History of Curling." USA Curling Association Web site, *www.usacurl.org/history* (March 10, 2001).

Worth, Sylvia (ed.). (1990). *The Rules of the Game*. New York: St. Martin's Press.

▦ Ice Hockey

Definition

Ice hockey is a fast-paced winter sport played on an enclosed rink between two teams of six players. Participants wear ice skates and use a long stick with a curved thin blade to propel a hard rubber disk, or puck, up and down the ice. The object of the game is to shoot the puck past the opposing goalkeeper into the goal for a score and to prevent the opposing team from scoring. Though ice hockey is believed to have European and Native American beginnings, the modern game developed in Canada during the late 19th century, where it has been regarded for close to a century as the national sport. Today, hockey is played in about 40 countries, principally in North America, Europe, and western and central Asia.

History

The exact origins of ice hockey are unknown, though the sport clearly has its roots in a number of stick-and-ball games that were popular in lands far from North America. Ancient carvings depict Greeks playing a hockey-like game as early as 500 B.C. At about the same time in Ireland the game of hurling, a sport similar to hockey, was being played (*see* Hurling). There is evidence that various games similar to hockey were played throughout the Middle Ages in Europe. A game called bandy was played on ice with a round ball and curved stick (*see* Bandy). A golf-like game on ice known as *kolven* was also popular in Holland during the 16th and 17th centuries.

In North America, the Native American sport of lacrosse was probably also a precursor of ice hockey (*see* Lacrosse). A variation of lacrosse, a fast-paced stick-and-ball game, was played during the winter on ice. French explorers who visited the St. Lawrence River Valley in the mid-18th century reported watching Iroquois Indians whacking a hard ball with sticks and reacting to misplaced blows by shouting "Ho-gee!," which meant, "It hurts!" More likely the name hockey is derived from the French word *ho-quet*, meaning a shepherd's crook or a bent stick.

There are also obvious similarities between field hockey and ice hockey (*see* Field Hockey). The Scottish game of shinty had also been imported to the United States in the early 1800s and was quite popular in the Northeast by century's end. In shinty, players attempted to control a ball or piece of wood with the ends of their sticks and then to evade defenders and shoot the object between stones set four or five feet apart.

An article in a London newspaper in 1862 confirms that "hockey on ice" was already played in England as early as the mid-19th century. Writing in defense of Victorian mores, the author produces what may be the first attack on ice hockey as a violent sport:

> Hockey ... ought to be forbidden, as it is not only annoying but dangerous. ... Any weak spot on the ice is sure to give way if the ball should happen to pass near or over it; for the concourse of fifty or a hundred personals all converging on the same point is a test which no ice, save the strongest is able to bear. ... It is more than annoying to have the graceful evolutions of a charming quadrille broken up by the interruptions of a disorderly mob, armed with sticks and charging through the circle of skaters and spectators to the imminent danger of all. I should be truly glad to see the police interfere whenever hockey is commenced.

While America and Europe played various primitive forms of hockey, Canada adopted the sport as its own, refining it to a game of strategy and teamwork. Legend has it that a group of soldiers known as the Royal Canadian Rifles developed the modern game in a series of contests on ice behind their barracks in 1855. Early games were disorganized and confusing, with as many as 30 players to a side. But the sport soon developed a uniform set of rules—first in 1879, when students at McGill University in Montreal wrote the first rulebook, and a short time later, when proponents of the game, calling themselves the Amateur Hockey Association of Canada, gathered in Montreal in 1885 to amend the rules and to adopt further guidelines for the game.

During the 1880s several amateur clubs and leagues were formed in Ontario and Quebec, and by the 1890s, men in colleges and athletic clubs all across Canada were playing hockey. The game had become so popular that in 1893 Frederick Arthur, Lord Stanley of Preston, Canada's Governor General, inaugurated the prized Stanley Cup, to be awarded annually to the national champion club. Valued at $48.50, Stanley's lavish Cup was initially awarded to the Montreal Amateur Athletic Association, which won the Amateur Hockey Association Championship in 1893. By 1895 there were more than 100 ice hockey teams in Montreal alone.

Though ice hockey was a favored pastime of college-aged men and young middle- and working-class athletic club members, its reputation as a national sport was founded on its widespread popularity among youth throughout the country. Canada's long, cold winter and abundance of frozen ponds provided ideal conditions for the development of the sport, as young boys by the thousands took to playing hockey in the late 1800s. For a nation whose society was still largely rural and agrarian, hockey provided an inexpensive form of exercise and entertainment. For pucks children would use pieces of wood or tin cans. Boards were built around the ice to keep the puck from getting lost in the snow, and wooden poles were bored into the ice to serve as goals. Sticks were quite often do-it-yourself models, and goaltenders wrapped their legs with newspapers to deaden the sting of the puck. Before skates were mass produced, many children would fasten or clamp steel blades to their work boots or street shoes.

Soon entrepreneurs in America and Canada realized that hockey could be a money-making venture. The boards surrounding the rink lent themselves to advertising, which at times was valued more than the revenue raised from admissions. While the first professional league was established in northern Michigan in 1904, it was short-lived, as were numerous pro leagues that came and went throughout the early 20th century. The National Hockey League (NHL), the highest level of professional hockey played in North America today, launched a four-team league in 1917–1918. Today, the NHL has teams in 30 U.S. and Canadian cities with players from over 20 countries.

Equipment

Though we are familiar with the concept of technology improving sports equipment and thereby enhancing an athlete's performance, we often fail to make a much more elemental connection between manufacturing capability, the mass production of sports equipment, and the rise in a sport's popularity. Canada in the latter half of the 19th century was undergoing an industrialization that had swept England and Western Europe in the late 18th and early 19th centuries. Hockey's rise in popularity in Canada mirrored the country's developing consumer goods industry. Therefore it comes as no surprise to learn that two of the most essential pieces of hockey equipment—sticks and pucks—were not manufactured in Canada until the 1880s, and that skates weren't produced in any quantity there until about the same time. Equipment manufacturers also began to produce leather leg pads and gloves for goaltenders, along with padded chest protectors. Prior to this time goalies had to be content with fielding gloves and the chest guards worn by American baseball players.

Though all players today wear much more protective gear than did earlier players, technology has made for lighter, stronger materials, which in turn has kept players and the game moving fast. Shoulder, hip, and thigh pads and shin, arm, and knee guards are standard equipment, as are helmets and heavily padded gloves. Goalies are of course the most protected players. Now all goalies wear face masks in addition to heavy leather leg pads and thick leg, chest, shoulder, and arm pads.

Like other sports, hockey has enacted several rules related to equipment to keep the sport competitive. Goalie gloves and leg padding are restricted in size and "must protect the goaltender, not the goal." A stick's size and material are also closely regulated. The curvature of a stick's blade is limited to one-half inch to lessen the curve of a shot.

Rules

Hockey is played on a rink which is 200 feet long and 85 feet wide, and surrounded by a wooden wall or fence known as the "boards" (see illustration). The boards extend not more than 48 inches above the ice surface. Goals measure 4 feet high and 6 feet wide and are placed at the center of a red line, 10 feet from each end of the rink.

A team consists of a goalkeeper, who usually plays directly in front of the goal to block shots by opponents, two defensemen, who pursue attacking players to disrupt their attack, and three forwards (a center and two wings) who are primarily offensive players. Players can only move the puck with their stick, though they are permitted to knock it down with their body or hands. "Checking" an opponent who has the puck or is about to have the puck is permitted, but players may not hold, trip, or charge an opposing player or use their stick to impede an opponent's

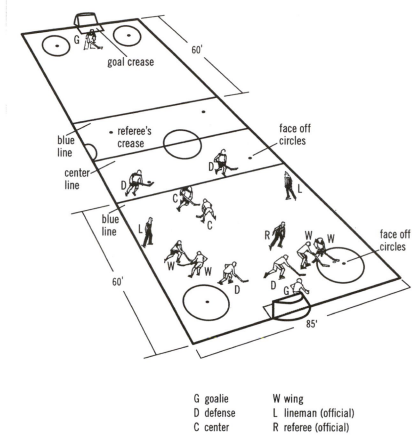

G goalie	W wing
D defense	L lineman (official)
C center	R referee (official)

Figure 29. Ice hockey rink, with an illustration of traditional offensive/defensive player alignments.

progress. For fouls such as charging, holding, high-sticking, and hooking, players are penalized by being sent off the ice for 2 to 5 minutes. In the interim, the team with a penalized player or players must play shorthanded.

Hockey is known as "the fastest game on ice" because play is continuous. A stoppage in play occurs only in the event of an infraction, foul, or time-out, or when the puck is unplayable. A team may substitute freely without stopping play, provided no more than six players are on the ice at any one time. The game is played in three 20-minute periods. Each period begins with a face-off at center ice. A face-off is also used to resume play after a goal is scored or after play has been stopped due to an infraction or penalty.

The ice is split into three parts: two blue lines, drawn 60 feet out from each goal line, demarcate defending and attacking zones. The space between the two blue lines is known as the neutral zone. The puck must precede each and every attacking player across an opponent's blue line—otherwise an attacking player or players are off-sides, play is suspended, and the puck is brought back to the neutral zone for a face-off.

Many of the rules that streamline play—uninterrupted substitutions, allowing goalies to sprawl on the ice to stop the puck, the introduction of the blue line and the concept of off-sides—were enacted by an innovative hockey family, the Patricks. Brothers Frank and Lester Patrick (the namesake of today's NHL Patrick Division), who were players, and father Joseph, an owner, headed west and organized the Pacific Coast Hockey Association in 1911. By making the game faster and more exciting, they were able to lure more fans and, in turn, pay higher salaries to players whom they coaxed away from eastern teams.

Bibliography

Dryden, Ken, and Roy MacGregor. (1989). *Home Game: Hockey and Life in Canada*. Toronto: McClelland and Stewart.

Ronberg, Gary. (1974). *The Hockey Encyclopedia*. New York: Macmillan.

Strachan, Al (ed). (1999). *One Hundred Years of Hockey*. Thunder Bay, Ontario: Thunder Bay Press.

▦ Lacrosse

Definition

Lacrosse is a game played on a rectangular field between two teams of 10 players using a ball and a long-handled netted stick, or *crosse*. The object of the game is to move the ball downfield by running with it in the crosse or by passing to a teammate. Goals are scored by sending the ball, using the crosse, into the opposing team's goal. Having originated among Native Americans of North America—perhaps as early as the 15th century—the game has been widely played in the United States since the late 19th century.

History

Lacrosse is believed to be the oldest sport in North America. Native Americans were playing a version of the sport at the time of the first European contact with the New World in the late 15th and early 16th centuries. Though Native Americans played a number of stick-and-ball games, lacrosse was unique because it used a netted stick or racquet, called a crosse, with which to handle the ball.

Lacrosse seems to have been confined to the eastern half of North America, played mostly by tribes in the Southeast, in the western Great Lakes, and in the St. Lawrence Valley area. The earliest accounts of the game date back to the 1630s and come from Jesuit missionaries, trappers, and French and English explorers. Legend has it that Jean de Brebeuf, a French missionary, likened the stick the Hurons used to a bishop's crosier, which resembled a shepherd's crook, or *crosse*. Eventually the term "la crosse" evolved to simply lacrosse. Yet *crosse* also translates as "bat," which is an apt description for a basic lacrosse technique. The Onondaga tribe referred to lacrosse as *dehuntshigwa'es*, meaning "men hit a rounded object." Lacrosse was also used as a war game by many tribes. In the Southeast, the Chippewa coined the term *baggattaway*, or "little brother of war," to describe a game that might be played by as many as several hundred braves.

Clearly lacrosse served important cultural functions for Native Americans. In addition to its warring undertones, lacrosse was also thought to have curative or medicinal powers. Stories abound of village or tribal leaders calling their young, able-bodied men together for a game of lacrosse upon the orders of the local shaman or sorcerer, who prescribed the game in the face of illness to preserve the health of the community. (Tribal shamans usually served as game officials.) Lacrosse was also used to vent frustrations between tribes, or to settle territorial disputes. A game between the Creek and the Choctaw in the late 1700s was held to settle rights over a beaver pond. Even though most of these games ended peaceably, the ceremony and ritual surrounding the players' preparations often mirrored the steps taken to ready a tribe for war. Monsieur de Sabrevois, a commandant of French Fort Pontchartrain (in modern-day Michigan/Great Lakes region) described a game played by the Potawatomi in 1719 where the players' "bodies are painted all over with all kinds of colors."

Early versions of lacrosse seem to have had few rules (see illustration). Differences in the game had more to do with equipment. Among southeastern tribes (e.g., Cherokee, Choctaw, Chippewa, Creek, and others), a double-stick version of lacrosse was played. A short 2½-foot-long stick was held in each hand, and a small deerskin ball was caught, held, and released between the two sticks. Aboriginal tribes from the Great Lakes (e.g., Potawatomi, Miami, Huron, Winnebago, and others) used a single 3-foot stick with a small wood pocket slightly larger than the wooden ball. The northeastern tribes (e.g., Iroquois, Onondagas, Mohawk, etc.) used much longer sticks, similar to modern-day equipment, with a flat triangular surface of webbing extending as much as two-thirds the length of the stick. Lacrosse balls ranged from hard wooden-core models which were wrapped in rawhide to larger leather sack-like bags stuffed with deer hair.

Distances between goals ranged from several hundred yards to two or three miles. Often, a large rock or tree was considered the goal and points were awarded for hitting the rock or tree with a ball. Though teams sometimes numbered a dozen to 20 players, there are accounts of mass games between teams of as many as 100 to 1,000 or more braves. Games lasted from sunrise to sunset and often stretched over the course of several days.

Figure 30. Native Americans playing a traditional game of lacrosse (© Bettmann/CORBIS).

Violence was part of lacrosse, and the players accepted it, as evidenced by the following account from Nicholas Peffot, an early 18th-century fur trader in the Great Lakes region:

> If a player keeps the ball between his feet and is unwilling to let go, he must guard against the blows his adversaries continually aim at his feet...legs and arms are sometimes broken, and it has happened that a player has been killed. It is quite common to see someone crippled for the rest of his life.... When these accidents happen, the unlucky victim quickly withdraws from the game, if he is in a condition to do so, but if his injury will not permit this, his relatives carry him home, and the game goes on till it is finished, as if nothing had occurred.

Clearly, lacrosse was strictly a man's game, though less rough versions of the game, such as shinny and double-ball, were played by women.

There is no evidence of non–Native Americans playing lacrosse until the mid-19th century, when English-speaking Montrealers adopted a version of the Mohawk game played by the local Caughnawauga and Akwesasne. W. George Beers, a Montreal dentist, is often referred to as "the father of lacrosse" for popularizing the sport among Canadians. In 1856 the Montreal Lacrosse Club was formed and a set of "civilized" rules was created. The number of players, size of the field, and dimensions of the goal were all standardized. Soon, lacrosse was played by thousands of amateurs in clubs throughout Montreal, Ottawa, and Toronto. Before the rise of ice hockey around the turn of the century, lacrosse was considered Canada's national pastime. So it is fitting that the Canadian National Lacrosse Association was established in 1867—the same year the Dominion of Canada itself was created. By the 1880s, the game had spread to the British Commonwealth countries of Australia and New Zealand and to the United States, where it became quite popular in northeastern colleges, universities, and public and private high schools. Today the game is played by both men and women in the United States at over 500 colleges and universities and by more than 1,500 high schools nationwide.

Ironically, the Native American game nearly died out between the late 19th and early 20th centuries. Though betting on games had always been a part of the Native Americans' interest and involvement in lacrosse, gambling, violence, and widespread cheating increased as traditional Indian culture was eroded by modernization and political disenfranchisement. Government officials and the religious community in Canada and America opposed the game for its "impoverishing effect" on Native Americans. In some native areas lacrosse was banned. Yet the game has made a resurgence among Native Americans in the last 20 to 30 years. Today, the game is played by the southeastern and northern Iroquois tribes, the latter fielding a world-class lacrosse team that encourages greater understanding of Iroquois culture through international competition.

Equipment

Lacrosse sticks and balls are a far cry from the man-made equipment of the 18th century. The crosse measures 40–72 inches long, with an aluminum, wood, or graphite shaft and plastic molding around the cupped "basket" at the end. The basket is usually strung with rawhide, gut, or nylon string. The lacrosse ball is made of hard "Indian" rubber and measures about 8 inches in circumference and weighs about 5 ounces.

Though not as violent as the original game, modern lacrosse is still rough, and participants require significant padding. Players typically wear helmets with face guards, shin guards, and light shoulder, knee, and arm pads. Padded gloves are worn similar to those used in ice hockey. Athletic shoes are generally the same as those worn in football: molded cleats of natural surfaces and rubber "turf" shoes for artificial grass. Uniforms consist of a mesh jersey and large, tightly woven nylon shorts.

Rules

Though all field dimensions vary slightly, most lacrosse fields are about 60 yards wide and 110 yards long, including 15 yards of open space behind each goal. Goals measure 6 feet by 6 feet and are positioned at each end of the field.

Games consist of two 30-minute periods. Each goal counts one point; the team with the most points wins the game.

Teams include a goalkeeper, three attackers, three midfielders, and three defensemen. The goalkeeper is permitted to deflect the ball with his hands, but otherwise the hands may not be used. A ball may only be picked up and passed with a stick. Checking is permitted, and players may strike an opponent's stick in an attempt to dislodge the ball. Striking an opponent with a stick or pushing, tripping, or holding an opponent is considered a foul. Players are assessed penalties of between 1 and 3 minutes, during which the offending team must play short-handed.

The ball is in play everywhere, and play is continuous except for penalty calls or when the ball is thrown or carried out of bounds. When the ball goes out of play, a player on the opposing team receives a "free throw." The ball is placed in his crosse and play is resumed.

There are several variations to traditional field lacrosse. Box lacrosse, also known as boxla, is an indoor game played on hockey rinks during the off-season, when the floor is covered with artificial turf. Teams consist of six players, and the game, in general, is much more physical, with more body contact and checking permitted. Today there are professional box lacrosse leagues in both the United States and Canada.

Women's lacrosse has become an increasingly popular game in the United States, particularly with the institution of Title IX of the Educational Amendments of 1972. The women's game is played under the same basic rules as the men's game except for the following key differences:

Women field 12 players instead of 10.

The women's game is shortened to two 25-minute halves.

No physical contact is permitted, and therefore women wear less protective gear.

No time penalties are assessed for fouls in the women's game. Instead, fouls result in the granting of a "free position" to an opposing player. Defenders must be 3 yards behind a player with a free position. This player may either attempt a shot on goal or pass off to a teammate.

Today, women's lacrosse is played at over 100 colleges and universities and more than 200 high schools nationwide.

Bibliography

Massie, Larry B. (1997). "Lacrosse: Michigan's First Team." *Michigan History Magazine* (September/October).

"More History of Lacrosse." (2001). LAXHISTORY.COM Web site, *www.laxhistory.com* (January 16, 2001).

Scott, Bob. (1976). *Lacrosse: Technique and Tradition*. Baltimore: Johns Hopkins University Press.

Vennum, Thomas Jr. (1994). *American Indian Lacrosse: Little Brother of War*. Washington, DC: Smithsonian Press.

▦ Powwow

Definition

Webster's dictionary defines *powwow* as "a social get-together" or "a meeting for discussion." Historically the term refers to the Native American tradition of a gathering of tribes at various times of the year to hunt, plant, harvest, and celebrate special occasions. Contemporary powwows have no tribal boundaries. Native Americans gather throughout North America to celebrate indigenous culture through such forms as song, dance, storytelling, native arts and crafts, games, and sporting competitions.

History

The term "powwow" came from the Algonkian-speaking Narragansett Indians from the region that is today the northeastern United States. The word originally had both collective and spiritual overtones, as it referred, not to a celebration, but to a shaman or teacher, a dream or vision, or a council or gathering. When English settlers met with Native American leaders, they would "powwow together," or one might visit a "powwow" to receive guidance or to overcome sickness. Today's powwows seem to trace their roots back to the Native Americans of the Great Plains in the early to mid-19th century, who came together periodically to renew family, clan, and tribal ties, forge political alliances, celebrate victories, and practice spiritual ceremonies. Marriages were often planned or agreed upon at powwows. Most powwows involved music and dance, and many held games and athletic competitions for young and old alike.

Powwows' significance to Native Americans was underscored by the Canadian and United States governments, which acted to suppress traditional Native American cultural practices in the late 1800s. In an attempt to erase the pride and spirit Native Americans felt for themselves, such ceremonies as the Potlatch (a ceremonial tribal feast) and the Sun Dance (a communal celebration centered around the solstice) were banned. As a result, powwows nearly died out. They weren't popular again until the mid-1940s, when communities began staging celebrations to honor the Native American veterans who returned to their reservations after World War II. Powwows continued to grow in popularity through the time of the 1960s civil rights movement in America, when more and more Native Americans began to discover anew their cultural heritage.

Contemporary Powwows

Native Americans stage over 100 powwows annually in North America. These events are held both on reservations and in urban areas. Some powwows are traditional, with dancing, games, and competitions staged for fun. Others conduct large competitions—most commonly dancing, but also rodeos, horse racing, and running events—and offer large cash prizes. Though powwows are usually held over a weekend, some last as long as a week.

A typical powwow might include the following:

Competitions and games like Native-style horse racing, lacrosse, stick ball, sprinting and cross-country running, and bow and arrow contests;

Storytellers who share Native American myths and legends with young and old alike;

Exhibits and seminars on stitching, weaving, tanning, and beadwork;

Carnival rides, clowns, and other games and amusements for children;

Rodeos featuring Native American cowboys;

Traditional dancing and singing for men and women.

Dance is central to most powwows. Contestants dress in colorful outfits that vary depending on the type of dance and the nation from which they originated. There are dozens of different dances, with names like Northern Traditional, Southern Traditional, Southern Straight, Grass, Fancy Shawl, Jingle, and so forth. Regalia for two of the most famous dances are described as follows:

Men's Northern Traditional: The dancer wears a bustle, often made of eagle feathers, a bone-bead breastplate, leggings, beaded moccasins, a beaded belt, ankle bells, a porcupine roach headdress, a breechcloth, and various beaded accessories, and carries an eagle feather fan. These dancers often paint their faces in accordance with the sign or symbol of their family or nation.

Women's Fancy Shawl: The dancer symbolizes the transition of a cocoon to a butterfly. A calf-length skirt is worn with a beaded or sequined cape or vest, and matching leggings and moccasins. The shawl is worn over the shoulders and spread out at the elbows. Much of the dance is improvisational, with dancers employing spins and freestyle footwork to express themselves.

Bibliography

Oxendine, Joseph. (1988). *American Indian Sports Heritage*. Champaign, IL: Human Kinetics.

White, Julia C. (1996). *The Pow Wow Trail*. Summerton, TN: Book Publishing Co.

Willard, Helen. (1990). *Pow Wow and Other Yakima Indian Traditions*. Prosser, WA: Roza Run Publishing Co.

▦ Sled Dog Racing

Definition

Sled dog racing is a sport in which teams of harnessed dogs compete. The team is driven by a "musher," who also cares for and trains the dogs year round. Today, the world's most famous sled dog race, Alaska's annual Iditarod, a supreme test of strength and endurance, covers some 1,100 miles from Anchorage across the Alaska Range to Nome on the Bering Sea.

History

Humans have used sled dogs to perform work for several thousand years. Anthropologists claim that human inhabitation of the Arctic regions of Siberia and North America would not have been possible without the assistance of domesticated dogs. Eskimos used dog sleds for hunting, travel, and recreation. According to the earliest Spanish explorers, Native Americans living in what is today the American Southwest and Mexico also used dogs as draft animals to pull carts. These cultures found dogs to be highly trainable, loyal, and reliable—all characteristics of what is considered to be a good dog today, and, not surprisingly, key traits for competitive sled dogs as well.

Though sled dog racing has probably existed for almost as long as humans and dogs have forged a working relationship in the Arctic, the first recorded sled dog races did not occur until the mid-19th century. Legend has it that travelers en route from Winnipeg to St. Paul, Minnesota, pitted their teams in an informal challenge race. A short while later, in 1886, the first St. Paul Winter Carnival featured sled dog races. By the turn of the century, the sport of racing teams of sled dogs over long courses was gaining popularity, particularly in Alaska, which had undergone rapid economic and social change as a result of the northern Gold Rush. Large settlements had sprung up overnight, and the adventuresome element in society—folks who were drawn to a harsh, distant land by the promise of riches—was probably greater in Alaska at the time than in almost any other area in North America. Thus it was fitting that Alaska play host to the first major sled dog races to receive worldwide attention—the All-Alaska Sweepstakes, which began as an annual competition in 1909. The event was a challenging round-trip race of some 400 miles between Candle and Nome. Many of the first mushers were either prospectors or suppliers or outfitters connected to the Gold Rush, and most of the sled dogs who took part in these early events were work animals, who freighted supplies into the remote mining camps.

When these prospectors returned to their hometowns in Canada, New England, and the northern Midwest, they brought sled dog racing with them. By the 1920s businesses in the Northeast were sponsoring professional mushers, who took their teams on the road to compete in a series of races that stretched from Maine to as far west as Idaho. In 1936 the Laconia, New Hampshire, Sled Dog Club organized the first World Championships. But sled dog racing waned between the 1940s and the 1960s, first as a result of World War II and then because snowmobiles and airplanes largely eliminated the need for sled dogs as transportation.

It wasn't until the 1970s and 1980s that the sport made a comeback. The International Sled Dog Racing Association (ISDRA), which was formed in 1966, began to develop and promote a series of races. Though the Open North American Championships and the Anchorage Fur Rondy became popular sprint events in the 1970s, the tradition of sled dog racing was essentially defined and preserved by one race, the Iditarod. Founded in 1973, the Iditarod has become known as "The Last Great Race on Earth," where humans and dogs test their mettle against the bitter Arctic cold and harsh, unforgiving wilderness terrain. Hundreds of teams compete in the race, which begins in downtown Anchorage, crosses the Alaska Range, and heads west along the Yukon River and up and around the Bering Sea coast to Nome—a total of 1,100 miles, which the leaders routinely cover in about 11 days.

While the Iditarod has gained worldwide fame, the event was inspired by a courageous real-life story that made global headline news when a diphtheria outbreak struck Nome in January 1925. Hundreds of inhabitants were seriously ill and could not be reached by air or road due to severe winter weather. With the nearest serum close to 1,000 miles away in Anchorage, health officials had to ferry medicine some 250 miles north to Nenana via railway, where volunteer dogsled drivers heroically took up the cause, carrying the serum the remaining 674 miles nonstop to Nome.

Today, several different forms of sled dog racing have gained prominence throughout the world, notably the sport of *pulka* in Scandinavia, where drivers accompany their dogs on skis. In 1992 the International Federation of Sled Dog Sports was created to focus the efforts of many regional, national, and international organizations on the goal of attaining Olympic recognition for the sport. Sled dog racing has appeared as a demonstration sport at the Oslo (1952) and Lake Placid (1980) Games.

Equipment

Sled dog racing equipment has, in general, grown more specialized. Sleds are extremely light, essentially made of aluminum, graphite, or composite framing, and are equipped with a basket and dog bag which is capable of safely carrying a dog that becomes injured or ill. In early races, dogs were aligned in a trapline tandem hitch, with a leather horse collar harness around each. Today, all mushers employ the Alaskan gangline, with dogs harnessed in pairs. Harnesses are made of light synthetic webbing.

Transportation to race sites is also a major concern, as most mushers and their teams need to drive hundreds of miles to get to an event. In the late 19th and early 20th centuries, competitors would need to drive their teams to a race. At times they would need to leave as much as a week in advance to make it to the starting line on race day. In modern times, dog trucks—typically a pickup truck and trailer—are equipped to carry individual dog boxes, small well-ventilated crates that keep dogs warm, dry, and comfortable.

Rules

The ISDRA sanctions a series of races which must all comply with rules and regulations regarding trail length and layout as well as mandatory safety equipment and canine fitness. Physical abuse of dogs is strictly prohibited, and such rules are sternly enforced; those convicted of animal abuse or neglect are barred from racing. A veterinarian is on call at all races to respond to emergencies and to prevent the spread of disease. The use of any substance that may affect a dog's performance (like steroids that enhance recovery, or drugs that mask pain) is prohibited. Dogs are periodically tested for performance-enhancing drugs like steroids, the presence of which will result in the disqualification of the driver and the dog. Choke collars, muzzles, and other similarly restrictive equipment that may harm a dog are also prohibited.

Training

Successful mushers need to have a vast array of knowledge and skill related to raising, caring for, and training dogs. Sled dogs are not only raised as puppies to race, but also, starting at around six months, they are socialized to run and work together as a team. Most sled dog teams number seven or nine dogs, with the dogs working in pairs behind a leader or lead dog. The driver must study his team, learning each dog's character, strengths, and weaknesses. By the time they are yearlings, sled dogs have usually been paired with a partner that they'll run beside throughout their entire careers.

The training cycle begins in the fall, when the weather is cool enough for dry land training. Dogs usually pull a cart or four-wheeler, the goal being to build up aerobic conditioning and muscle strength and to learn to run as a team. Young dogs must learn how to ignore distractions and respond to commands. As the weather turns cooler, the dog's fitness progresses and they are able to do longer, harder workouts. Snow cushions a dog's feet, and the colder weather helps regulate a dog's body temperature.

Bibliography

Cabelas Staff. (2000). "History of the Iditarod." Cabelas Iditarod Web site, *www.cabelaiditarod.com/history.html* (January 22, 2001).

International Federation of Sleddog Sports. (2000). "Mushing: A Brief History of the Sport." Cabela's Iditarod Web site, *www.cabelaiditarod.com/history.html* (January 22, 2001).

International Sleddog Racing Association. (2000). "An Introduction to Sleddog Racing." International Sleddog Racing Association Web site, *www.isdra.org/* (January 22, 2001).

▦ Softball

Definition

Softball is a game similar to baseball that is played on a smaller field using a larger ball which is pitched to the batter underhand. Though softball was created in the late 19th century as an indoor game, it soon moved outdoors. Several versions of softball are played today in the United States, where the game is extremely popular on scholastic and intercollegiate levels for women, and as both a competitive and recreation sport for men and women.

History

Softball's origins are very much like baseball's, rooted in the English game of rounders and the American folk sport of town ball (*see* Baseball). Softball was originally played indoors; the first game took place in the gymnasium at Chicago's Farraguat Boat Club on Thanksgiving Day in 1887. A group of young men were reportedly awaiting the results of the Harvard-Yale football game when an impromptu pick-up game of softball ensued. The sport, which used a larger, softer ball to deaden its liveliness, soon caught on all over Chicago, as it filled both a void in the sports calendar and was a more enjoyable alternative to the dry exercises and calisthenics that many athletes pushed themselves to do over the winter.

George Hancock, a member of the Farraguat Boat Club, moved the game outdoors in the spring of 1888, calling it "indoor-outdoor" and adapting the game to a smaller diamond. Hancock published the first set of rules in 1889, and the sport continued to grow, particularly in the northern Midwest. Lewis Rober, a lieutenant in the Minneapolis Fire Department, is generally credited with popularizing the game among working men. Rober, who used softball to keep his men in shape between emergency calls, made several changes to Hancock's rules, calling this adaptation to the game "kitten ball" or "kitten ball league." (Rober organized several leagues throughout the Minneapolis area.)

Though softball was originally an elite club sport, it quickly became a game that was played by people of all ages and socioeconomic classes. Perhaps this is because much of the competitive game has for many years been organized around the workplace. Businesses, manufacturers, municipal employers—all recognized the value of sponsoring teams of working men and women who would represent them in regular league and tournament competition. Softball also became a popular sport for schoolchildren, as it could be played on a smaller field, equipment was cheap, and in general the sport was safer than baseball. (In earlier days, balls were so soft that, in most cases, players didn't use gloves.)

The sport also accompanied the rise of municipal government in the United States, as villages, towns, and cities were created to deliver basic services to local populations. One such municipal service, or amenity, was recreation. Many American towns around the turn of the century developed parks with beaches or pools, picnic areas, and playing fields—all suitable for a weekend family outing. Softball grew to be an extremely popular park or playground game. In fact, the game came to be known as "playground ball" in the early 20th century when in 1908 the National Amateur Playground Association of America issued a rulebook on softball.

The term "softball" really wasn't used until the 1920s, when the YMCA began touting the sport as a game for all ages. While the YMCA can be credited with popularizing softball in the Northeast, the game got a tremendous boost nationally when Leo Fischer, a sportswriter for the *Chicago Tribune*, and M. J. Pauley, a sporting goods retailer, promoted a softball tournament at the World's Fair in Chicago in 1933. Sixteen men's and eight women's teams from 16 different U.S. states competed in the event, which was attended by over 350,000 spectators—a significant number for a tourney staged in the depths of the Great Depression. Fischer and Pauley capitalized on this success by forming the Amateur Softball Association (ASA), which, in turn, created the Joint Rules Committee on Softball (JRCOS) in 1934. JRCOS not only standardized the game with its rules, but also legitimized softball and strengthened its popularity by issuing separate guidelines for fast pitch, slow pitch, and women's play.

Though the game's rules have changed many times over the past century (see following page), its popularity has continued to grow, both in the United States and internationally. By the close of the 20th century, softball was being played in nearly 100 countries under the direction of the International Softball Federation (ISF), the sport's worldwide governing body. Softball is now a women's medal sport in the Summer Olympics; the United States won the gold in Sydney in 2000. In the United States, more than 650 National Collegiate Athletic Association (NCAA) universities and colleges sponsor women's softball programs, and annual championship tournaments are held on Division I, II, and III levels. The game is also extremely popular among men and women all across America—an estimated 25 million people, or about 1 of every 5 or 6 adults in the country, have at one time played the game on a regular basis.

Equipment

Today's game has many variations—fast pitch, slow pitch, modified, and so on (see following page)—and the equipment reflects this diversity.

The softball, which generally measures 11 inches in circumference, may be made of kapok (tightly woven fiber strands), a mixture of cork and rubber, a polyurethane composite, or other combinations of cork and fiber-like material. A larger ball measuring 16 inches in circumference has been used for play by both the very old and very young. This variation is known as "monster ball."

The bat used in softball may measure no more than 34 inches in length, nor weigh more than 38 ounces. Most players use bats made of aluminum, which last longer than wooden bats and hit the ball farther. Softball uniforms and footwear are generally the same as those worn by baseball players, although softball players wear plastic rather than metal cleats.

Rules

Softball played at the turn of the century was very different than today's game, as the 1908 National Amateur Playground Association rules show:

The first batter to get a hit in an inning could run either to first or third base; the batters who followed had to run in the same direction.

Teams could choose whether they wanted to play five, seven, or nine innings.

Points rather than runs were counted, with a point scored every time a runner reached a base.

Bases were just 35 feet apart, and the pitcher's mound was a mere 30 feet from home plate.

Just three balls were needed for a base on balls.

In general, the rules of softball have changed fairly often, usually from a desire to make the game more exciting. While we tend to differentiate softball from baseball by the larger ball and the pitcher's delivery (which is always underhand in softball), there are actually three different kinds of softball, all with their own rules:

Slow-pitch Softball: This is the most popular form of recreational softball, played by millions of men and women throughout the country. The distance between the bases is 65 feet, while the distance from the pitcher's mound to home plate is 50 feet. Pitchers are allowed to deliver the ball in an arc that may reach as high as 12 feet, and must exceed 6 feet. Though the game is based on a lot of hitting and scoring, batters must get used to timing their stroke to a slower pitch and swinging with either a slight or pronounced upper cut, depending on whether they want to hit a towering fly or a line drive. To counter the advantage enjoyed by the offense in slow-pitch, batters are not allowed to bunt, runners can't steal bases, and teams field 10 rather than 9 positions.

Modified-pitch Softball: This game is played on a smaller field—bases are 60 feet apart and the distance from the pitcher's mound to home plate is 46 feet—and isn't as high scoring as slow-pitch. Though pitchers don't need to follow an arc in delivering the ball to home, they are not allowed to begin their windup at a point higher than their waist. As a result, pitching is fast, but pitchers are limited regarding the amount of movement and deception they can create in a short windup. Modified-pitch men's leagues are popular in the Northeast and Midwest. Women also play the game.

Fast-pitch Softball: This form is extremely popular, played by millions of interscholastic and collegiate women around the country. While the base paths in fast-pitch are the same as in modified, pitchers are allowed to take a windmill windup, and the distance from the mound to home plate is just 40 feet. Therefore, fast-pitch is very much a game of pitching and defense, with the ability of the pitcher often making the difference in whether a team wins most of its games or loses most of them. Batters are allowed to bunt and base runners can steal any base (as they can in modified-pitch), leading to another dimension of excitement.

Bibliography

Leonardt, Cheryl. (1998). *Official Rules of Softball 1998: USA Softball*. Chicago: Triumph Books.
Plumber, Bill. (1998). "The Origins of Softball." Steve Dimitry's Slow Pitch Softball History page, *www.angelfire.com/sd/slopitch* (February 9, 2001).

▦ Volleyball

Definition

Volleyball is a game played on a rectangular court between two teams of six players. An inflated ball is volleyed back and forth across a high net, as each team attempts to ground the ball on the opponent's court, while preventing the ball from being grounded on its own court. Today, volleyball enjoys global popularity, where it ranks behind only soccer among participation sports.

History

Volleyball's origins and development mirror basketball's. William G. Morgan invented the game in 1895. Morgan, an instructor at the YMCA in Holyoke, Massachusetts, created volleyball as an indoor game that could augment the spare regimen of gymnastic exercises that constituted late 19th-century physical education in America (*see* Gymnastics). Volleyball was to be accessible to the average YMCA client, many of whom were middle-aged, unathletic businessmen and professionals. Thus the sport, in its earliest form, was a slow game, where participants batted a large oversized ball back and forth over the top of a net that was set just 6½ feet above the floor. Originally the game was called "mintonette," because a badminton net was used. But the term "volleyball," indicative of the game's principal action, was coined in 1897 when Morgan wrote volleyball's first set of rules for the YMCA handbook.

With a network of YMCA gymnasiums across the United States and in an increasing number of cities worldwide, volleyball quickly spread. By 1915 the game had been introduced to Canada, South America, India, China, Japan, and the Philippines. During World War I, YMCA instructors were inducted into the army as physical education teachers. In 1919 the American Expeditionary Forces distributed 16,000 volleyballs to its troops and allies, and soon the game was being played throughout Europe. During the 1920s hundreds of clubs were formed in France, and in 1931 Paris hosted the first international volleyball championships. The sport grew popular in the Soviet Union as well. The International Volleyball Federation was founded in 1947 in France and consisted largely of France, the Soviet Union, and a number of Eastern bloc nations.

The United States, which had founded its own national organization in 1937, did not promote volleyball at the highest levels of competition. During the 1940s and 1950s, participation in the American collegiate game was sparse. This didn't change until the 1960s, when volleyball was introduced as an Olympic sport at the 1964 Games in Tokyo and the National Collegiate Athletic Association (NCCA) sanctioned volleyball as a competitive Division I sport in 1969. Modern international competition has been dominated by the Russian, Czech, Polish, Japanese, Chinese, and American teams.

Equipment

The standard volleyball uniform consists of shorts, T-shirt, knee and elbow pads, and court shoes. Today's volleyballs are about half the size of the original game's monsters. Now a ball weighs between 9 and 10 ounces and is inflated to about 6 pounds of pressure. A modern net is much sturdier than the badminton nets used in the original game. The net is also strung much higher—7 feet, 11⅛ inches for men and 7 feet, 4⅛ inches for women.

Rules

The court measures 29 feet, 6 inches wide by 59 feet long. Players on each team are aligned in two rows of three facing the net. Play begins by one team serving the ball to the other team, with each team thereafter allowed to hit the ball three times before it must cross the net. The first two hits are usually used to set up a teammate, who may attempt to "spike" the ball, or drive it downward into the opposing team's court. Players in the Philippines in the early 20th century are generally credited with developing the set and spike maneuver, where the ball is passed in a high trajectory to be spiked by a player in the front line. The Filipinos call this hit a "bomba" or "kill," and refer to the hitter as a "bomberino."

Points are scored only by the serving side; if the serving side fails to make a good return, the service passes to the other side. A single player serves during a team's turn; when the team regains service, all players move clockwise to the station to their right so that each player may have an opportunity to serve during a game. But players are required to stay in position only until the ball is served. The modern practice at higher levels of competition is to have spiking and set-up specialists change places on the court as soon as the ball is served.

The game is played until one team scores 15 points and has at least a 2-point advantage over the other.

Two-person beach volleyball emerged during the 1980s and 1990s as a popular form of recreation for many and as a professional sport for an elite few, who have corporate sponsorship and compete on a pro circuit. Men's and women's beach volleyball became an Olympic sport in 1996.

Bibliography

Federation Internationale de Volleyball. (2000). *Official Volleyball Rules (2001–2004)*. Paris: Federation Internationale de Volleyball.

"The History of Volleyball." (2000). Volleyball World Wide Web Site, *www.volley ball.org/* (December 22, 2000).

▦ OCEANIA

HISTORICAL OVERVIEW

Oceania is the region in the South Pacific that includes Australia, New Zealand, and the islands throughout Polynesia, Micronesia, and Melanesia. During the 18th and 19th centuries, people indigenous to these areas clashed with Western cultural institutions. Though the Dutch had preceded the British to Australia, it was England that aggressively settled the continent, first using it as a penal colony in the late 18th century, then granting land to soldiers and settlers as a British "frontier" of sorts. By the early to mid-19th century, the Aboriginal culture that had existed there for thousands of years had been either pushed to the continent's desert-like interior or effectively destroyed by contact with settlers. A similar pattern occurred with the Maori in New Zealand. British explorers also "discovered" many of the South Pacific islands during the late 18th century. British, European, and later American (in Hawaii) business interests soon established a presence on these islands, accompanied by Christian missionaries, who considered it their moral duty to break the native population of its heathenish ways and to convert the masses to Christianity. As a result, many traditional cultural practices, including sports and games, were banned. It has only been since the mid- to late 20th century that traditional folk culture in Oceania has begun to be revived by a concerted, organized effort.

THE LEGACY OF 18TH- AND 19TH-CENTURY SPORTS AND GAMES

Some of the region's oldest sports are utilitarian in nature. Swimming, diving, canoeing, and boating are activities that have been engaged in by native peoples since ancient times, with the organized, competitive aspects of these sports only relevant for about the past century. Other sports engaged in purely for fun—for example, the Polynesians did surfing and dry land sledding (*holua*), and natives of the Melanesian Islands engaged in a land diving activity similar to bungee jumping—were usually forbidden by European and American missionaries, whose strict Protestant work ethic led them to label many of these traditional sports and games as immoral. As a result, **surfing** nearly died out during the 19th century, along with many **traditional Polynesian sports and games** discussed in this chapter.

Traditional Aboriginal sports and games were also discouraged by British settlers in Australia, though, in this case, many of these popular folk sports and games were preserved when Aboriginal peoples moved to the isolated interior. One factor in whether or not a sport is preserved is how often it is used and for what purpose. Many Aboriginal sports and games are related to skills inherent in hunting. Though the Aboriginal culture became marginalized and isolated, fragments of it continued to function as a hunter-gather society, and thus many traditional sports and games were preserved. **Boomerang throwing,** though not directly related to hunting, is an offshoot of similar "throwing woods" with which Aboriginals used to hunt. Many boomerangs were also adorned with scenes related to native spiritual concepts, and their popularity was augmented by their practicality—many doubled as digging implements or as musical instruments.

Because of the pervasive influence of Western culture in Oceania from the late 18th century on, many organized sports from England, Europe, and later the United States gained popularity in the region, largely with either transplanted British subjects (e.g., cricket, rugby, and tennis in Australia and New Zealand) or with the smaller class of native professionals who were intent on adopting Western ways and institutions (e.g., tennis and croquet in Indonesia). Cricket and rugby in both Australia and New Zealand were soon played at a level equal to the British. Both these sports, along with netball, soccer, and field hockey, were introduced on a mass scale in schools throughout Australia and New Zealand. All played an important role in socializing the Aboriginal and the Maori. Sports like swimming and running/athletics (track and field) were also embraced by a broader segment of indigenous society in Australia and New Zealand, perhaps because these sports embodied traditional day-to-day activities or had significant aspects that were related to folk sports.

The two most popular organized sports indigenous to the region today have been heavily influenced by Western sport. **Netball** is a women's version of basketball which was actually created in England in the late 19th century and exported to New Zealand. Its acceptance there has been pervasive, as evidenced by a recent survey in which Maori girls named netball as their third most popular sport behind aerobics/running and swimming.

Australian Rules football has also been embraced by a broad segment of society. With rules similar to rugby and soccer, Aussie Rules football was originally played as a cold-weather substitute for cricket. Today it is viewed on television by more Australians than any other sport.

▦ Australian Aboriginal Sports

Definition

Aboriginal Australians were native peoples to the Australian continent. They survived by hunting animals and foraging for food like nuts, roots, and berries that grew naturally in the wilds. Aboriginal Australians engaged in a number of traditional sports and games that sharpened the skills they needed to survive as hunter-gatherers. Though their culture was decimated by the English, who colonized much of Australia in the late 18th century, a strong native Australian movement exists today which celebrates the Aboriginal culture and its practices.

History

Aboriginal Australian oral tradition places the birth of their culture some 40,000 years ago. Their religion, which they referred to as a "meaning of life," was based on a concept of creation called the "Dreamtime." During Dreamtime, humans were created along with animals, birds, insects, plants, trees, and so on. All things on earth are interrelated, or part of a plan. There is also interconnectivity between the present, past, and future, which are bound together by, among other things, creative ancestral spirits. These spirits play an active role in the life of each generation. Thus traditional Aboriginal culture was based on strong family ties and rooted in nature.

This culture experienced cataclysmic change in the mid- to late 18th century when the British established a penal colony on the southeastern coast of Australia and began importing settlers to farm the land. Soon, Australia took on a political and economic importance for the English, who in 1788 founded the colony of New South Wales at Sydney Cove. In order to control the land and its inhabitants, the English embarked on a plan to "civilize" the Aboriginal. They wished for the natives to become good Christian subjects of the British Empire and industrious farmers. This plan failed miserably. Aboriginal peoples and British soldiers and settlers clashed in a number of small battles. Aborigines also began to catch diseases from the English. Because they had no immunities to European infections, seemingly mild viruses like colds and flu in many cases proved fatal. Weakened by warring and sickness, the Aboriginal people were ultimately crowded off the land. By the early 1800s, those who remained in the British settlement were largely marginalized, made to take the lowest jobs and given the worst land to live on. Others were driven into the Outback, the hot, arid interior of Australia.

Today the plight of Aboriginal people in Australia is similar to that of the Native Americans. Though they are a distinct minority whose members have been discriminated against for generations, they are at the same time fighting to gain political and economic power and to reassert their cultural heritage. Traditional sports and games are a part of that heritage.

TRADITIONAL ABORIGINAL SPORTS AND GAMES

Many of the Aboriginal games stress speed, quick reflexes, sharp hand-eye coordination, and excellent throwing ability. These skills were readily transferable to European team and individual sports like track and field, swimming, soccer, and cricket. Several Aboriginal sprinters bested English and Australian champions in the late 19th century (see page 241), and an Aboriginal cricket team toured England in 1868, winning 7 games, losing 7, and playing 19 draws. The following are among the most common Aboriginal games.

Catchball. This game involves at least three players and sometimes as many as five or six. Two players pass a ball back and forth, while one or a group of opponents stands between the two and tries to intercept the ball.

Drop Trap. This game has a direct correlation to hunting. Players attach a heavy stick, stone, or bone to the end of a rope and toss it—usually from a fair distance and from behind an obstruction or obstacle—at a large hole dug in the ground. The hole may or may not be covered with netting, which would simulate an animal trap.

Field Hockey. Both sexes played a field hockey–type game similar to the European stick-and-ball game of shinty. A premium was placed on cooperation and teamwork, symbolic of the interdependencies Aboriginal peoples established among one another.

Football or Kickball. Traditional Aboriginal culture included several games involving kicking a ball for height and for distance. The Aboriginal people's facility for kicking games translated to modern organized sport. Though Australian Rules football (see entry) began as a white man's sport, a number of Aboriginal players have become stars in today's professional league. And both the Australian national men's and women's soccer teams have Aboriginal members.

Kangaroo Rat. This game is similar to an American child skipping a flat rock across the water. Named after a small indigenous animal that hops about, kangaroo rat involves skipping a flat piece of wood or a wooden disk along the ground. The object is to either record the most number of hops, or to skip the wood for distance.

Mungan-Mungan. This game is analogous to "guard the flag" in America. A stick is painted white and placed in the center of a round playing area. One team defends the stick, pushing and tackling the opposing team, which tries to steal the stick. Cultural anthropologists suggest that this game was often socially symbolic. The stick would represent a young girl. The group guarding the stick was made up of boys, while men were in the group trying to capture the stick.

Spear the Disk. One Aboriginal game that is directly related to hunting is called spear the disk. A log segment is rolled down a hill and a participant attempts to spear the log from a distance before it comes to a stop.

Sprinting. In most hunter-gatherer cultures, the ability to run fast—to draw on short bursts of speed—is favored over endurance and staying power. Certainly the element of surprise and explosive strength are essential in overpowering an animal, particularly when one hasn't the aid of firearms. Aboriginal athletes have excelled in international sprint competition, beginning as early as the mid-19th century, when a professional runner named Manuello defeated the best British runners on tour in Australia. In the 1880s, Aboriginal athlete Charles Samuels defeated the Australian sprint champ, Jim McGarrigal, over 50 and 130 yards, and by the mid-20th century, Aboriginal athletes were accepted on national teams. Kathy Freeman, an Aboriginal Australian, won the gold medal in the 400 meters at the 2000 Olympic Games in Sydney.

Throwing Wood. Aboriginal people are experts at throwing the boomerang (*see* Boomerang), having invented the implement out of the ancient throwing wood, which they called a *Kylie*. *Kylies* were about 2½–3 feet long and slightly bent. Thrown from a three-quarter overhand delivery, the *Kylie* would rotate at a high velocity and cover as much as 200–250 yards. Though the throwing wood was used to kill or stun small game, it was also a popular piece of traditional sporting equipment. *Kylies* would be thrown for distance and accuracy. By the 18th century, the boomerang was also being used in a similar fashion.

Bibliography

Howell, Reet. (1999). "Traditional Sports, Oceania." In David Levinson and Karen Christensen (eds.), *Encyclopedia of World Sport*. New York: Oxford University Press.

Howell, Reet, and Maxwell Howell. (1987). *A History of Australian Sport*. Sydney: Shakespeare Head Press.

Lenoch, J. E. J. (2000). "Throwing Wood and Boomerang." Crystal Links Web site, *www.crystalinks.com/boomerangs.html* (March 4, 2001).

Moore, Geoff (ed.). (2000). "Aboriginal Culture and Adaptation." Australian Aborigine History and Culture Project Web site, *www.aaa.com.au/bizzskills/* (March 14, 2001).

———. (ed.) (2000). "Aborigines and Sport." *Australian Aborigine History and Culture Project Web site, www.aaa.com.au/bizzskills/* (March 14, 2001).

▦ Australian Rules Football

Definition

Australian Rules football developed in Melbourne, Australia, during the latter half of the 19th century. The game is played on a large oval field by two teams of 18 players, who attempt to move the ball across the opponent's goal line. Known as a game of constant movement, Australian Rules football allows players to move the ball forward, backward, or sideways by kicking, punching, or dribbling it.

History

Thomas Wentworth Wills, an accomplished cricket player and captain of the soccer team at Rugby School, is generally credited with "inventing" the game of Australian Rules football. In 1857 the 22-year-old Wills returned to Australia advocating for a winter game to keep cricketers in shape during the off-season. Wills, along with a handful of his friends, formed the Melbourne Football Club in 1858. Initial rules for the game were established and the first official Australian Rules football match was contested in August 1858 between Scotch College and Melbourne Grammar School. Accounts of early games suggest that Australian Rules football was a mix between soccer, the developing game of rugby, and Gaelic football. (*See* Soccer; Rugby. Gaelic football is an ancient Celtic game where players kick, punch, and run/bounce the ball toward a goal that resembles a hybrid of a soccer goal and a rugby goalpost.)

Between the 1860s and the 1880s, the rules of the Australian game were modified several times. Initially players could run with the ball, and points were scored by carrying the ball over the goal line. Later, rules stipulated that players needed to dribble the ball in order to move with it, and points were to be gained only by kicking the ball through the goalposts rather than running with it. In general, the sport developed into a nonstop, action-filled game in which the ball is in almost constant contention. This has made Australian Rules football an exciting spectator sport. Early on, important games in Melbourne were drawing 10,000–20,000 spectators. Such a following supported a professional league, which was founded in Victoria Province in 1896. Eight teams made up the initial Victoria Football League, which is today known as the Australian Football League (AFL). The AFL now has a team in every major city throughout the country.

Australian Rules football has never really caught on outside Australia, though teams from other countries have played the sport well. A visiting

English team toured Australia in 1876 and won 14 of 25 matches. England was keen to spread the game throughout Europe and the Commonwealth—as it would do with so many sports in the mid- to late 19th century—but those in control of the game in Australia were reluctant to let their imperial betters take over. Though Australian players were scheduled to tour England following 1876, a repeat series between the two countries never took place. Aside from teams in South Africa and New Zealand (which by 1901 sported over 100 Australian Rules football clubs), the sport had little more than esoteric or passing appeal for players in Europe, Asia, and America until the 1980s and 1990s.

Over the past 15 to 20 years, Australian teams have played "test" matches against teams from Ireland, Japan, New Guinea, Canada, Denmark, and the United States. Due to worldwide cable television, Australian Rules football games have been shown to millions of enthusiastic viewers in Western Europe, Japan, and America, and this activity, more than anything else, has sparked international interest in the sport. In 1995 the International Australian Football Council was founded to promote the sport worldwide. In 1997 the United States Australian Football Association (USAFA) was formed. Today the game is played on an amateur level in a number of large U.S. cities.

Equipment

Though the ball is oval-shaped, it is much rounder than an American football, measuring 720–730 millimeters long and 545–555 millimeters wide and weighing between 450 and 500 grams.

Players wear shorts, sleeveless shirts, and very little padding. Low-cut soccer cleats are worn. Due to the wide-open nature of the game—participants are constantly moving to either create space on the field (offense) or to guard players in flight (defense)—a player's uniform must afford him mobility.

Rules

The game is played on an oval-shaped grass field, measuring between 135 and 185 meters in length and between 110 and 155 meters in width (see illustration). Two goalposts set 6.4 meters apart and measuring at least 6 meters in height are set at each end of the playing field. Two behind posts are set at a distance of 6.4 meters to the outside of each goalpost and in a straight line with them. The minimum height of these posts is 3 meters. The line between the goalposts is called the goal line. The lines between each behind post and goalpost are called behind lines.

Each team fields 18 players, who play in positions all over the field and are matched with a specific opponent. Players are allowed to move the ball by hand or by foot forward, backward, or sideways. Players may not run with the ball, though dribbling it to move into position for a kick is

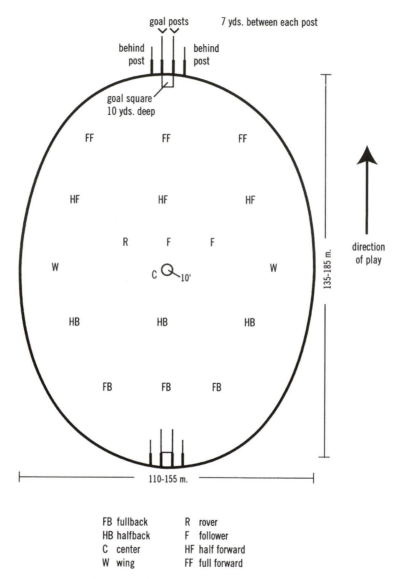

FB fullback   R rover
HB halfback   F follower
C center   HF half forward
W wing   FF full forward

Figure 31. Australia Rules football field, with an illustration of traditional offensive/defensive player alignments.

permitted. Throwing the ball is also not allowed. In general, players move the ball by punting it, or by holding it in the palm of one hand and punching it with the other (called a "handball"). If a player catches a ball that has been kicked without being touched in flight, this is known as a "mark." After "marking" the ball, a player is allowed to take a free kick.

Players can move to any position on the field, at any time, as there is no offside rule. As a result, there is a great deal of movement by the offense to create space in which plays may unfold, and by the defense to guard the opposing offensive players. Speed, strength, and elusive movement are premium skills for the Australian Rules football player. Though there is much tackling and bumping of opponents for the ball, players also resort to unorthodox acrobatic plays like using a teammate as a springboard on which to step and leap high in the air to mark a kick.

Despite the game's wide-open nature, a number of plays result in the opposing team being awarded a free kick:

Holding an opponent who does not have the ball.

Tackling an opponent around the neck.

Holding the ball after being tackled. (A player must release the ball quickly.)

Throwing the ball.

Pushing an opponent in the back.

Running more than 15 meters with the ball without dribbling it.

Kicking the ball out-of-bounds without the ball touching the ground.

The game is divided into four 20-minute quarters. Teams swap sides of the field at the end of each quarter. The object of the game is to score the most total points. Goals count six points and are awarded when the ball is kicked between the two goalposts without being touched by any player. One point is awarded when the ball passes between a goalpost and a behind post, or hits one of the goalposts, or is "rushed" (either comes off a player's hands before crossing the goal line, or is kicked by a defender through the goalposts to thwart a goal).

Bibliography

International Australian Football Council. "Australian Football FAQ." IAFC Web site, *www.iafc.org.au/* (March 15, 2001).
———. "Laws of the Game." IAFC Web site, *www.iafc.org.au/* (March 15, 2001).
Vamplew, Wray, Katherine Moore, John O'Hara, Richard Cashman, and Ian Jobling. (1992). *The Oxford Companion to Australian Sport*. Melbourne: Oxford University Press.

▦ Boomerang Throwing

Definition

Boomerang throwing is the practice of tossing a curved, aerodynamic "throwing wood" that returns to the thrower. The boomerang was invented by Australian Aborigines, who seem to have used it solely for pleasure or sport. Earlier nonreturning throwing sticks were used as hunting weapons by many ancient cultures. Today millions around the world enjoy boomerang throwing. Some even compete in national and international events involving throwing for distance, time in the air, accuracy, height, and so on.

History

Though anthropologists are certain that the boomerang developed in Australia—the only place on earth where ancient boomerangs have been found—its connection to the nonreturning throwing stick is a bit of a mystery. Throwing sticks, called *Kylies* by the Aborigine, were used for hunting small game like rabbits, prairie dogs, or birds. Measuring about three feet long and a half-inch thick, *Kylies* were shaped in a slight curve much like a banana. A *Kylie* could be thrown for great distances—as far as 200 yards. A *Kylie* would spin end-around-end, hovering over the ground as it cut a much wider swath than a spear or an arrow. The nonreturning throwing stick was around for many thousands of years, used by hunters in Egypt, West Africa, Eastern Europe, Scandinavia, and North America. A throwing stick made out of woolly mammoth tusk was found in Poland and carbon-dated back some 20,000 years.

All throwing sticks were made from one piece of wood, and it has been speculated that the first boomerang was an accident of sorts, made from lighter wood, shaped smaller and with more of a bend than normal. When this mutant throwing stick was thrown, it came back. Chances are its thrower was fascinated with this discovery and in no time had modified the boomerang into an instrument similar to the one used today.

It should be noted that boomerangs, like almost every other tool used by Aborigines, had multiple purposes. We know that boomerangs were also used to dig roots to eat and as cooking tools. By clacking two boomerangs together, they were probably also used as musical instruments. The importance of boomerangs to the Aborigine culture is underscored by the rich art that adorned each one. This is true for the very earliest boomerangs found, up to instruments that were used in the 18th and 19th centuries. Religion for the Aborigines was defined by "the Dreamtime," an event similar to Christianity's Biblical Creation. Aboriginal carvings, paintings, and many everyday items, including boomerangs, depict characters and scenes from the Dreaming. The Rainbow Serpent can often be seen winding its way down and around a boomerang.

The boomerang was one of the few pieces of Aboriginal culture that was adopted by English settlers to Australia in the 18th and 19th centuries. Today, Australians continue to be among the best boomerang throwers in the world, though national boomerang clubs and associations have developed in many countries throughout Europe, Asia, and North America. Many national and regional competitions are held, with the Boomerang

World Cup staged every other year. In the United States, nearly 50 tournaments are held annually. The United States Boomerang Association lists several thousand members. Americans have proven to be among the best throwers in the world, having beaten the Australian national team in the first international boomerang competition in 1981.

Equipment

Modern boomerangs are much different from those which were made even 100 years ago. Until recently, all boomerangs were carved out of the same piece of wood. Newer boomerangs use composite materials, which enable designers to make them with smaller, more acute angles. Smaller angles (less than 90 degrees) mean more spin, which provides greater stability and produces longer flights. Common materials used to make boomerangs today include carbon fiber, fiberglass, kevlar, and plywood laminate.

How a Boomerang Works

A boomerang's spin and return are governed by principles set forth by an 18th-century scientist, Daniel Bernoulli. "Bernoulli's effect" states that "the pressure of a gas decreases as its velocity increases." A good way to understand this concept is to imagine the wings of an airplane that are curved on top and flat on the bottom. As the wing of the plane moves through the air, the air must move farther on the top than on the bottom, and must therefore move faster. This higher velocity forms a low-pressure area on the top of the wing, which in turn creates lift.

A boomerang works on the same principle as the airplane wing. A boomerang's ends are like wings—each is shaped, or beveled, on its trailing edge (the left edge for a right-handed thrower, the right edge for a lefty). While an airplane's wings are laid flat—creating upward lift—a boomerang is thrown end over end—nearly vertical to the ground. This means that a right-handed boomerang will be creating lift to the left, essentially pulling itself around in a circle, while the left-handed boomerang lifts to the right and circles around.

Rules

Australian Aborigines enjoyed the practice of throwing a boomerang. To them, the object of the game was fun. Western sports have created objective competition out of boomerang throwing. The following are the most common boomerang-throwing events:

Accuracy: Similar to darts, a boomerang is thrown from a bull's-eye on the ground and allowed to return to the target untouched.

Trick Catch: Competitors attempt to make catches one-handed, behind the back, under the leg, etc.

Australian Round: A kind of all-around competition, where throwers are tested for distance, accuracy, and throwing ability.

Fast Catch: Competitors make five throws and catches as quickly as possible with the same boomerang.

Endurance Boomerang: Tests one's fast-catching ability over a five-minute period.

Dual Events: Throwing and catching two boomerangs at the same time, or "juggling" two boomerangs in the air—keeping both aloft with alternating throws.

Long-Distance Throwing: Throwing for distance.

Maximum Time Aloft: Times the longest of five throws to stay in the air. John Gorski, of Delaware, Ohio, holds the record for the longest flight. In 1993 Gorski threw a boomerang and caught it an amazing 17 minutes and 6 seconds later—just 40 meters from the point from which he had thrown it.

Bibliography

Bailey, Ted. (2000). "How Does it Work?—The Science of the Boomerang's Return Flight." United States Boomerang Association Web site, *www.usba.org* (February 17, 2001).

"Boomerang History." (2000). J & N Boomerangs Web site, *www.jnboomerangs.com/* (February 17, 2001).

Lenoch, J.E.J. (2000). "Throwing Wood and Boomerang." Crystal Links Web site, *www.crystalinks.com/boomerangs.html* (March 4, 2001).

United States Boomerang Association. (2000). "The Sport of Boomerang." United States Boomerang Association Web site, *www.usba.org* (February 17, 2001).

▦ Netball

Definition

Netball is a court game played by two teams of seven players each, the object of the game being to place an inflated ball through an opponent's goal from within a 16-foot shooting area. Originating in England as a variation on basketball, netball is played predominantly by women in 25 to 30 countries throughout the world, particularly in New Zealand, Australia, and England.

History

Netball's early history has as much to do with American basketball, the game from which it is derived, as it does with Victorian England's views concerning a woman's proper character and role in society. When basketball crossed the Atlantic in 1895, men at universities and clubs in England began playing the sport with very little skill. An American physical education instructor at Luton Teachers College in London created the game of netball to teach skills such as passing, shooting, and rebounding. Though netball was initially played in a number of local and regional variations, the game in general was characterized by a staccato rhythm of stop, start, catch, and shoot. As a result, netball, by nature, lacked the fluidity of basketball. Around the turn of the century, the Ling Association, an organization founded to advance the professional and academic interests of physical educators in England, drafted standardized rules for netball. Goals gave way to points, a 16-foot semicircle from which to shoot the ball was introduced, and a ring with a net replaced the basket. In 1905 the English rules were introduced to the British Isles as well as the United States, Canada, France, Australia, and South Africa.

As an organized game, netball was played almost exclusively by women. Athletic administrators and educators hailed the sport for the sense of "control" it developed among participants. Lacking rhythm, speed, contact, and aggressive behavior in general, netball epitomized a reserved, rational game with calculated, moderate movement. Players had to come to a complete stop on the court to set and shoot, and plays unfolded in an orderly fashion, with the ball being passed between all teammates and no one relying on an individual's burst of energy and athleticism. In this sense, the game reaffirmed society's perception of how women should behave. Women could run, catch, and be competitive to a degree, but the unrestrained athleticism of sports like soccer and field hockey was largely forbidden.

During the 1920s the All-England Women's Netball Association was founded, and many local clubs and county associations were formed during the 1930s. Though World War II arrested netball's growth, the game picked up where it left off in postwar England. The BBC had its first radio broadcast of a game in 1947—the same year that the British national team traveled to Prague in a rare East-West cultural exchange.

Today, netball enjoys great popularity in New Zealand, Australia, and the West Indies—all former Commonwealth countries or territories that were controlled by England. Once popular in schools and colleges, netball has gained acceptance on a community level and in cultures very different from the British. Results of a 1991 survey conducted nationwide in New Zealand found that 26 percent of the country's females aged 15–18 years participated regularly in netball. Among aboriginal Maori females, 25 percent played netball. For this group, netball was the third most popular activity after aerobics and swimming.

In Australia and New Zealand, coed and men's netball is becoming increasingly popular as a form of recreation. In the United States, the game of netball has been taught from time to time in high school physical education classes to develop coordination and teamwork skills. But the competitive game is virtually nonexistent in America, probably because of its reputation as a less stressful form of basketball.

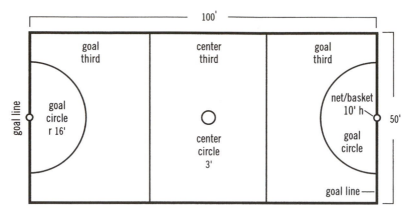

Figure 32. Netball court.

Equipment

Traditional netball wear has consisted of a blouse, polo shirt, or T-shirt with matching skirt. Uniforms must include the initials of a player's position, worn both front and back above the waist. A low-cut tennis or court shoe is worn for start-stop motion and lateral movement. A netball is about the same size as a basketball, covered with leather or rubber casing, and inflated to similar pressure. Sometimes a smaller Size 5 regulation soccer ball is used instead.

Rules

A netball court measures 100 feet long by 50 feet wide (see illustration). The game is based on each team trying to score as many goals as possible. Each team defends its own goal, which consists of an open-ended net placed atop a 10-foot-high post at the end of the court. The game consists of four quarters of 15 minutes each. The position of each player has a designated area on the court, which is divided into thirds. In general, there are two attacking players, who are confined to the forecourt, and two defensive players, who are positioned in the backcourt. A center is stationed at midcourt and is involved in both the offensive and defensive flow of the game. A goalkeeper defends the goal, while a goal scorer is restricted to the 16-foot semicircle around the net.

The main rules of netball are as follows:

After catching the ball, a player may take only two steps.

A player can hold the ball for only three seconds.

A defending player must be at least three feet away from an attacking player with the ball.

Only two positions on the court (the goal scorers) can shoot.

Shots can only be taken from within the semicircle.

Bibliography

Galsworthy, Betty. (1997). *Netball: The Skills of the Game*. Doune, England: Crowood Press.

Nauright, John, and John Broomhall. (1994). "A Woman's Game: The Development of Netball and Female Sporting Culture in New Zealand, 1906–1970." *International Journal of the History of Sport* Vol. 1, No. 3, pp. 387–407.

Vamplew, Wray, Katherine Moore, John O'Hara, Richard Cashman, and Ian Jobling. (1992). *The Oxford Companion to Australian Sport*. Melbourne: Oxford University Press.

▦ Polynesian Sports and Games

Definition

Polynesian sports and games were pastimes played by the inhabitants of the Polynesian Triangle, a group of Pacific islands located east-northeast of Australia and bounded by New Zealand and Easter Island in the south and the Hawaiian Islands in the north. These activities were popular through the early to mid-19th century, when a combination of disease and religious conversion imposed on the native peoples by European missionaries served to wipe out much of the ancient Polynesian culture.

History

Polynesians are descended from the ancient sailing peoples of Southeast Asia, who were known as Austronesians. From about 2000 B.C., they began sailing eastward, populating the Solomon islands, Vanuatu, and, by 200–300 B.C., Fiji, Tonga, and Samoa. Throughout these islands, the Polynesians established stable communities organized around fishing and raising fruits and vegetables. Though the Polynesian Island region had been visited by Spanish, Portuguese, and Dutch voyagers in the 16th and 17th centuries, there was no lasting European presence until the arrival of English captain James Cook in the 1770s.

Impressed by the beauty and richness of the area, the British immediately set about colonizing Polynesia and teaching the "heathen" natives European ways. As has happened with so many similar clashes of cultures, the Polynesians, who had lived in isolation from other societies for many hundreds of years, succumbed to all sorts of European illness and disease for which they had no immunity. Tens of thousands of native islanders died. Those who survived found their way of life radically altered by Christian missionaries, who accompanied British traders and soldiers. Sports and games were considered idle diversions, and many, like surfing and sledding, were banned. Missionaries also forbade many of the traditional celebrations at which sports and games were played. As a result, it is estimated that over 100 ancient sports and games disappeared from Polynesian culture. Ironically, as these islands have become a tourist attraction (particularly Hawaii), many of the traditional sports and games have been revived, including the Makahiki Games, an ancient Hawaiian Olympics of sorts which is now part of an annual cultural festival.

The Makahiki Games were conceived as a multisport festival staged each year throughout the four months between mid-October and mid-February. Similar to the European harvest festival, folks danced, feasted, and engaged in sports and games. Though the Makahiki Games were no longer held in the 18th and 19th centuries, many of the sports that had been a part of the celebration had become established in Polynesian culture. These include:

Surfing (*see* Surfing).

Sledding: Called *holua*. Participants would slide headfirst down a steep hill on short sleds made from the wood of the breadfruit tree.

Wrestling: Polynesian wrestling is highly symbolic, accompanied by dancing and linked to the harvest celebration. Wrestlers start to grapple from a standing position, the objective being to trip or throw an opponent on his back.

Bowling Disks: Called *maika*. Participants roll spherical disks along the ground in a rectangular playing area similar to bocce or lawn bowling. The object of the game is to place one's disks closest to a marker or target.

The following are some of the most popular sports and games Polynesian Islanders played through the early to mid-19th century.

Animal Games. Polynesians domesticated dogs, chickens, pigs, and rats, which they kept for pets. Cockfighting was and still is an extremely popular pastime in many parts of the region. Aggressive breeds of birds are raised to be fighters. Bouts are conducted essentially until the death of one of the birds. Cockfights are accompanied by much betting and, for trainer and spectator alike, are considered social events.

Stick-and-Ball Games. Men and women throughout much of Polynesia played a game similar to shinty or field hockey. Balls were made of dried plantain leaves, twisted together and bound by vines.

Stick Fighting. Much of the culture engaged in a form of fighting with wooden sticks. Though this sport had warring antecedents, there is no evidence that Polynesians met in duels or fought to settle differences. Long sticks were used to row or pole boats, to pick fruit, and to build houses. Being proficient in the use of sticks was an important skill, and it is likely that fencing-type sports reflect this.

Tree Climbing. Another activity that was directly related to day-to-day life. Polynesians climbed trees for speed. A variation of climbing trees involved racing up ropes or vines suspended from a high tree branch.

Tug-of-War. Groups of men would engage in tug-of-war, similar to the version played by our culture, though there was also a reverse version of the sport. Two teams of at least 10–12 men would line up facing one another, each about 5 yards in front of an end line or boundary line. The object of the game was to push the opposing team back over its end line.

Water Sports. In addition to surfing, Polynesians were also proficient at swimming, canoeing, and diving. Competitions were held in all of these sports. When Europeans set down the rules to organized swimming and diving in the late 19th century, they found that Polynesians were far advanced in terms of swimming strokes and diving form. In fact, Polynesians were probably using the freestyle stroke for several hundred years before the Europeans.

Bibliography

Houston, James D., and Ben R. Surfin Finney. (1996). *Surfing: A History of the Ancient Hawaiian Sport*. Beverly Hills, CA: Pomegranate Press.

Howell, Reet. (1999). "Traditional Sports, Oceania." In David Levinson and Karen Christensen (eds.), *Encyclopedia of World Sport*. New York: Oxford University Press.

⬜ Surfing

Definition

Surfing is the act of riding on waves as they break over a shallow segment of shoreline. Though surfing is typically done by lying, kneeling, or standing on a surfboard, some surfers use only their bodies (bodysurfing). The sport developed on islands in the Pacific Ocean and was popular upon the arrival of British explorers in the 18th century. Today the sport is practiced in warm coastal areas—primarily in California, Hawaii, Australia, and South America. Though challenging and exciting, surfing requires no formal training and can be done anywhere a wave is breaking.

History

The famed British explorer James Cook made the first recorded mention of surfing, in 1778. According to Cook, practically all Polynesian Islanders, including men, women, and young children—even kings—were experts at the sport (see illustration). However, surfing's mass appeal rapidly declined in the early 19th century, when Christian missionaries suppressed what they considered to be a frivolous and immoral activity. It wasn't until the early 20th century that the sport reappeared. Hawaiian swimming great Duke Kahanamoku, a gold medal winner at the 1912 Olympics, is generally credited with reintroducing the sport to an international audience. An accomplished surfer, Kahanamoku would bring his board with him as he traveled to championship swim meets and exhibitions. During the Roaring Twenties, America's new pleasure culture was

Figure 33. Surfing was a leading pastime for Polynesian Islanders in the 18th century. This historic illustration depicts a group of native Hawaiians catching a wave. (© Bettmann/CORBIS)

drawn to thrill-seeking and hedonistic activity. Surfing fit the bill, and the sport was soon being practiced on the beaches of California and Hawaii.

A different style of surfing developed in Australia, where surf clubs were given control of the waves at local beaches in exchange for providing rescue services for beachgoers. Most Australian surfers were "lifeguards" on boards, with little time to ride the waves for sport. Therefore the sport was more disciplined there.

Changes in technology have greatly affected the sport of surfing throughout the 20th century. Lighter boards are easier to maneuver, and, as a result, the range of surfing styles and tricks has changed accordingly (see following). A surfing craze in California in the late 1950s turned the sport into a subculture unto itself. Surfers developed their own slang, humor, and dress, and Hollywood spread their influence worldwide by producing a host of surf films.

Competitive surfing also developed in the 1950s. In 1954 the Waikiki Surf Club organized the first International Surfing Championships at Makaha, Hawaii. Points were awarded for length of ride, number of waves caught, and overall skill, sportsmanship, and grace. The first World

Surfing Championships were held in Manly, Australia, in 1964. Today the Association of Surfing Professionals (ASP) sanctions men's and women's World Championships tours. Several hundred professional men compete at 60 "feeder" or qualifier events, which lead to a 10-event grand prix circuit. The Women's World Tour is composed of 15 events. Despite the lure of professionalism, most surfers engage in the sport for fun and the search for the "perfect" wave.

Equipment

Reduced to its essentials, surfing requires a good wave and a board. In early times, a native Hawaiian board was typically one piece of wood, anywhere from 8 to 12 feet long and weighing as much as 160 pounds. The bottom of the board was flat; an early board tended to slide down the face of the wave rather than "trim" along on top of the wave running at the same speed. To change direction, a 19th-century surfer had to drag one foot in the water.

Boards today are much lighter. Most are made of a plastic foam core covered with a hard shell of polyurethane or fiberglass. A top-of-the-line board used for competition is typically just 6–6½ feet long, 18½ inches wide, and less than 2½ inches thick. These boards—known as shortboards—are fast, highly maneuverable, and light, weighing in at just 6–7 pounds. Recreational surfers usually opt for a longer board. Longboards are 9 feet long, as much as 22 inches wide, 2½–3 inches thick, and about twice the weight of a shortboard. All boards have a fin device on the bottom toward the tail, or back. The three-fin, or thruster, design is most common. Fins provide the board with stability and drive, enabling the surfer to both change direction and take advantage of a wave's propulsive power. The archetypal picture of the surfer—knees bent, back arched, and arms outstretched—came into vogue with the advance of surfboard technology, replacing the traditional rigid, upright stance.

Rules

A surfer usually paddles away from the shore beyond a point where waves are breaking and waits for a suitable wave to ride. To catch a wave, the surfer paddles hard in the direction the wave is moving and essentially tries to match the speed of the wave. The basic objective of surfing is to ride the unbroken portion of a wave for as long as possible, using an array of maneuvers to speed up, slow down, and steer around the breaking portion of the wave.

Surfing requires a great deal of agility and stamina as well as excellent swimming skills, for even the best surfers are occasionally knocked off the board. Normally, a surfer stands with his or her left foot forward, maneuvering the board by constantly shifting his or her weight. By leaning to one side, a surfer can cut diagonally across a wave. By leaning forward, a surfer causes the board to sit lower in the water and move down the line of the wave faster. To pull out of a wave, the rider either shifts his or her weight to the rear and lets the wave break over the board, or turns the board, and, using the impact of the rising wave, rides back over the top of the wave and into the calm water behind.

In competition, surfers are required to ride a specified number of waves and are judged on how soon they catch the wave, the distance ridden, and their ability to maneuver the board on the wave. Surfers can catch a maximum of 10 waves, but only the best 4 are counted toward the overall score. There are judges for all heats and finals. According to ASP rules, competitors are to be judged on "the most radical controlled maneuvers" executed with "speed and power in the most critical section of the wave."

Bibliography

Booth, Douglas. (1995). "Ambiguities in Pleasure and Discipline: The Development of Competitive Surfing." *Journal of Sport History* Vol. 22, No. 3, pp. 189–206.

Houston, James D., and Ben R. Surfin Finney. (1996). *Surfing: A History of the Ancient Hawaiian Sport*. Beverly Hills, CA: Pomegranate Press.

Lueras, Leonard. (1984). *Surfing: The Ultimate Pleasure*. New York: Workman Publishing Co.

▦ BIBLIOGRAPHY

GENERAL REFERENCE

About.com Web site, *http://www.about.com/*. Provides basic topical information (e.g., instruction and rules) and links to specific sports and games Web sites.

All Star Sites Sports History Web page, *http://www.allstarsites.com/links/Sports_ History*. Provides links to Web sites devoted to sports history.

Barton, John (ed.). (1996). *Sports Encyclopedia: Index and Reference Book of New Information*. Washington, DC: ABBE Publishers Association.

Brown, Gerry, and Michael Morrison (eds.). (2000). *The 2001 ESPN Information Please Sports Almanac*. New York: Hyperion Books.

CBS Sportsline, *http://www.cbs.sportsline.com*. A comprehensive list of chronological historical summaries for different sports.

Corbett, Doris, John Cheffers, and Eileen Crowley (eds.). (2001). *Unique Games and Sports Around the World: A Reference Guide*. Westport, CT: Greenwood Publishing Group.

Cox, Gerry (ed.). (1999). *The Dictionary of Sports*. London: Carlton Books.

Friedlander, Noam (ed.). (1999). *The Mammoth Book of World Sports*. Berkeley, CA: Publishers Group West.

Gratch, Bonnie, Betty Chan, and Juditch Lingenfelter. (1983). *Sports and Physical Education*. Westport, CT: Greenwood Publishing Group. A source for publications and documents on sports.

HandiSearch Web site, *http://ahandyguide.com/Directory/Sports/History*. Provides links to sports history Web sites.

Hickok Sports.com, *http://www.hickoksports.com/history*. Information on the beginnings and history of various sports, with links to other Web sites.

Information Please Sports Almanac, *http://www.infoplease.com/sports.html*. Online version of annual reference source.

Knight, Thomas, and Nick Troop. (1988). *The Sackville Illustrated History of Athletics*. Sackville, UK: Sackville Book.

Levinson, David, and Karen Christensen (eds). (1999). *Encyclopedia of World Sport.* New York: Oxford University Press. This is a condensation of a three-volume edition of the same name which was published in 1996.

Lokesh, Thani. (1992). *The Encyclopedic Dictionary of Sports.* Columbia, MO: South Asian Books.

Merriam-Webster. (1976). *Webster's Sports Dictionary.* Columbus, OH: Weekly Reader Books.

Microsoft Encarta Encyclopedia, *http://www.cncarta.msn.com/.* Individual sport and game entries include origins, history, and basic rules.

Shoebridge, Michele. (1992). *Information Sources in Sport and Leisure.* Munich: KG Saur Publishing. A guide to international sources for study on sports.

Sports Quest.com Web site, *http://www.sportsquest.com/.* Provides a directory of resources and links on various sports.

Washington Post.com, *http://www.washingtonpost.com/.* Provides overview, rules, history, and glossary of terms for numerous sports.

Worth, Sylvia (ed.). (1990). *The Rules of the Game.* New York: St. Martin's Press. Easy-to-follow rules and diagrams for common sports and games.

Wukovits, John F. (2000). *The Encyclopedia of the World of Sports.* London: Franklin Watts.

Yahoo! Sports Section, *http://www.yahooligans.com/content/ka/almanac/sports.* Detailed information on indoor and outdoor games for all seasons.

TOPICAL REFERENCE

Brown, George (ed.). (1979). *The New York Times Encyclopedia of Water Sports.* Danbury, CT: Arno Press.

Clark, Thomas L. (1988). *The Dictionary of Gambling and Gaming.* Hyde Park, NY: Lexic House.

CNNSI.com Olympic Sports Almanac, *http://sportsillustrated.cnn.com/olympics/.* Information on evolution of events and medal winners.

Corcoran, John, Emil Farkas, and Stuart Sobel. (1993). *The Original Martial Arts Encyclopedia.* Los Angeles: Pro Action Publishing.

Cox, Richard, Grant Jarvie, and Wray Vamplew (ed.). (2001). *The Encyclopedia of British Sport.* Santa Barbara, CA: ABC-CLIO.

European Sports History Review Web Site, *http://www.frankcass.com/jnls/eshr.htm.* Provides resources and links to scholarly and popular works on the history of various European sports and games.

Findling, John E., and Kimberley D. Pelle (eds.). (1996). *Historical Dictionary of the Modern Olympic Movement.* Westport, CT: Greenwood Publishing Group.

Frederic, Louis. (1991). *A Dictionary of the Martial Arts.* Rutland, VT: Charles Tuttle Press.

Journal E Olympic History Web Page, *http://www.journale.com/kodak/olympics /olympichistory/.* Provides summaries, timelines, and photos on Olympic sports history.

Oglesby, Carole A., Doreen L. Greenberg, and Karen Hill (eds.). (1998). *The Encyclopedia of Women and Sports in America.* Phoenix: Oryx Press.

Osborn, Kevin. (1997). *The Scholastic Encyclopedia of Sports in the United States.* New York: Scholastic.

Porter, David L. (1995). *Biographical Dictionary of American Sports*. Westport, CT: Greenwood Press. Contains biographical sketches and bibliographical resources on notable American sports figures.

St. Lawrence County (NY) AAUW Web Site, *http:www.northnct.org/stlawrenceaauw/ sports.htm*. A women's sports history resource, including a comprehensive history of women in sports timeline.

Sparano, Vincent. (2000). *The Complete Outdoors Encyclopedia*. New York: St. Martin's Press.

Taylor, A.R. (1992). *The Guinness Book of Traditional Pub Games*. London: Guinness.

Washington Post.com Winter Olympic Web page, *http://www.washingtonpost.com/wp*. Provides general history and background of Winter Olympic sports in addition to Olympic history.

GENERAL AND TOPICAL STUDIES

Adelman, Melvin. (1986). *A Sporting Time: New York City and the Rise of Modern Athletics, 1820–1870*. Urbana: University of Illinois Press.

Arbena, Joseph L. (ed.). (1988). *Sport and Society in Latin America*. Westport, CT: Greenwood Press.

Baker, William J. (1982). *Sports in the Western World*. Totowa, NJ: Rowman and Littlefield.

Baker, William J, and James A. Mangan (eds.). (1987). *Sport in Africa: Essays in Social History*. New York: Africana Publishing.

Burke, Peter. (1978). *Popular Culture in Early Modern Europe*. London: Temple Smith.

Costa, D. Margaret, and Sharon R. Guthrie (eds.). (1994). *Women and Sport: An Interdisciplinary Perspective*. Champaign, IL: Human Kinetics.

Cross, Gary. (1990). *A Social History of Leisure Since 1600*. State College, PA: Venture Books.

Culin, Stewart. (1907). *Games of the North American Indians*. Washington, DC: Government Printing Office.

De Nayer, P. P., M. Ostyn, and R. Renson. (1976). *The History, the Evolution and Diffusion of Sports and Games in Different Cultures*. Brussels: BLOSO.

Derek, Sir Birley. (1993). *Sport and the Making of Britain*. Manchester, England: Manchester University Press.

———. (1995). *Land of Sport and Glory: Sport and British Society, 1884–1910*. Manchester, England: Manchester University Press.

Dulles, Foster Rhea. (1965). *A History of Recreation: America Learns to Play*, 2nd ed. New York: Appleton-Century-Crofts.

Dunning, Eric, and Kenneth Sheard. (1979). *Barbarians, Gentlemen, and Players*. Oxford, England: Martin Robertson. On the development of English sports.

Durant, John, and Otto Bettmann. (1973). *Pictorial History of American Sports*. 3rd ed. Cranbury, NJ: A. S. Barnes and Co.

Edwards, Harry. (1973). *The Sociology of Sport*. Homewood, IL: Dorsey Press.

Eitzen, D. Stanley (ed.) (1996). *Sport in Contemporary Society: An Anthology*. New York: St. Martin's Press.

Elias, Norman, and Eric Dunning. (1986). *The Quest for Excitement: Sport and Leisure in the Civilizing Process*. Oxford, England: Oxford University Press. A sociological interpretation of the development of English and European sport.

Endrei, W., and L. Zolnay. (1986). *Fun and Games in Old Europe*. Budapest: Corvina Press.

Fitz-Barnard, L. (1983). *Fighting Sports*. Surrey, England: Saiga Publications.

Gorn, Elliot J., and Warren Goldstein. (1993). *A Brief History of American Sports*. New York: Hill and Wang.

Grover, Katheryn (ed.). (1989). *Fitness in American Culture: Images of Health, Sport and the Body, 1830–1940*. Amherst, MA: University of Massachusetts Press.

Guttmann, Allen. (1978). *From Ritual to Record: The Nature of Modern Sports*. New York: Columbia University. Press.

———. (1988). *A Whole New Ball Game: An Interpretation of American Sports*. Chapel Hill: University of North Carolina Press. Essays on the history of American sports.

———. (1991). *Women's Sports: A History*. New York: Columbia University Press.

———. (1992). *The Olympics: A History of the Modern Games*. Urbana: University of Illinois Press.

———. (1994). *Games and Empires: Modern Sports and Cultural Imperialism*. New York: Columbia University Press.

Hargreaves, Jennifer. (1994). *Sporting Females: Critical Issues in the History of Sociology of Women's Sports*. London: Routledge Books.

Kelly, J. R., and G. Godbey. (1992). *The Sociology of Leisure*. State College, PA: Venture Press.

Knuttgen, Howard G., Qiwei Ma, and Zhonguan Wu (eds.). (1990). *Sport in China*. Champaign, IL: Human Kinetics.

Lowerson, John. (1994). *Sport and the English Middle Classes, 1870–1914*. New York: St. Martin's Press.

Loy, J. W. (1989). *The Social Significance of Sport: An Introduction to the Sociology of Sport*. Champaign, IL: Human Kinetics.

Lueschen, G. (1967). "The Interdependence of Sport and Culture." *International Review of Sport Sociology* Vol. 2, pp. 127–142.

Mandell, Richard D. (1984). *Sport: A Cultural History*. New York: Columbia University Press.

Mangan, James A. (ed.). (1992). *The Cultural Bond: Sport, Empire and Society*. London: Frank Cass.

Massengale, John, and Richard Swanson (eds.). (1997). *The History of Exercise Science and Sport*. Champaign, IL: Human Kinetics.

Naul, Roland (ed.). (1997). *Contemporary Studies in the National Olympic Games Movement*. Oxford, England: Peter Lang Publishing.

Oxendine, Joseph. (1988). *American Indian Sports Heritage*. Champaign, IL: Human Kinetics.

Rader, Benjamin. (1990). *American Sports: From the Age of Folk Games to the Age of Spectators*. Englewood Cliffs, NJ: Prentice-Hall.

Reid, A. H., A. W. Reid, Kendall Blanchard, and Alyce Cheska. (1985). *The Anthropology of Sport: An Introduction*. South Hadley, MA: Bergin and Garvey.

Reiss, Steven A. (1989). *City Games: The Evolution of American Urban Society and the Rise of Sports*. Urbana: University of Illinois Press.

Schaap, Dick. (1975). *An Illustrated History of the Olympics*. New York: Alfred A. Knopf.

Spears, Betty, and Richard Swanson. (1995). *The History of Sport and Physical Activity in the United States*. Madison, WI: Brown and Benchmark.

Struna, Nancy. (1977). "Puritans and Sport." *Journal of Social History* Vol. 4, pp. 1–21.

Twombly, Wells. (1976). *Two Hundred Years of Sports in America*. New York: McGraw-Hill.

Van Dalen, D., and B. L. Bennett. (1971). *A World History of Physical Education*. Englewood Cliffs, NJ: Prentice-Hall.

Vertinsky, Patricia Anne. (1994). *The Eternally Wounded Woman: Women, Doctors, and Exercise in the Late Nineteenth Century*. Urbana: University of Illinois Press.

Wagner, Eric A. (ed.). (1989). *Sport in Asia and Africa: A Comparative Handbook*. Westport, CT: Greenwood Press.

Yalouris, Nicolaos (ed.). (1979). *The Eternal Olympics: The Art and History of Sport*. New Rochelle, NY: Caratzas Bros.

Yiannakis, Andrew, Thomas McIntyre, Merrill J. Melnick, and Dale P. Hart (eds.). (1991). *Sport Sociology: Contemporary Themes*. Dubuque, IA: Kendall Hunt.

▦ INDEX

Swimming, 1, 2, 119, 125, 130, 168, 170, **174–79**,185, 189, 237–38, 240; Classical Greek and Roman influence on, 175; and club movement, 175–76; definition of, 174–75; and English Channel crossing, 176; equipment for, 176–77; events of, 177–78; history of, 175–76; Native American influence on, 175–76; and Olympic Games, 176, 178; rules of, 177–78; strokes of, 178–79; in United States, 175–76

Table tennis, 2, 13, 45, **112–14**; Asian influence on, 113; definition of, 112; equipment for, 113–14; history of, 112–13; origins in British military, 112; rules of, 114
Tae kwon do, 12, **37–39**; definition of, 37; equipment for, 38; history of, 38; Korean origins of, 38; and Olympics, 38; rules of, 38–39, spiritual origins of, 38; tenets of, 39; "Trinity" of, 39
Tai chi, 12, **39–42**; attitudes of, 40; Chen style of, 41; Chinese origins, 40–41; definition of, 39; history of, 40–41; and I Ching, 40; philosophical essence of, 40–41; postures of, 40; Yang style of, 41; and yoga, 41
Tailteann Games: and early track and field competition, 123–24
Tamil Nadu, India: as birthplace of silambam, 32–33
Tarahumara Indians, 188
Tennis, 45, **115–18**, 168, 191, 195, 238; and amateur ideals, 116–17; definition of, 115; equipment for, 117; history of, 115–17; rise of professionalism, 117; royal origins of, 115; rules of, 118; and social class, 115–16; in United States, 115–16
Tenzing, Norgay, 160
Thames Rowing Club, 64
Thoroughbred racing, 89
Throwing wood, 241. *See also* boomerang throwing
Ti Juan Zu, 46

Title IX of the Educational Amendments of 1972: and popularity of rowing, 99; and women's lacrosse, 225
Tlachi, 190
Tobogganing, **179–183**: as club sport, 180; definition of, 179; European origins of, 180; history of, 179–80; Native American origins of, 179–80; variations of, 180–82. *See also* bobsled; luge; skeleton
Town ball, 201–2
Track and field, 2, 7–8, 44–45, 94, **118–25**, 131, 148, 168–70, 195, 238, 240; and amateur ideals, 120; definition of, 118–19; and distance running; 121–22; evolution of events of, 120–24; and gambling, 119–20; general history of, 119–20; and hurdle, 122–23; and jumping events, 123–24; and Olympic Games, 120, 124; and rise and fall of professionalism, 119–20; and sprinting, 120–21; and throwing events, 124; in United States, 121, 124
Trail orienteering, 174
Tree climbing, 252
Triple Crown: of horse racing, 88
Tsu Chu, 105
Tucuna Indians, 190
Tug-of-war, 189, 252
Turnen: as precursor of modern gymnastics, 147
Tutsi, 9

United States Bobsled and Skeleton Association (USBSF), 182
United States Bocce Federation, 135
United States Canoe Association, 212
United States Handball Association, 84
United States Wrestling Federation, 144

Virgin, Craig, 66
Volkssport, 131–32, **183–85**; definition of, 183; folk origins of, 183–84, history of, 183–84; and nationalism,

About the Author

ROBERT CREGO is an accomplished sportswriter and long distance runner. This is his first book.